ROBERT, EARL O

Robert Lacey, a former magazine editor and journalist, is the author of many best-selling works of biography and history. Following his success with *Robert, Earl of Essex* and *Sir Walter Ralegh* (Phoenix Press) Robert Lacey wrote *Majesty*. Published on the occasion of the Queen's Silver Jubilee in 1977, it is the definitive study of the British monarchy, on which subject Lacey continues to lecture around the world.

Winning renown for his original and painstaking research, Robert Lacey has gone on to write authoritative and successful works on Saudi Arabia, the Ford family, the gangster 'Little Man' Meyer Lansky, Princess Grace of Monaco and Sotheby's. He also wrote and presented the BBC television series *Aristocrats*. Most recently his fascinating description of life at the turn of the first millennium in *The Year 1000* has been a best-seller on both sides of the Atlantic.

Also by Robert Lacey

Aristocrats
Elizabeth II and the House of Windsor
Ford: the Men and the Machine
The French Revolution
God Bless Her! Queen Elizabeth, the Queen Mother
Grace
The Kingdom
The Life and Times of Henry VIII
Little Man Meyer Lansky and the Gangster Life
Majesty
The Queens of the North Atlantic
The Queen Mother's Century
Sir Walter Ralegh (Phoenix Press)
Sotheby's: Bidding For Class
The Year 1000

ROBERT, EARL OF ESSEX

An Elizabethan Icarus

Robert Lacey

**PHOENIX
PRESS**

5 UPPER SAINT MARTIN'S LANE
LONDON
WC2H 9EA

A PHOENIX PRESS PAPERBACK

First published in Great Britain
by Weidenfeld & Nicolson in 1971
This paperback edition published in 2001
by Phoenix Press,
a division of The Orion Publishing Group Ltd,
Orion House, 5 Upper St Martin's Lane,
London WC2H 9EA

A CIP catalogue record for this book is available from
the British Library.

Printed and bound in Great Britain by Clays Ltd, St Ives plc.

ISBN 1 84212 285 1

To my parents

Contents

CONTENTS

Illustrations

Preface

'I was ever sorry your Lordship should fly with waxen
wings, doubting Icarus' fortune.'
                        – *Francis Bacon to Essex, September* 1600.

Robert Devereux, Earl of Essex, has long fascinated me both as a
man and as the parable of an eternal dilemma. When Francis
Bacon compared him to Icarus, his soaring flight destroyed by the
sun, he captured not only the spirit of the man but the essence of
the historical tragedy in which he was trapped. His political power
was based on the personal attraction he exercised over Queen
Elizabeth I, but when he presumed to pursue that attraction he
was struck down.

It is over forty years since Lytton Strachey first published his
monograph *Elizabeth and Essex*, and over thirty since G.B.
Harrison completed his more scholarly *Life and Death of Robert
Devereux Earl of Essex*. Since then the methods and materials
available to students of Tudor history have extended enormously,
and this reinterpretation attempts to take account of some of
them.

It draws on no documents that have not been published or
studied in recent years, but it does for the first time apply their
new evidence to the relationship between Queen Elizabeth I and
Robert Devereux, 2nd Earl of Essex, and also reassesses the significance of court politics at the end of the sixteenth century.

The love affair between Elizabeth and Essex was non-existent,
if 'love' is understood by its conventional meaning. The young
Earl's wooing of the Queen was, in the first instance, a calculated
exercise in financial survival and later an instrument of political
ambition. Elizabeth, old enough to be her suitor's grandmother,

was in love with the idea of an *affaire*, but experienced towards Essex the man nothing more than a calculated, wilful infatuation whose main constituent was fear of old age. The Queen with whom Essex had to deal was failing – she was not the woman who had flirted in earlier years with Hatton and Leicester. It suited the purposes of both the needy young suitor and the ageing monarch to weave around their relationship a tissue of romance which subsequent generations have embroidered; but the core of it was hollow.

The essential reason for this emptiness was the cold, flawed nature of their own personalities. And the explanation of the rich, elaborate husk which they and others pieced together around their deficiencies lies in the nature of society at the end of the sixteenth century – and particularly in life at the royal Court, which was in the 1590s closer to destruction in the Civil War of 1642 than it was to the glorious certainties of the high Tudor Age. And I also examine in some detail the three great military expeditions of the Earl of Essex to Cadiz, the Azores and Ireland. These shed considerable light on the Earl's own personal qualities and, though often neglected in the shadow of the Armada of 1588, they were in fact the most costly and ambitious English military ventures of the century. In a sixteenth-century context their scale can be compared to the sending of British expeditionary forces to the Crimea, South Africa or Korea.

With the general reader in mind I have kept footnotes and references to a minimum, but have provided a guide to sources.

I should like to express my gratitude to Professors Owen Chadwick, Geoffrey Elton and Joel Hurstfield for the advice they gave at the outset of my research; to Charles Peter Hill, Maurice Isaac, John Millward, Professor William Brock and Doctor Harry Porter for the historical instruction and encouragement that dared me to venture; to my parents for inspiring me to start and for their painstaking help along the way; to Sandi and Sasha for helping me to finish; to Barbara Osborne, Jane Kingdon and Peter Coxson for relieving me of the labour of typing; and to John Cushman and Jacqueline Reynolds whose faith and criticism turned ambition into reality. Napoleon attempted a crude study of the Earl of Essex before his energies were turned in other directions. I hope I match him in this enterprise at least.

Robert Lacey
February 1970

I

'He desired nothing more
than to die in public'

She sent two executioners, and sent them secretly. His death
was to be a private affair. No crowds nor cheers nor
scaffold harangues, but a brief dawn quietus in a prison
courtyard. The romance between a rash young earl and a queen
old enough to be his grandmother had occupied the centre of
English politics and gossip for over a decade and now the gossip
would have to stop.

But it did not, of course. The few eyewitnesses who were
present in the Tower of London on the morning of Ash
Wednesday 1601 were participants in too sad a ceremony to
keep it their own secret. The destruction of a man who bestrode
his narrow world like a Colossus was a tale made for the telling.
It was told within hours by the street ballad-sellers – and, with the
history of the accidents that led up to the block, it has been told
ever since.

Robert Devereux, 2nd Earl of Essex, had first come to court as
the protégé of Queen Elizabeth I's favourite, Robert Dudley,
Earl of Leicester. He had brilliantly outdazzled his patron. He
had fought for Queen and country in seven foreign expeditions
and had commanded four of them. He had organized an
intelligence network that few could rival. He had known and
patronized Francis Bacon and Edmund Spenser, possibly William
Shakespeare as well. He had himself written, composed and

danced with a skill all admired. He had loved the most beautiful women of the Elizabethan Court and had succeeded in keeping his Queen's love longer than most men. He had captured the imagination and affection of the English people as no other royal favourite has done before or since. He was the reflection and example of his age. But his glory had fostered pride and his pride had fathered rebellion. So now he was to die.

The executioners came secretly, for fear that London set upon them – as London did once the news of the execution had spread. And there were two 'because if one faint, the other may perform it,' explained the letter to the Lieutenant of the Tower. A precaution which proved unnecessary, for no one fainted. History's book of unlikely and useless records lists Robert Devereux, 2nd Earl of Essex, as the only man ever to suffer formal execution inside the walls of the Tower of London. All other male prisoners were taken outside to meet death in an arena of jeers and execration. But Elizabeth was unsure of her people's sympathies – and gave out that the Earl of Essex had asked for private execution as a special favour. A fairy story which did not convince his friend the King of France, for one. 'Nay, rather the clean contrary,' he chuckled to the British ambassador, 'for he desired nothing more than to die in public.'[1]

The Earl of Essex had to make do with a limited audience. When he heard on 24 February 1601 that he was to die next day he opened the casement to his chamber and asked the guards outside to pray for him. 'Tomorrow you shall see in me a strong God in a weak man,' he told them, 'for I have nothing left but that which I must pay to the Queen tomorrow in the morning.' And by their account he did not sleep that night, but prayed on his knees 'the long hours through that his soul might participate of Heaven, freed from the miseries of this wicked world'. It was a pious end to a life that was in some need of piety to redeem it.

And it was in pious mood next morning that he walked to the scaffold a little after seven. The block waited for him on a raised, railed platform three yards square in the Tower courtyard. Through the dark chill February dawn a damp wind whipped off the Thames. The Earl was huddled in a black, wrought velvet cloak worn over a black satin suit. A tall, ginger, stooping figure, he bowed to the clerics who had come to minister to his last minutes, then turned to the nobles who had risen early to witness his end. Most had come to this bleak grey courtyard to watch an enemy die. A few mourned the foolishness that had brought an over-impulsive friend to the block. But all were there for duty's sake, present at the Queen's command to observe for the record that a rebel had indeed met the end rebellion warranted. Elizabeth could risk a totally secret killing no more than she could a public execution, for Essex was the stuff of which legends were made. Already the street rhymesters were composing:

> I have deserved to die, I know:
> But never against my country's right
> Nor to my Queen was never foe:
> Upon my death, at my goodnight,
> Farewell, Elizabeth, my gracious Queen!
> God bless thee and thy Counsell all![2]

That doggerel bore a fair resemblance to the Earl of Essex's last speech, but it took little guessing at. Sixteenth-century prisoners all knelt to the block acknowledging both the guilt of their actions and the innocence of their intentions. The one graced their exit from this world, the other smoothed their entry to the next.

The wide, spare figure was speaking. He was begging pardon for his rebellion that had turned the streets of London into a battlefield less than three weeks earlier: 'this my last sin, this great, this bloody, this crying and this infectious sin, whereby so many, for love of me, have ventured their lives and souls, and have been drawn to offend God, to offend their Sovereign and to offend the world.' Some of his hearers must have shivered to think how close they had come to standing there, heads bowed with Essex. Others must have expected his reproaches. Sir Walter Raleigh had come ready to rebut the accusations he feared the condemned man would lay to his charge. But he need not have worried: 'I confess I have received an honourable trial and am justly condemned. And I desire all the world to forgive me, even as I do freely and from my heart forgive all the world.'

Blown on the wind his words must have been difficult to catch, and if his hearers shuffled their feet as damp from the cold Tower cobblestones seeped up through their shoes, they had little longer to wait. Essex was unfastening his gown and ruff. More confused than he wished to appear, he called without thinking for his serving man Williams to help him. But this final unfastening was work the Earl had to tackle alone. He turned to face the block. Many times he had been in danger of his life, he murmured to a chaplain, but never had death been so certain and inevitable. He prayed for strength against the weak fears he had felt in the trials of the past.

Then he knelt down on the straw and repeated the Lord's Prayer. Some of the onlookers joined in. Others looked away. He stripped off his black satin doublet to reveal beneath it the scarlet waistcoat with which his life's blood was soon to be stained. He would not shiver and he would not be bound. Outstretching his arms he lay flat on the board and fitted his head to the notch in the block. He refused a blindfold. A chaplain began the 51st Psalm:

> Have mercy upon me, O God, according to thy loving kindness:
> According to the multitude of thy tender mercies, blot out my transgressions,
> Wash me thoroughly from mine iniquity
> And cleanse me from my sin.

The words steamed a pall in the cold air over the block and its prostrate victim. The executioner struck. The first blow drove into the condemned man's shoulder. The second also missed the neck. It was not until the third stroke that the Earl of Essex's head lay severed from his body and the executioner could brandish it in the air. 'God save the Queen.'

The Queen was saved – but she had not long to live herself. In three years' time young James VI of Scotland would be cavorting in Whitehall with his boyfriends. In 45 years' time, the number of years Elizabeth had ruled England, the first Civil War would have run its course and a scaffold would be going up for a monarch to walk upon.

The world was in dissolution. And the drama of Essex and his Elizabeth was played out against a backcloth from which the great certainties of the sixteenth century were fading fast. Essex's Elizabeth was a very different woman from the Gloriana who had steered England through the epic years of Drake's discoveries and victory over the Spanish Armada. And Essex himself was not the traditional soldier-poet-courtier, prepared idly to gild his sovereign's court, for his o'er-vaulting aspirations made the customary charade between monarch and favourite impossible to sustain. Ahead of his time, he appealed for popular support and sought an eminence over his sovereign no man of the sixteenth century had dared to claim. Behind his time, he laid claim to that eminence with a motley crew of household servants and clients prepared to brandish their swords for their Lord in 'Wars of the Roses' fashion. That both anachronisms came so close to success betokened the schizophrenic uncertainty of the age. And nothing epitomized that uncertainty better than the glittering, spiteful, tragic relationship between the Earl of Essex and Queen Elizabeth I.

2

The Devereux

obert Devereux was born on 10 November 1567, at
Netherwood in Herefordshire, first son of Walter
Devereux, Viscount Hereford, Lord Ferrers of Chartley,
Bourchier and Lovaine, and of his wife Lettice. In 1567 the
Devereux were not yet Earls. And one hundred years previously
they had not even been Viscounts. Their rise was a typical Tudor
success story.

Robert was named after the first of the Devereux, Robert of
Evreux, a hard-drinking, freebooting Norman who came to
England with William the Conqueror. D'Evreux's descendants
settled in Herefordshire, and as rough squires living close to
Wales they both farmed their lands and kept their weapons
handy to fight for their king in the battles of the border wars.
Robert's great-great-great-grandfather, Sir Walter Devereux,
fell on Bosworth Field in the summer of 1485 defending
Richard III against the armies of Henry Tudor – the grandfather
of Elizabeth I. But before his death, Sir Walter had set the
Devereux on the upward path with a shrewd marriage to the
heiress of Lord Ferrers of Chartley. The alliance won for Sir
Walter the Ferrers title. And his son, John, succeeding to the new
dignity in 1485, equalled his father's skill in advancement through
matrimonial alliance. He married Cecilia, sister and heiress to the
last Bourchier Earl of Essex and had by her a son, another Walter,

who inherited through his mother the lordships of Bourchier and Lovaine to string behind the Ferrers title that he inherited on John's death in 1501.

This Walter, the great-grandfather of Robert, was a fighting man like the Devereux before him, and since his grandfather's last battle had failed to prevent Henry Tudor capturing the crown of England, it was for the new Welsh dynasty that Walter fought. He upheld their name in the Welsh border valleys and sailed in 1512 to Guipuscoa on the first expedition to the Continent England had launched for sixty years. He went at the behest of the young King Henry VIII who had been persuaded by his Spanish wife, Catharine, and her father, Ferdinand of Aragon, to give English assistance to a Spanish attack on France. But once despatched and landed the English troops became simple tools of a Spanish plot to conquer Navarre. They were left by their supposed allies to moulder near Bayonne where ill-disciplined wine consumption followed by dysentery destroyed the morale of those it did not kill. The English commander, the Marquis of Dorset, Walter Devereux's brother-in-law, proved feebly indecisive, and after a month or so of chaos, sickness and death the expedition defied his orders and sailed home, without honour or glory. Yet somehow Walter salvaged enough credit from the fiasco to be appointed Captain of the *Imperiall Carrik* on his return. And on 1 August 1513 he was appointed a member of the Council of Wales.

Theoretically an arm of the London government, the Council of Wales was in practice the sovereign government of Wales and the border Marches. Its members, as more than one Welshman complained to London, were like local princes who could exercise their power with little reference to the royal government so many days' ride away. Henry VII had tried to mollify such complainers by giving his heir the title Prince of Wales, and Henry VIII kept up the pretence. In the absence of a legitimate son he conferred the Welsh title on Mary, his gentle daughter by Catharine of Aragon.

Walter Devereux, freshly made a Knight of the Garter, was appointed in 1525 Seneschal Chancellor and Chamberlain of the

7

Household of this young lady, and was given by her father two further positions as Chamberlain and Chief Justice of South Wales. Walter had little legal training and less experience, but that was more than counter-balanced in Henry VIII's eyes by his loyalty to the Crown. And that loyalty was needed in the next dozen years as Henry changed wives and advisers, broke off England's religious links with the Pope and confiscated the vast monastic properties of the Roman Church in England. Thousands of pounds' worth of land changed hands, more than a little of it staying with officials like Walter Devereux who administered the great upheaval. And Walter went to battle one last time, joining in 1544 Henry's final expedition against France, as miserable an enterprise as its predecessors. After Henry's death he was sworn in as a member of the Privy Council of Edward VI, the dead king's sickly son. And with the new oath went a new title. On 2 February 1550 Walter Devereux, Lord Ferrers of Chartley, Bourchier and Lovaine was created Viscount Hereford, and though now one of England's more powerful peers, he remembered in his title the green countryside his forebears had farmed and fought over for some dozen generations and where the bulk of his possessions still remained.

A very old man in sixteenth-century terms – he was by 1550 at least sixty years old – Walter lived quietly through the turmoil that attended the sickness and death of young Edward VI, avoided destruction with the poor nine-day Queen, Lady Jane Grey, and meekly swore obedience to his former charge, Princess Mary, when she came to the throne in 1553 restoring Popery to England the following year. Protestants died in the fires of Smithfield through the twilight of Walter Devereux's long life until he died on 27 September 1558, less than two months before Mary's death and the accession of her sister Elizabeth to the throne of England. Since Walter's son Richard had died back in the reign of Henry, in 1547, it was his grandson, another Walter, who acceded to the Hereford title, and the old Welshman was laid to rest in the parish church of Stowe, near Stafford.

Young Walter, the father of Robert, was to earn the Devereux the Earldom of Essex by methods similar to those his grandfather had employed. He came to Court, a new young lord anxious to serve attendant on the new young Queen, and true to family tradition he soon made an advantageous match. In 1561 he married Lettice, the eldest daughter of Sir Francis Knollys, one of Elizabeth's chief advisers, and he promptly retired with her to the country. For seven years young Lord Hereford and Lettice enjoyed each other's company among the Staffordshire orchards around their Chartley home, and during this time their five children were born. Penelope was their first, born in 1563: she was to become the 'Stella' of Sir Philip Sidney's sonnet sequence. In 1564 came Dorothy whose involvement in Irish affairs, through her husband's family, the Perrots, was to be as disastrous as other Devereux entanglements in that land of mist and bogs. Then came Robert on 10 November 1567 as heir to the Devereux titles: through his mother's side of the family he was Queen Elizabeth's first cousin once removed; and after Robert came Walter in October 1569. It was a well balanced Tudor family: two daughters to bestow in marriage: two sons to double up against the risks of sixteenth-century illness and medicine, risks underlined when a fifth infant died under the care of the family physician. Lord Hereford could count himself lucky that, of his five offspring, four outlived him.

At Chartley he occupied himself with the affairs of the family estates and local administrative duties on the Crown's behalf. And he was called to more than administrative service in 1569 when a plot was suspected to spring Mary Queen of Scots from her captivity at Tutbury not far from the Devereux home. Walter was ordered to keep in readiness a body of cavalry that could fight off Catholic rescuing parties, and the cavalry saw action two years later when the Catholic earls of the north rose in revolt. Lord Hereford marched to join the royal forces at Leicester and as High Marshal of the Field he served with the distinction it was hard to avoid in the suppression of a most feebly organized and brutally destroyed rebellion. Seven hundred and fifty insurgents were executed.

On 23 April 1572 Walter Devereux was admitted to the company of the Knights of the Garter and on 4 May that year was

created an Earl, taking the title of Essex, not through any substantial connection with that county but because of his descent
through his great-grandmother from the Bourchier family who
had held the title previously. The Devereux had arrived. In just
over a century they had risen from the ranks of the Welsh
squirearchy to stand equal with the greatest in the land. But
Walter wanted more. For despite his earldom, his English and
Welsh estates were not vast, nothing compared to the domains of
Earls like Suffolk and Leicester. And since he lacked the money to
buy more land, he would have to win it by force of arms – which
in 1572 meant an expedition to Ireland.

That strange and treacherous land lurked mysterious behind
the squalls of the Irish Channel. Nominally an English possession,
it remained an unruly battleground for local chieftains who only
paid heed to the Queen of England's deputies when it suited the
purposes of their campaigns against each other. It would have
been a country better left to frolic in its own self-destruction had
it not steadfastly resisted all English attempts to spread the
Protestant Reformation among its peoples. Ireland remained
defiantly Catholic – and since Spain, along with England's other
greatest enemies, was Catholic too, there were dangers in Irish
chaos that no English government could ignore.

In 1573, therefore, Walter Devereux, the new Earl of Essex,
volunteered to take troops to Ireland and colonize its northern
parts on Elizabeth's behalf. Ulster should be English – and Essex's.
The agreement the Queen signed with Walter was typical of the
fashion in which she employed private enterprise to do the work
of State. Similar agreements made possible – and patriotic – the
escapades of adventurers like Drake. An army of 1,200 men was
to be raised, Walter and Elizabeth sharing the cost. To help meet
his share of the expenses the Queen extended the earl a £10,000
loan and became first mortgagee of his English estates: and she
granted him almost all the county of Clandeboyne (now County
Antrim) if he could capture it. The Devereux could sell parcels
of their land to Englishmen as they wished, and were guaranteed
free trade with the mainland for seven years.

Whole new horizons seemed opening for Walter as he sailed

out of Liverpool Bay one sunny day in July 1573. But the misfortunes that were to bring disaster on every Irish enterprise his family attempted began as soon as his fleet left port. A storm blew up and the ships were scattered, some as far south as Cork. With a few survivors Walter limped into Carrickfergus, the one town in Clandeboyne excluded from his royal agreement.

Sir Brian MacPhelim was the native Irishman who owned the land Elizabeth had granted to Essex – and not surprisingly the chieftain was disinclined to yield up his estates without a fight. After a feigned submission MacPhelim drove away cattle he had offered to Walter, and mustered troops. A fierce raid by the English salvaged a few animals to eke out their dwindling provisions, but the English soldiers were already discouraged by the obvious difficulties of the task ahead of them. Fitzwilliam, Elizabeth's representative in Dublin, had from the first deplored the whole expedition, which could only diminish his own position in Ireland as a whole, and he withheld all assistance. Walter sent his secretary back to England to explain his position to the Queen and ask for orders compelling Fitzwilliam to assist his northern enterprise. But only a handful of troops were sent, and in March 1574 the 1st Earl of Essex had no choice but to negotiate a truce with the local Irish. His son Robert was to be reduced to a similar humiliation a quarter of a century later.

Still bottled up in Carrickfergus, Walter had nothing to show for nearly a year on the threshold of the land promised to him, except a mortgage on his English lands which the Queen could claim if her £10,000 were not repaid within three years. Disease and famine began to take their toll of the English garrison and the death rate reached fifteen or twenty a day. Walter showed characteristic Devereux bravery and stupidity by working and sleeping in the rooms of the dead and dying, but by May 1574 he was driven to admit the hopelessness of his enterprise. He escaped to Dublin with the two hundred invalids who were the sole remnants of his proud invasion force of 1,200 warriors.

After a summer of inconclusive raids he resorted to trickery. In October 1574 he invited his Irish opponent, Brian MacPhelim, to confer with him in Dublin and greeted the chieftain with a banquet worthy of the Borgias. For when MacPhelim, his wife, his brother and attendants reached the midstage of the feast the curtains were flung back to reveal armed hordes of English soldiers who seized the three principal guests and butchered the rest as they struggled to rise from their food: and the principals were spared but a short time. Walter had MacPhelim, his wife and brother executed in Dublin, boasting 'this little execution hath broke the faction and made them all afeared'.

But he was wrong, for the struggle dragged on into 1575. The Queen appointed Essex Earl Marshal and granted him more land in County Monaghan, praising his efforts on her behalf. Walter took her encouragement as a cue for more brutality – as it most probably was – and when his ships, one of them commanded by Francis Drake, captured the Isle of Rathlin, all its inhabitants were put to the sword. Old women and children who attempted to hide in the caves of the island were rooted out and ruthlessly massacred one by one.

It was Walter Devereux's parting gesture to a country that had ruined him and his family. After two years of campaigning he had scarcely an acre of land he could call truly his own – and a mountain of debts and mortgages in England. He returned home and petitioned the Queen and Council to compensate him for the valiant efforts on their behalf which had left him besieged by creditors. But the Queen had paid enough. Through the winter and spring the haggling went on until 9 May 1576, when Elizabeth reappointed Essex 'Earl Marshal of Ireland' and confirmed his grant of lands in County Monaghan. To pay off some of his debts Walter sold estates in Staffordshire, Cornwall, Essex, Wiltshire and Yorkshire, before embarking again for Dublin. But a month after he arrived he was poleaxed by an attack of dysentery. And a few weeks later, on 22 September 1576, Walter Devereux, 1st Earl of Essex, died in Dublin Castle at the age of thirty-five. His last days had been dragged out in agony and piety: 'He never let an hour pass without some sweet and excellent prayers grounded on God's word,' wrote one observer who was so overcome in reminiscence that he had to lay down his pen: 'I blott the page with tears as I write'.[1] As bowel spasms racked his body, Walter sang fervent hymns to the deity who had looked on him with so little favour.

The miseries of his end cannot have been eased by thoughts of the poverty in which he was leaving his wife and children. A pathetic letter to the Queen two days before his death begged her to favour his eldest son, and next day he implored her Lord Treasurer, Burghley, for similar assistance. It was all he could do. The Devereux destiny – and debts – were left to a nine-year-old boy, Robert, 2nd Earl of Essex, Viscount Hereford, Lord Ferrers of Chartley, Bourchier and Lovaine: empty titles without the wealth and influence that his father Walter had squandered. Young Robert was the poorest Earl in England.

3

The Boyhood of Essex

Of the boyhood of Essex we know little. Young Robert spent his early years with his sisters Penelope and Dorothy playing in the soft fields and orchards around their timbered home at Chartley in Staffordshire. Until he was four he probably saw quite a lot of his father, but once Walter had sailed to Ireland father and son were separated for good, and it would have been hard for Robert, when he heard the news of his father's death in 1576, to recall precisely whom he had lost, or, indeed, to feel any real sense of loss at all.

His education was entrusted to Richard Broughton, a pedantic local gentleman of Welsh-speaking Shropshire stock who laid claim to being an antiquarian. No records have survived of the course of instruction through which this tutor put the heir to the Essex title, but a time-table drawn up a few years earlier by Lord Burghley gives a fair idea of the general range of proficiencies a young Elizabethan nobleman was expected to acquire before his tenth birthday. There was a lot to cram into every day:

7.00–7.30 a.m.	Dancing
7.30–8.00 a.m.	Breakfast
8.00–9.00 a.m.	French
9.00–10.00 a.m.	Latin
10.00–10.30 a.m.	Writing and Drawing

10.30 a.m.	Prayers, Recreation, Dinner
1.00–2.00 p.m.	Cosmography
2.00–3.00 p.m.	Latin
3.00–4.00 p.m.	French
4.00–4.30 p.m.	Writing
4.30 p.m.	Prayers, Recreation, Supper

On holidays, the Roman religious festivals still celebrated by the Church of England, the young pupil had to read the epistle of the day in Latin or English before the midday meal and the gospel of the day in Latin or English afterwards. His holiday recreations were a carefully regulated programme of riding, shooting and dancing.[1]

Old Richard Broughton was a fastidious tutor, and on the death of Earl Walter he became young Earl Robert's trustee as well, but he had little personal impact on the boy. The one adult who really shaped the young Earl of Essex, if anyone did, was his forceful, flirtatious mother Lettice. She was a beautiful woman in the dark sullen fashion that can infuriate men with desire – and women with jealousy. She flaunted her beauty shamelessly, first to capture Walter Devereux, but soon after her marriage to capture other lovers. Wilful and impetuous, she insisted always on having her own way, dominating her son Robert in his youth and then dogging his footsteps at Court. She was to have a more than casual involvement in the plottings that led up to the Essex rising of 1601, and in the revolt she lost not only her son but Christopher Blount, her third husband.

Her second husband was Robert Dudley, Earl of Leicester, and she was campaigning to capture him long before her first spouse, Walter Devereux, 1st Earl of Essex, was dead. It was not for nothing, whispered her many detractors, that her grandmother had been the lascivious Mary Boleyn, a mistress of Henry VIII, and that her grandmother's sister Ann had also graced the royal bed – among others. It was not considered politic to point out that that connection with the Boleyns made her a second cousin of Queen Elizabeth, Ann Boleyn's daughter. For Queen Elizabeth hated Lettice Devereux bitterly, and it was all because of Robert Dudley, Earl of Leicester.

A tall, fine-featured man, Robert Dudley had long wooed Queen Elizabeth and had pushed her, most thought, almost to the point of accepting him as a husband. But in urging any cause upon the Queen, most of all causes that concerned her own person, it was the final hurdle of decision that proved a million times more difficult to cross than all the long course of obstacles she had been coaxed over to reach that point – as the 2nd Earl of Essex was to discover. Marriage to an Englishman proved a stumbling block the Queen absolutely refused to approach. Marriage to some foreign prince would have carried risks enough to her authority and independence. Marriage to a mighty subject would encourage all the perils of overmightiness in those who were already difficult enough to keep subdued. And it would also lack the glamour of the royal alliance that her lesser subjects expected their Queen's marriage to possess. So Elizabeth would not marry Leicester, but neither would she release him from her toils. It was the same tactic she was to employ with Essex. She kept him teetering on the brink, an eternal suitor for favours she intended eternally to deny.

Lettice Devereux and Leicester had met while Walter, Lettice's husband, was still alive, and through the autumn of 1565 they had carried on a wild flirtation of which Walter was most probably unaware but which infuriated Elizabeth to the point of a blazing quarrel between Queen and favourite. It was not until Walter went chasing his fortune across the bogs of Ireland that the affair really developed, and then to such a point that Leicester used his Privy Council position to keep Lettice's husband in foreign employment as long as possible. So strenuous were his attempts to maintain the Earl of Essex abroad that when Walter died horribly in Dublin Castle there were not lacking those who ascribed his death to poison administered at the Earl of Leicester's instructions. The Earl's first wife, Amy Robsart, had died in mysterious circumstances: so had Lord Sheffield soon after he discovered Leicester's liaison with his wife: why should not the Earl add the Lord Lieutenant of Ireland to his list of cuckolded victims? In Dublin Sir Henry Sidney ordered a post-mortem to scotch the rumours that sprang up immediately. And though the medical report confirmed that Walter Devereux had died from terrible but ineluctably natural causes the rumours went on.

By September 1578, two years after her husband's death, Lady Essex was unmistakably pregnant. And her father, Sir Francis Knollys, was not a man to be bought off or brushed lightly aside. An earnest Puritan, he was a relative of the Queen's, a Privy Councillor and Treasurer of the Royal Household. To see his young daughter a widow was unpleasant enough: but to see her a pregnant widow was intolerable. In vain did Leicester assure him that a secret marriage had already been contracted. Sir Francis wanted to see for himself. And so, on Saturday, 20 September 1578, he rode out to the Earl of Leicester's rural retreat at Wanstead. There he took supper with his daughter, the Earl her lover, the Earl of Warwick (Leicester's brother), the Earl of Pembroke and Lord North. Next morning the party rose early, for they had a dawn visitor. Mr Tindall, a chaplain of Leicester's, performed a brief marriage service whose secrecy all swore to preserve – but which thanks to Sir Francis' insistence had, this second time, at least, been witnessed by sufficient confidants to ensure that it could not remain secret for ever.

Two days later the Queen arrived at Wanstead in the last stages of her summer progress and all traces of the wedding had vanished. Leicester threw an enormous feast for his guest, but he had enemies enough to ensure that his indiscretions could not remain for ever concealed. And despite the most elaborate precautions, within thirteen months Elizabeth had been told. Her rage was terrible and it was all her councillors could do to save the Earl of Leicester from the Tower. Leicester was warned to steer clear of Court until Elizabeth's fury was abated, and he did so, occupying his time playing the proper husband to Lettice – and stepfather to her son Robert, the young Earl of Essex.

Young Robert had been kept well in the background by his mother while her affair with the great Leicester proceeded. He was left in the care of Richard Broughton at Chartley, and his overall guardian was Lord Burghley, Elizabeth's Lord Treasurer and Master of the Court of Wards. As Master of the Wards old Burghley had control of all minors like Robert who came into their inheritance before their majority – and in response to Walter Devereux's pathetic deathbed petition from Dublin Castle, he had kept the young Earl of Essex in his own care instead of selling his wardship to the highest bidder.

Burghley sent Waterhouse, Walter's former secretary, to Chartley to see whether the nine-year-old lad could attend his father's funeral as chief mourner. But the boy seemed frail, and the weather down in the wild west corner of Wales was treacherous. So Robert's uncle George walked at the head of the funeral procession through the windy winter streets of Carmarthen. Waterhouse attempted some description of the young earl for his new guardian's interest: 'He can express his mind in Latin and French, as well as in English, very courteous and modest, rather disposed to hear than to answer, given greatly to learning, weak and tender, but very comely and bashful.'[2] Richard Broughton had taught young Robert well.

With his letter Waterhouse included a note of excuse written by the little Earl 'without help or correcting of one word or syllable':

Whereas I am appointed of the Queen's Majesty and your lordship, together with my Lord Chamberlain, to do my lord and father the last service, I would be willing to do not only this service, but any other in my power, if that my weak body could bear this journey, and that all things were convenient: Wherefore I most humbly desire Her Majesty and your lordship to pardon me: and thus wishing your lordship prosperous health, I bid your lordship farewell.[3]

It is ironic that Robert Essex's earliest surviving letter pleaded bodily frailty as an excuse for non-appearance, as so many of his later epistles were to do. He remained at Chartley until early the following year when he moved to spend a few months in the Burghley household in the capital. And it was probably then, at the beginning of 1577, that Essex met for the first time great Burghley's son, the little hunchback Robert Cecil with whom his adult life was to be so closely entwined. Though Essex was younger than Cecil he must even then have overtopped the stunted cripple – and he far outshone him in beauty.

Erect and wiry with a handsome head of curly hair, the nine-year-old Robert Devereux charmed everyone he met. His beauty was breath-taking. And he met too for the first time his Elizabeth, the Queen, who wished immediately to kiss him. But the boy was untrained to the attentions of bewigged ladies of forty with blackened teeth and strange-smelling breath, and, prophetically perhaps, he backed away abruptly. Elizabeth was not amused, and though Robert learned more politic manners in later life the first trace of a pattern had been established: success through his physical attractions spoilt by his own involuntary lack of judgement. He was never to be a great man of policy.

The young Earl may in Burghley's household have glimpsed for the first time what true policy involved, for the old Lord Treasurer, the most influential man in England, spared no pains to educate the youths that sat at his table. 'Bring thy children up in learning and obedience,' was his motto, and he carried it out with the same conscientious duty he applied to his responsibilities for the Queen's affairs of state. He set frequent and gruelling general knowledge tests and demanded dissertations from eleven-year-olds on subjects like 'All are incited to the study of virtue by the hope of reward' – in Latin. Any hours unoccupied by instruction were filled with Bible reading – and tested subsequently by impromptu questions. He himself read the Psalter and the Old and New Testaments through from beginning to end in the course of every year.

But young Essex did not stay long enough in London to derive any permanent benefit from Burghley or his deformed, brilliant son Robert. He went on his way to Cambridge, and from Trinity College in the spring of 1577 he wrote a well turned bread-and-butter letter to thank his guardian for his hospitality.

My very good lord: I am not only to give your lordship thanks for your goodness toward me in your lordship's house, whereby I am bound in duty to your lordship, but also for your lordship's care in placing me here in the University where, for your lordship's sake, I have been very well entertained, both of the University and the town. And thus desiring your lordship's goodness towards me to continue, I wish your lordship health, with the continuance of your lordship's honour. From Trinity College, Cambridge, the 13th May 1577.[4]

Not ten years old and a Cambridge student. The Earl of Essex was to stay at Trinity four years, taking his Master of Arts degree on 6 July 1581, by no means the youngest of Cambridge students, but certainly privileged as a nobleman in being allowed up at an early age. He took his studies seriously and worked his way steadily through the bachelor's and master's curriculum that was little changed from the Middle Ages: theology, civil law, the philosophy of Aristotle and Plato, medicine according to Galen or Hippocrates, mathematics, arithmetic, geometry, astronomy, dialectic, rhetoric, Greek and Hebrew. The only book on his reading list in the English language was an edition of the chronicles of Holinshed. He wrote letters to his guardian Burghley in Latin, and, if his time at University was like that of other young aristocrats, he probably received much personal tuition from the Master of his college, with whom he also lodged. In the late 1570s the Master of Trinity was Dr John Whitgift, an earnest cleric who had made a name for himself defending the Church of England against the attacks of Puritans who felt that too many Anglican rites retained damning, residual traces of Popery. Queen Elizabeth had suspended her Archbishop of Canterbury, Edmund Grindal, in the same year that the Earl of Essex went up to Trinity, precisely because he refused to prosecute Puritans for their undermining of Anglican authority, and in 1583 she was to name Dr Whitgift of Trinity as Grindal's successor. Whitgift did not disappoint her, proving a veritable scourge of Low Church practices; and as Archbishop of Canterbury he was to remain a true friend to his former pupil, Robert Devereux. A bond of affection was established at Cambridge between Whitgift and Essex which was to survive the Earl's headstrong antics at Court – and even the Earl's encouragement of certain Puritan ministers that he invited to preach in Essex House.

Through the biting winters of the Fens young Robert lodged in College, but most summers he had to evacuate his rooms when the plague came to town. Lectures and exams would stop and students quit Cambridge for the health of the countryside's wooded walks and ripening cornfields, to relax, perhaps, by the river up which trading vessels sailed to the Cambridge wharves. The town 'standeth very well,' wrote William Harrison, but 'somewhat near unto the fens, whereby the wholesomeness of air is not a little corrupted'.[5]

Town regulations of the time make the wholesomeness of the Cambridge air sound more than a little corrupted: the city fathers were much worried by the mire and dung in the streets, the pigs, cattle and geese that wandered loose through the lanes and even the colleges, and they tried unsuccessfully every device to remove the odours of the carcasses mouldering in the King's Ditch open sewer: the lane behind the Augustinian Friary was also a bother; running with blood from the slaughterhouse it was littered with rotting entrails.

But such mundane concerns do not appear in Robert Devereux's letters from Cambridge. Mostly his epistles to Burghley and Richard Broughton discussed 'friends of the family' who pestered him for favours – among them Hugh Broughton, Richard's brother, noted at Christ's College as one of the country's leading Hebraists and rumoured to spend twelve to sixteen hours every day in prayer and study.[6] And it was while he was at Cambridge that Essex also established the firmest of the curious relationships that were to run as a strand through his life before becoming interwoven with the tissue of the 1601 revolt.

A young Welshman presented himself to the Earl as the academic year began in October 1579. He had a strange name, Gwyllyam Meyrick, so wild and Welsh that Englishmen laughed at him and called him Gelli. Gelli's father was a clergyman, the Bishop of Bangor, and that too was a cause for ridicule: for only a few years earlier priests were still forbidden to marry, as they had been forbidden since the early years of the Roman Church, and to be a priest's son was to be a particularly shameful form of love child. But Gelli was a quickwitted youth, who shrewdly decided that his own surest path to profit lay with the young Earl of Essex, noted for his Welsh possessions and connections. And he was right. Robert Devereux was attracted to this dark sharp-talking Welshman, some ten years his senior, who seemed so anxious to pay him homage. While at Cambridge he could offer little, but in 1587 he made Gelli Meyrick his steward, in 1596 he helped him to a knighthood, and in 1600 he was to rely on him to whip up support in Wales for his rebellion. Though in London Gelli was laughed at – particularly after he acquired his knighthood, chose himself a strange coat of arms, 'two porcupines passant', and took over a small Welsh castle – in Wales he became almost a Viceroy, riding round the farmsteads of the Essex tenants bearing the warrant and executing the orders of his Lord. Men offered him as much as £100 to win the favour of the Earl, his master.[7] And great were the celebrations in the valleys when Gelli Meyrick, who had risen with his Lord, fell with his Lord and was executed in 1601: 'They do not only rejoice at his fall but curse him bitterly,' reported Sir Richard Lewkenor to Robert Cecil in 1601.[8]

But that all lay in the future. At the beginning of the 1580s Robert Devereux was just like any other Cambridge student about to go down with his degree and having to arrange for the transport of all the books and other impedimenta he had gathered from his four years up. He found a young carrier called Hobson prepared to shift his 'stuff': it was the same carrier the poet John Milton was to hire in the next century, for 'old Hobson' lived to the incredible age of eighty-seven before his death in 1631.

In July 1581 Robert Devereux left Trinity, a Master of Arts at the age of fourteen. And one letter sent to his guardian from York in December of that year confessed to the prodigal habits that were to dog the Earl of Essex to his death – and his family beyond it: 'I hope your lordship in courtesy will pardon my youth if I have, through want of experience, in some sort passed the bounds of frugality.'[9] Extravagance was the very sort of indiscretion Lord Burghley was least inclined to overlook, and he must have concurred in Lettice's decision to send her son to the country for a spell to imbibe some sound rural virtues.

Down to Lamphy in Pembrokeshire went young Robert to an old family house that the Atlantic gales lashed as they came stinging through the dunes. It was isolated. It was quiet. And with

Robert was his eighteen-year-old sister Dorothy and her raw husband, Tom Perrot. The couple were in deep disgrace, for they had broken into a church with a Bachelor of Divinity accomplice, who had converted their liaison into a marriage only moments before angry relatives had galloped into the church porch in vain pursuit. Dorothy's impulsiveness came from her father and her wilfulness from her mother, who was, of course, infuriated by the escapade. It reflected, as did the marriages of her other children, the inadequacies of Lettice's own relationship with her first husband. Penelope had just given herself without love to the prosperous but spineless Lord Rich, whom she was openly to cuckold first with Sir Philip Sidney and later with Sir Charles Blount, Lord Mountjoy. Earl Robert himself was to treat marriage as a social convention that placed him under no obligation to the woman who gave up her life to him. Having witnessed no warmth or strength of affection in either of their parents, the young Devereux were emotional cripples. Rash gestures like Dorothy's elopement were not tokens of deep feeling but excuses for the lack of it.

In later life Robert was to remember Lamphy with affection protesting he 'could well have bent his mind to a retired course'. But he was through and through a Devereux, as ambitious and wayward as his ancestors, and an Elizabethan, living under the spell that Gloriana still cast. Besides, there was a family fortune to be redeemed, and the surest way to win that back was to capture favour in the royal palace of Whitehall. So in 1584, in his seventeenth year, Robert Devereux, 2nd Earl of Essex, came to Court.

4

At the Court of Queen Elizabeth

It was at the Court of Queen Elizabeth I that the young Earl of Essex was to rise to heights which neither his father Walter nor even his stepfather the great Earl of Leicester achieved. And he succeeded so brilliantly not through any greater wisdom or effort or skill but simply through the power which his personal attractions exercised over one elderly, vain and capricious woman, the Queen herself.

Not that Elizabeth was alone in finding young Robert Devereux attractive. He was only seventeen when he first began seriously to attend to the ritual of work, ceremony and play that made up the daily routine at the royal palace of Whitehall, but already the ladies of the Court found his charms irresistible. He was tall, long-faced, with a broad forehead from which he brushed back his fierce red hair. His nose was aristocratic, with a high bridge, almost Roman, his fingers slender but manly. When his stubble permitted he ventured to sprout a fine ginger beard and moustache. He shambled somewhat as he walked, but there must have been a tension, an excitement in his gait, for the slight clumsiness with which he manoeuvred his large frame was never laughed at. Despite his eastern counties title, he was very definitely a Celt, speaking, probably, with lilting Welsh intonation, and certainly behaving with all the roughness and impetuosity of the Welsh warrior lords who had quarrelled and fought over the Marcher lands since the Conquest. His deep soft eyes would flare at the mention of battlefields and feats of arms, and it was obvious that though financial necessity might drive him to sue for favour at Court, he would never be a carpet knight. His concepts of honour and social values were simple matters of swords and trumpets, battles and challenges, hangovers from a past age of imagined chivalry. You could see how he might become a man of blood.

And yet he was more than an unlicked bearcub from the wastes of Wales. His animal magnetism was tempered by his Renaissance instruction and by his years at Cambridge. He could read and write fluent English – no mean achievement for a Welshman or for anyone in the sixteenth century – and he had mastered Latin. He could compose little verses to the ladies he courted, and had a smooth, pleasing voice when it came to singing. He danced well too when ceremony expected it, swaying tidily through the detached formalities of Elizabethan ballroom technique. A pious churchgoer who had imbibed the vocabulary of theological dispute at Cambridge, he measured up exactly to the polished, educated norm set out in *The Courtier*, the treatise by Balthazar Castiglione which had been published in 1561. That manual of social accomplishment had articulated the courtly ideals of the Renaissance, and Robert Devereux twisted his Celtic energies to its Italianate stereotypes.

The twisting did not always work. At times the young Earl would break out in rages or sink into deep black sulks. And women, particularly older women, found the unpredictable, overflowing mystery of these sudden passions fascinating. They thought they were facets of his enthusiastic youth, outbursts of frustration by a boy impatient to become a man. If they were, then Robert Devereux was to remain a boy till he died, for his wild, irrational rages were to dog him all his life, becoming more and more frequent until they finally exploded in the hopeless, fatal fury of his rebellion. They seemed at first to set in contrast, but in time they came to cancel out, his charming, winning ways.

In later years there occurred a possible medical explanation of his fits. But the flaw was deep in his character before disease aggravated them. And when it comes to probing his personality one can only speculate. Robert Devereux was an enigma to his contemporaries, a question mark who first intrigued, then baffled and ultimately annoyed Queen Elizabeth, her Court and the world beyond it. He could be as mercurial and inspiring as Henry v, as amorous and captivating as Anthony, but then too he could be haughty and domineering as Coriolanus, uncertain and moody as Hamlet, ambitious as Macbeth and obtuse as Othello.

Where did the components come from? Partly from his Celtic stock and partly by imitation of the straining, baroque world in which he sought his fortune. But the truth must lie deeper, in the relationship between the cuckolded father he hardly saw and the intense, unfaithful mother busy stalking her new lover. The labyrinth that was Essex was knotted up in his superficial eagerness to please and his wary reluctance to commit himself, his constant testing of new friends and acquaintances. He allowed no one really close to him. Was he incapable of genuine love and friendship? He could only relax in the transparent insincerity of Court alliance or the crude platitudes of battlefield comradeship. Ever ready to slap drinking companions on the back, he was suspicious of men who asked and offered more. It was strange, for he was not incapable of subtlety, indeed sometimes he seemed overcome by the impossible contradictions he could sense in himself, succumbing to vast waves of panic, tumbling head over heels, arms flailing into a void of despair. For he could grasp no middle in himself that he could come to terms with, acting out the bluff warrior, the courtly lover, the grave man of affairs, but floundering from one persona to the next with no idea of what lay between.

The one simple thing about him was why he came to Court – to make money. Being left the poorest Earl in England by his father meant he was not simply short of resources, he owed large sums – £10,000 cash to the Queen and £25,473 on his lands in 1576.[1] His father had mortgaged his English estates and many of his Welsh possessions to finance his Irish adventures, so young Robert had to build up a fortune simply to pay off what his creditors demanded. Since by far the largest single creditor was the Queen, it was logical for him to seek her favour. But even if he had not owed her so much, her Court was the sensible resort for a penniless young nobleman, for at the end of the sixteenth century pursuit of the royal presence could provide the shortest cut to prosperity.

In later centuries the royal Court was to become a gilded pimple on the body politic – glamorous, opulent but irrelevant to the real financial and political concerns of the nation. It spent money but did not make it. It displayed power but lacked its substance.

In the reign of Queen Elizabeth I that was definitely not the case. The Earl of Essex went to Court initially to make money, later to win political influence, and only incidentally to engage in the clichéd charades that were the appearance but not the reality of life at Court. For real history was made there. Sixteenth-century England was an autocracy and the Tudors were despots. Elizabeth's Court was the dazzling mesmeric embodiment of her power, the cornucopia from which she spilled out the kingdom's wealth, the market place where everyone who mattered was seen – and had to be seen to matter. It buzzed with the latest news, it glittered with the latest fashions, it tut-tutted at the latest scandals, and it revolved around the Queen. In the Middle Ages the great of the land served their monarch by bringing troops to his battle standard: in the 1580s and 1590s they brought their clothes and jewels to Court. And if they did not, they were no longer great.

It was far more than a matter of status – though most of the great Tudor titles were awarded to those who won Court favour: Burghley, Russell, Southampton, Leicester, Rich and Essex were all titles awarded for carpet and council capers, not military exercises. It was the wealth of the nation passing through the hands of one old woman that attracted courtiers to Whitehall. Elizabeth needed men to help administer her revenues, and she could choose her administrators only from the men she met. So the royal presence was the focus of an institution that was itself the focus of national activity. 'Where is the court but here?' asked Edward II in Marlowe's play. 'Here is the King.' Entrance to the presence was life – exclusion living death. A nod, a flicker of the eyelid, the ghost of a smile from Elizabeth, these were occasions for jubilation and the basis of the position that the Earl of Essex hoped to win for himself. A frown, a swift, blank indifference, these were the danger signs that suddenly cut your friends away and brought your creditors knocking on your door – as Essex later discovered to his cost. A word, a sentence from the royal lips could make or break a man for life. 'Four lagging winters and four wanton springs end in a word,' marvelled Bolingbroke, the Essex figure in *Richard II*. 'Such is the breath of Kings.'

It lay in the power of Queen Elizabeth I to dispose of all the great offices of state, not to mention the positions of authority in the royal household. They carried status, they carried salaries, but, far more important, they gave access to a whole spectrum of private profit that, properly managed, could redeem debts like Essex's in a couple of years. One contemporary observer, for example, estimated that though the Lord Keeper of the Great Seal of England had an official income of only £919 a year, the office was in fact 'better worth than £3,000 per annum' when bribes and gratuities were added in: the post of Lord High Admiral with an official salary of £200 per annum was worth a dozen times that from income on the side; and the official Principal Secretary, whose fixed fee was only £100, made two or three thousand per cent profit from selling his favours to suitors. There were supply contracts, warrants, delays of justice, special priorities, administrative short cuts, a dozen ways a high officer of state could help those who won or bought his friendship. To arrive at a late-twentieth-century equivalent of the sums that changed hands the figures should be multiplied thirty or forty times. Men would bid up to £400 to secure apparently worthless positions like the Clerkship of the Court of Wards, nominally valued at £10 a year but 'worth some thousands of pounds to him who, after his death, would go immediately to heaven: twice as much to him who would go to purgatory: and nobody knows what to him who would adventure to go to hell.'[2]

The Mastership of the Court of Wards was still more remunerative, for the holder of the position was the guardian of all young nobles, like Essex himself, who inherited their estates before their twenty-first birthdays. The Master of the Wards administered their lands and incomes, or farmed out his charges to other guardians, for a suitable consideration. Substantial profits could be made from noble estates before their youthful owners came of age, and the heir had little opportunity of redress if, for example, his guardian chose to cut the trees on his land for short-term income. Lord Burghley made himself a comfortable living as Master of the Wards until 1598, and then, on his death, the Earl of Essex tried for the position. He made discreet enquiries as to the sort of income the Master of Wards could expect, and was shown a list of nine official payments made to Burghley which totalled £906. 3s. 4d. But with the official list went a secret estimate of the gratuities that Burghley had received from the suitors to whom he had granted those nine wardships, and those gratuities totalled £3,016. 13s. 4d.[3]

That was the sort of money Essex was after – though not in any anti-social or fraudulent way. The contradiction between private and public interest that twentieth-century eyes see in such practices did not trouble Elizabethans, or Elizabeth herself. It was the way jobs got done. To prevent men offering and receiving gratuities for favours rendered would have meant increasing official salaries to levels the Queen simply could not afford. Bribes paid to her servants were indirect taxes, freely offered, especially welcome in the later years of her reign when war taxes grew heavy. Besides, allowing administrators these opportunities for personal profit was the only way Elizabeth could hope to organize anything resembling modern bureaucracy. Customs dues levied on goods entering and leaving the country were administered by 'farms' or private companies which guaranteed to pay the Crown a certain sum of money. They had to organize and pay the tax-collecting machinery to meet this guarantee, but they were allowed to pocket whatever profits they made. And those profits could be considerable. The ascendancy of the Earl of Essex all through the 1590s was to be based on the 'Farm of Sweet Wines' granted him by Elizabeth. The Earl's fortune and opportunities to gain further credit were derived directly from the duties levied on the sugar-heavy wines of the Levant, and when he fell from favour and Elizabeth refused to renew his licence to collect those duties, then he was ruined. That was the ultimate importance of his relationship with the Queen. Other nobles had lands and houses, perhaps even ships or mines of their own, resources on which they could fall back if things went badly at Court. But Essex did not possess that independence, he could not afford to sue for royal favour in a detached or leisurely fashion. So, in addition to his personal intensity, he was impelled by pressing factors beyond his own control in all his dealings with the Queen. His relationship with her was more than a matter of caprice or love, it was a matter of crude economic survival.

And he first came to Court as part of another man's strategy of survival. His stepfather, the Earl of Leicester, was ageing fast, and his hold on the Queen was being disputed by younger, more agile men. Chief among the rival suitors was Walter Raleigh, a swarthy, arrogant warrior with a rough Devon accent who had first won the Queen's favour in 1582. Whether or not he had ever laid down his cloak to keep muddy water from his sovereign's feet is uncertain, but he had certainly gathered in the few years since he caught Elizabeth's fancy sufficient tokens of royal favour to finance a whole wardrobe of cloaks. Leicester could not hope to compete with Raleigh on his own terms, and so he brought to Court his stepson Robert, whose youth and good looks could jostle with the attractions of other young rivals and bring new vigour to the connection between Elizabeth and the Leicester faction.

Besides, poor Leicester must have reflected that it was time a Devereux did him some good at Court. The dead Earl Walter was a continuing reproach to Leicester's good name. And Walter's widow Lettice, Leicester's new wife, was causing nothing but trouble with the Queen. Ostentatious and extravagant like her son Robert, she had taken to riding to Court in a coach drawn by four milk-white steeds with four footmen in black velvet jackets, preceded by two knights and thirty gentlemen and followed by coaches of other friends, retainers and servants. Thinking this procession was accompanying the Queen or at least some foreign prince or ambassador, crowds would gather round to cheer – as Lettice intended them to, and to Elizabeth's intense annoyance. When Lettice then deliberately started wearing in the royal presence dresses that were finer than the Queen's own garments,

Elizabeth exploded. She called Lady Leicester before her, told her 'that as but one sun lighted the east, so she would have but one Queen in England,' boxed her soundly round the ears and told her never to return to Court again. Lettice went, never fully to be forgiven for her arrogance; and it was fortunate for Leicester that her son, though equally arrogant, was able to handle the Queen more diplomatically in these early days. Indeed, when Elizabeth caught sight of this tall, handsome young man she was attracted by him instantly. He stood a clear head above the other courtiers who crowded round her, seeming somewhat distant and aloof from the common ruck. He inflamed rivals like Raleigh with jealousy – an emotion Elizabeth dearly loved to see smouldering among the men who pursued her. And he fought outstandingly in the jousting tournaments that were the Court's great holiday entertainment. Elizabeth revelled in sitting above the jousting ring watching her men cross lances and swords in dispute for her honour. The situation symbolized the only method by which she, a woman, could rule over a man's world. She was transported by a physical, almost sexual excitement.

It was strange, the degree to which sexual factors influenced her political behaviour. There was her cousin Mary Queen of Scots, expelled from Scotland in 1568 and kept a prisoner by Elizabeth ever since. Mary's powers of seduction were both legendary and well-proven, so Elizabeth took a special interest when the Privy Council proposed that the Scottish queen be moved to Chartley. Mary had not only been involved in plots aimed against Elizabeth, there were now rumours of a plan to spring her from her present place of captivity, Tutbury. Chartley with its moat and fortifications was a much securer place of captivity.

But Chartley was the residence of the young Earl of Essex, who protested vigorously at the proposal to lodge the Queen of Scots in the home where he had grown up. He complained that all the trees on his estates would be cut down to warm the uninvited guest and the retinue necessary to guard her. He would not be able to call his house his own. And he took swift evasive action, instructing his steward 'to remove all the beds, hangings and such like stuffs to your own house for a while, and if she come to

Chartley it may be carried to Lichfield'. His grandfather, Sir Francis Knollys, wrote to the Queen pointing out that Chartley was the one house that the mortgage-laden young Earl could call freely his own. Could not the prisoner be shifted somewhere else?

What Elizabeth thought of all the protestations is unknown, but the most potent advocate of young Essex's case must have been the note his grandfather scribbled in the margin of his petition: 'it is no policy for Her Majesty to lodge the Queen of Scots in so young a man's house as he is.' The hint was most subtly calculated. Mary, with her lascivious reputation, was kept at Tutbury until the Earl of Essex was safely out of England, and she was moved on again from Chartley before young Robert returned. Elizabeth did not care greatly about the trees on the Essex estates, but she had already developed a keen personal interest in their owner.

5

'To my beloved and much honoured lord, the Earl of Essex, my best sword'

On 8 December 1585, after just over a year's initiation in the ways of the Court, Robert Earl of Essex was introduced to the other accomplishment that rounded off the complete Renaissance nobleman – the art of war. He sailed with his stepfather, the Earl of Leicester, and an English army raised to fight the Spanish forces occupying the Netherlands. The reasons for Essex's involvement in the enterprise were simple: a youthful enthusiasm for military glory, an antiquated but common faith in the special virtues of martial honour, and complete ignorance of what real war involved. The reasons for the enterprise itself were more complicated.

In the high summer of 1584 had occurred the assassination of Prince William of Orange, the inspirer and organizer of the Netherlands provinces' revolt against the Spanish forces claiming sovereignty over them. William, nicknamed the Silent, had been the backbone of the Protestant burgher towns' efforts to drive Spanish soldiers out of the Netherlands, and Englishmen had applauded his fight for both religious and strategic reasons. Spanish Catholic troops occupying the harbours of the Low Countries posed an obvious threat frighteningly close to London. There had been frequent suggestions both in Parliament and the

Privy Council that England should provide armed assistance to
the Dutch forces in a battle that so directly concerned the English
national interest. Dutch independence and English survival were
one and the same thing.

But Elizabeth had set her face against helping the Dutch rebellion. She could see the convenience of keeping Spanish men,
ships and treasure embroiled in demoralizing guerrilla skirmishes
among the dykes of Holland, Zeeland, Gelderland and the other
Netherlands provinces. But she had a horror of rebellion and could
not bring herself to endorse the Dutch insubordination, even
though it was aimed against England's greatest enemy. A cynic
when it came to religion, she had the greatest reverence for
crowned monarchs, whom she believed to have been set in their
places by God. She knew Mary Queen of Scots was involved in
plots to assassinate her and seize the throne for herself, but she
could not bring herself to have the woman executed. She knew
King Philip of Spain had also hired assassins: one of them had
killed William of Orange and others were intended for her: but
she shrank from any action that might assist rebellion against his
divinely instituted authority. Open warfare was permissible – if
she could afford it. Supporting rebels was not.

So the Earl of Leicester's proposal to lead an army to the
Netherlands met with the fiercest resistance from the Queen, even
though every post brought further evidence that the Dutch will to
fight had crumbled since the death of William. The Spanish
armies were making fresh progress every month. If Elizabeth did
not act soon the Netherlands would become a Spanish colony
again, a springboard for an overwhelming invasion of England.
Not until August 1585 did the Queen's obstinacy weaken, for in
that month the Duke of Parma led his Spanish armies through the
shattered walls of Antwerp. The danger became too explicit to
ignore, for few ports in Europe provided better facilities for an
English-bound fleet to assemble and equip in safety.

Leicester offered to supplement whatever Elizabeth could afford
for an army. The argument was decisive, as it was to sway the
Queen when in future years the Earl of Essex wished to lead
expeditions abroad. English military commitment to the tune of

4,000 foot, 1,000 horse and £125,000 annual maintenance was agreed. And among the young courtiers who leapt at the chance of military adventure in a foreign land was Robert Devereux, Earl of Essex.

Ignoring his existing debts, he ran up bills for the best part of £1,000 in the course of recruiting and equipping a train of some 700 gentlemen and 1,585 common soldiers to follow him into battle. In vain did his grandfather, Sir Francis Knollys, reproach him for his extravagance: 'wasteful prodigality hath devoured and will consume all noble men that be wilful in expenses,' he warned in a long letter that pointed out that even if Essex sold the portion of his lands that he was free to sell, he would still be hopelessly in debt. He concluded with a prayer beseeching 'our Almighty God so to assist you with His heavenly grace, that youthful wilfulness and wasteful youth do not consume you before experienced wisdom shall have reformed you.'

The prayer was never answered, for though the Earl of Essex was to win from Queen Elizabeth the means of re-establishing his fortunes, never was he to acquire the moderation sensibly to husband and build on his resources. What he got, he spent, partly through generosity, partly through ostentation and partly in the pursuit of winning more – the eternal over-reacher.

He must have been glad to clatter over the cobbles of the Dutch towns that fêted Leicester, far from the carpings of captious grandfathers, at the head of his train of followers. His stepfather had appointed him General of Horse, and though the title was largely honorary – his cavalry were under the effective control of Sir William Russell, his second-in-command – it meant that Essex rode in prominence through The Hague, Rotterdam, Amsterdam and Delft as bells pealed, cannon saluted, fireworks exploded and mummers danced welcome beneath the triumphal arches that foretold future victories. The Dutch crowds gathered in their thousands to cry 'God save Queen Elizabeth'.

Elizabeth herself was infuriated that such personal adulation should be attached to the Earl of Leicester, particularly when he accepted from the grateful Netherlands the title of Governor-General. It made him a semi-sovereign in his own right, and when Elizabeth heard that the hateful Lettice was planning to sail out to join him as some Queen across the water, she was with difficulty restrained from calling the whole army home. Her only consolation was that the expedition had succeeded in avoiding battle, marching and countermarching but evading direct confrontation. If her forces came home relatively unscathed she could not complain too fiercely.

But the Earl of Essex was not so pleased with the weeks of fruitless manoeuvrings that lengthened into months without a sniff of the enemy. His men were falling prey to the strange marsh fevers of the Low Countries and were dying or deserting in dozens. The fact that the very presence of the English army had checked the Spanish advance was no comfort to him. He wanted battle – and not the pretence of it, the jousts which had been his only excitement since the day of disembarkation. On 23 April 1586 the Earl of Leicester had held a special feast in Utrecht to celebrate St George's Day. Essex rode in the ceremonial parade with the Bishop of Cologne, and after the banquet in the old Hall of the Knights of Rhodes the party moved outside to the jousting ring. There the Earl 'behaved himself so towardly that he gave all men great hope of his noble forwardness in arms.' Hope, but no proof until five months later, in September 1586. And even then the hero of the one slight confrontation of the sad indecisive Netherlands campaign was not the Earl of Essex but Sir Philip Sidney, the quiet young warrior who had fallen in love too late with Penelope Devereux, Robert's sister, and embalmed his tragic passion in the sonnet sequence *Astrophel and Stella*.

The skirmish – it was hardly a battle – took place on the River Yssel near Zutphen, a town Leicester was besieging. The town's defences were strong – they had successfully resisted a ten-month siege by 14,000 men two years earlier – but the Duke of Parma decided to rush to it a convoy of extra supplies before the English force had settled firmly in its attacking positions. The besiegers were just completing their network of trenches around the town when, on Wednesday, 21 September 1586, a captured Spanish soldier betrayed Parma's revictualling plan to Leicester. The Earl decided to intercept the convoy next morning. Yet so inefficient were his scouts that he had no idea of the Spanish relief party's size, and he allocated only 300 horse and 200 foot to deal with the enemy force.

The sounds that came through the mist next morning indicated a Spanish convoy far larger than that, and sure enough, when the mist rose, the English found themselves facing some 3,000 infantry and 1,500 cavalry. But it was too late for second thoughts, and the English charged – the Earl of Essex among the leaders of the sally. He shattered his lance on the first Spaniard he met, but rode on into the enemy hacking to both sides of him with an axe. Twice he reformed his cavalry and charged hard at the Spanish. He showed no fear, shouting encouragement to his men and seizing an enemy weapon when his own was struck from his hand. Sir Philip Sidney was only just behind him – having cast off his heavy thigh armour to increase the speed of his attack. Yet it was in the thigh, just above his unprotected knee, that Sidney was struck by a musket ball on the third charge. And the weight of Spanish numbers slowly pushed the English back until the town gates were close enough for 2,000 of the garrison to emerge and escort the convoy to safety.

As Sidney was being carried back to his tent, his wound streaming blood, he called for a water flask. But just as he was lifting the bottle to his lips he caught sight of a wounded soldier crying out from thirst. 'Which Sir Philip perceiving, took it from his head before he drank and delivered it to the poor man with these words: "Thy necessity is yet greater than mine." '[1] It was the incident that was to make the sorry skirmish of Zutphen memorable. For two weeks later, Sidney, the young shepherd knight, lifted his hospital blankets and sniffed the sweet putrefaction of gangrene from his wound. A week later he was dead.

The bravery the young Earl of Essex had shown in the skirmish was quite forgotten in the sorrow that engulfed the English army and England as a whole on the news of Sidney's death. His body was brought back to London for burial in St Paul's, though the funeral was delayed three months while the dead hero's creditors were satisfied. It was not until his father-in-law Walsingham had paid out some £6,000 of his own money that the black-draped cortège could proceed to the Cathedral: the 'streets all along were so thronged with people that the mourners had scarcely room to pass: the houses likewise were as full as they might be, of which great multitude there were few or none that shed not some tears as the corpse passed them by.'[2] The procession itself was some 700 strong, composed of all the great in the land, prominent among them being the Earl of Essex.

Zutphen had ended Leicester's Dutch adventure on the note of sad futility it deserved. Essex came home with the title of Knight Banneret bestowed on him for his valour in the final skirmish – and with the martyred Sidney's sword, left to him in the dead man's will: 'I give to my beloved and much honoured lord, the Earl of Essex, my best sword.'

The legacy was taken to symbolize the transfer of some special heroic mantle to Robert Essex's shoulders, a transfer completed a few years later when the young earl took to wife the slain hero's widow Frances. Sir Philip Sidney had seemed to represent an Elizabethan ideal: the literate, gentle, courageous all-round courtier at ease writing verses, fighting battles, on his knees at prayer or on his toes in courtly dances. How well Robert Devereux would live up to that example still remained to be seen.

6

'Till birds sing in the morning'

Fifteen-eighty-seven was the year in which the relationship between Essex and Elizabeth became firmly established. They laughed through their first lovers' idyll and stormed through the first of their quarrels. But things got off to a bad start.

It stemmed from the execution of Mary Queen of Scots on 17 February 1587, a couple of months after Essex returned from the Netherlands with his stepfather, and the day after he had marched in the black-draped procession to Sir Philip Sidney's funeral. Elizabeth had been persuaded by evidence that Mary had organized yet another plot against her, to sign a warrant for the Queen of Scots' execution. But she gave no orders for it to be sent to Fotheringay Castle where her royal captive was lodged. She still could not bring herself finally to countenance her cousin's death. It was her Privy Council who took matters into their own hands and sent Mr Secretary Davison riding north to see that the warrant was carried out. They said nothing to Elizabeth.

The Queen was returning from one of her vigorous rides in Greenwich Park a few days later when the sound of pealing bells wafted downstream from her capital. She asked what the occasion for such celebration might be, and was told.

Horrorstruck, she broke down, and the weeks to come were consumed by her hysterical tears and rantings. She had indeed signed the execution warrant, but only the knowledge that it was not the final and irrevocable step had taken her resolution that far. How could she ever cut off the head of a fellow sovereign, a woman, a relation of her own? She refused to admit that she had half-hoped her hand would be forced in this way, that she had edged towards commitment, that Burghley, Leicester, Davison and the other councillors were only pursuing the logic of her earlier actions. She vented her fury on the men who had dared to divine – and bring to pass – what she had in the dark recesses of her mind always wanted. Burghley was banished from her presence: Leicester and the others were screamed at: and Davison, who had been but the instrument of the general conspiracy, was sent to the Tower and fined heavily. Never, vowed Elizabeth, could she forgive the man for what he had done.

Yet it was on behalf of this broken victim of the royal choler that Essex decided to take up the cudgels. It was his first attempt to intervene in major Court politics – and a prophetically fore-doomed one, for Davison's case was hopeless. He was as much the victim of his own colleagues as of Elizabeth. And he had done nothing for Essex that placed the young Earl under a special obligation to help him. To take his part was pure chivalry – and gratuitous provocation. Essex could do nothing to help Davison – or himself. For though the Queen had continued to smile on him since his return from the Netherlands, he was still far from being a favourite entrenched with the security of a Leicester or a Hatton. He had received no gifts, no definite tokens of affection beyond kind words. He still had very limited reserves of royal good will to his credit, with nothing to spare to squander on others. He was asking for trouble. And yet he plunged into the fray with charming fecklessness.

Feckless was the operative word, for Robert Essex decided not to approach Elizabeth initially. He wrote instead to the dead woman's son, James, King of Scotland, asking him to take up Davison's cause. Essex was compounding his stupidity, for by any calculation James was unlikely to come to the assistance of the man responsible for his mother's execution. Either he was smouldering with thoughts of filial revenge against Elizabeth – and Davison, or else he was simply concerned to do nothing that might endanger his claim to the English throne. Neither way was he likely to take the part of the never powerful and now completely powerless secretary – even if he had the slightest influence over events at the English Court. Which he did not.

But Robert Devereux plunged in regardless: 'Mr. Davison, fallen into Her Majesty's displeasure and disgrace, beloved of the best and most religious in this land, doth stand as barred from any preferment or restoring in this place, except, out of the honour and nobleness of your royal heart, your Majesty will undertake his cause.'[1] Robert was to learn in later years that appealing to the 'honour and nobleness' of people's motives was irrelevant, not to say laughable, in the context of high-level Renaissance politics. But he never became a true Machiavellian, for he was incapable of concealment. He acquired a deeper understanding of his own self-interest and that of others, but he was for ever blurting it out. When he suspected the worst, he said it. When he wished harm to others, he told them.

Yet just as the transparency of his ambition was to bring him to ruin in future years, so the unconcealed naïvety of his hopeless good intentions saved him from trouble in 1587. For Elizabeth must have known of his letter to James – which James, of course, ignored. Many wrote from Whitehall to Courts in other countries, but few letters escaped the attention of the agents Sir Francis Walsingham had working on Elizabeth's behalf. Essex's epistle was a youthful indiscretion best ignored as such. Besides, the Queen was developing a serious interest in this earnest, headstrong young Earl. The spring of 1587 saw their relationship flower.

Essex was so predictable, so eager, so anxious to please. And Elizabeth knew he was completely at her mercy. There was no need for her to mention the vast mortgages his father had pledged to the Queen, which could be called in at any moment. Just as young Robert's wooing was impelled by the knowledge that his financial survival depended upon royal favour, so Elizabeth knew she could afford to allow this suitor liberties other men could not be trusted with. Courtiers like Leicester, Raleigh, old Burghley and young Robert Cecil were prosperous to different degrees. Raleigh had little to his name. But all were comparatively independent, none were so loaded down with debts as the Earl of Essex. None owed the Crown so much.

So confident that in the last resort Essex was her creature, Elizabeth felt free to venture with him into escapades she had let no other man share. 'Gratify your nobility and the principal persons of your realm,' Burghley had advised her in 1579, 'whereby you shall have all men of value in the realm depend only upon yourself.'[2] Here in Essex was a noble who appeared the very embodiment of Elizabeth's court system, a principal person, a man of value in the realm who depended only upon her. By raising him up to power the Queen could emphasize her own might – and cleverness. Essex could prove the culmination of half a century's hard political work.

There was also the difference in age. In 1587 the Earl of Essex was in his twentieth year: Elizabeth was in her fifty-fourth. She was old enough to be his grandmother – and realized it acutely. That too gave her freedom, for no longer was the offer of her hand in marriage a useful weapon in international diplomacy. She had never intended to yield it to anyone, but the possibility of it had been power. She no longer had to worry about what construction might be put by others on the intimacy of her male companions. Leicester had got close to her and marriage had been in the air. But the suggestion was preposterous when it came to the Earl of Essex: he was a boy, a mere child.

And then there were her own personal emotions, though they took second place to her political rationalizations – Essex's financial and political dependency and the disappearance of the possibility of marriage. Elizabeth was never a warm-blooded woman. Her father had cut off her mother's head when she was two years and eight months old. When she was fifteen Lord Admiral Seymour, the one man with whom she was romantically involved in her youth, was also beheaded. She learnt at an early age how cruelly emotion could betray. It made her canny and mistrustful, for as a woman ruling a nation no woman had successfully ruled before, she knew she could never afford to surrender to her feelings – except when her reason assured her it was quite safe to do so. And it was only after she had worked

out the logic of Essex's dependency upon her that she indulged
herself.

Even then it was not affection she indulged. She took up young
Robert Devereux not for his own sake but for what he stood for.
He was a toy, a diversion that took her mind away not simply
from the worries of state but from the decay of old age. She could
laugh and flirt with him in simulation of the carefree youth she
had never allowed herself. His real attractions – his good looks,
his impetuosity, his charm – captivated her, but only because she
wanted to be captivated. She knew she had nothing to lose.

And so, through the spring of 1587, Elizabeth and Essex saw
more and more of each other. Each time the Court danced the
young Earl seemed to spend just a little longer at his sovereign's
side: before long the Queen danced with no one else. Robert
Devereux went hunting with her, he rode through the streets at
her side. At masques and mummings he was placed in the front
row near her Majesty, or in the very next seat. She would draw
him aside, touch him fondly or whisper ostentatiously in his ear.
And he himself grew more confident, shaking off the uncertainties
of a diffident Welsh squire. In May 1587 his servant, Anthony
Bagot, wrote excitedly to his father in Shropshire about the
attention the Queen was paying their master: 'When she is
abroad, nobody near her but my Lord of Essex and, at night, my
Lord is at cards, or one game or another with her, that he cometh
not to his own lodging till birds sing in the morning.' Whatever
the night games were, they augured well for the strained Essex
finances: 'he told me with his own mouth,' wrote Bagot, that 'he
looked to be Master of Horse within these ten days.'[3] It was a post
worth some £1,500 a year in addition to the stabling and entertainment facilities that went with it – a most healthy step in the
right direction. And Elizabeth bestowed it on the young Earl on
18 June 1587. Robert Essex's enterprise at Court was beginning to
pay off.

Yet within weeks of this first great success, the award of a rich
office for which a dozen courtiers must have sued long years, the
Earl of Essex had done his best to get himself banished from Court
for ever. No sooner had the pattern of his intimacy with Elizabeth

been established than he sought to destroy it with the first of the succession of quarrels and misunderstandings that led him ultimately to the block. The perversity of it lay largely in the contradictions of his own character – the charm and mistrustfulness, the eagerness to please and the refusal to commit himself. But the fault also lay in Elizabeth, for Essex took her at face value. Unable to sense the cold logic behind her apparently most carefree actions, he assumed that the coquettish, loving face she turned towards him reflected some genuine gift of feeling, some pledge of affection he could redeem in concrete terms. Wooing through self-interest himself, he could not see that his partner's motives were no more altruistic than his own. And Elizabeth either could not see that her suitor was taken in, or enjoyed the deception.

At the end of July 1587 the couple had a flaming row. The Queen was on progress, eking out her finances with a summer round of self-invited hospitality at others' expense. As her train of servants and courtiers approached North Hall, the seat of the Earl of Warwick, Essex told her that his sister Dorothy was staying there. He knew that the Queen disliked on principle the sort of runaway marriage Dorothy and Tom Perrot had contracted a few years earlier. Apart from a certain jealousy, Elizabeth also felt that such undignified elopements among the upper ranks of her society set a poor moral tone.

The Queen showed no obvious reaction to Essex's warning. But no sooner had she dismounted at North Hall than she ordered Lady Warwick to stay the offensive female Devereux in her chamber.

The young Earl exploded. He interpreted Elizabeth's action as deliberate provocation – as perhaps it was. But he sought an external, mechanistic explanation of her behaviour, the malevolent influence of Sir Walter Raleigh. This was another of Essex's traits, to explain the actions of others in terms of extraneous interference: they might act on good advice or bad advice, at the behest of friends or of enemies, never on the basis of a unilateral decision. It betrayed the lack of respect he had for other people's independence – and his own insecurity.

It was merely to please that knave Raleigh, cried Essex, that the

Queen was slighting his sister: it was to please Raleigh she was disgracing him and his family honour. She let that man have too much influence over her.

Elizabeth was delighted by his touchiness. On the contrary, she replied, it was Essex whom she allowed to have far too much influence over her actions. If she were meekly to overlook his sister's former offence, then people would start whispering. She saw no reason why Essex should disdain Sir Walter Raleigh.

The young Earl was stung to the quick. He poured out his long pent-up jealousy of Raleigh, the things the man had done and was alleged to have done, a passionate garbled mishmash of fact, gossip and insinuation. He had every reason to disdain the man, he exclaimed, particularly as Raleigh dared to compete for the affection of the Queen. Essex raised his voice so that Raleigh, standing just outside the door, could hear his every word. And he continued to complain, casting aspersions on any woman who spared time and attention for such a worthless individual.

He had gone too far. Elizabeth lost her temper – and dignity. For every insult Essex had flung at Raleigh, she flung one back at Essex's mother Lettice, screaming to his face like a Billingsgate fishwife.

Essex suddenly realized his mistake. If his sister troubled the royal presence, he mumbled, then she would be sent away, and rather than disgrace his family name he would go with her. 'I had no joy to be in any place, but loth to be near about her, when I knew my affection so much thrown down,' he said later.

So there and then, in the middle of the night, he set his servants to pack his sister's belongings, and as they rode away from the castle, Essex galloped past them into the darkness. He was angry and hurt. His mind was made up. He would leave England immediately, taking ship for the Low Countries to which his stepfather had returned with another army. There he would venture on the battlefield in search of the glory that gilded the name of his dead cousin Philip Sidney. 'If I return, I will be welcomed home; if not *una bella morire* is better than a disquiet life.'[4] Arriving hollow-eyed and sleepless in London, Essex paused only long enough to breakfast briefly and gather his armour, then he was in the saddle again riding down through Kent towards Sandwich where the Netherlands ships put in.

But his romantic escapade ended before he could find a vessel to sail in. He was overtaken by another dusty cloaked rider, Robert Carey, the fourth son of Lord Hunsdon, despatched post haste at the Queen's express command to bring Essex back to Court. All was forgiven. The young Earl had won a victory more glorious than any he could have achieved in the Netherlands. Elizabeth had not given in to him over Raleigh, but she had reacted rapidly to his attempted departure, his gesture of rejection. He was recalled to her side and after a tender reconciliation the two of them progressed to nickname terms – Bess and Robin seemed closer than ever. Bewitched by his daring, she could not see she was encouraging him habitually to bluster, rage and sulk when he did not get his own way. Intoxicated by his triumph, he could not see it had cost Elizabeth nothing to respond to his little act of melodrama, for the feelings she was toying with were not her real ones. Essex was a new game to her in which the setbacks added to the fun, since she knew she could not be defeated.

7

The Armada

In 1588 Queen Elizabeth faced up to much tougher sport, with no guarantee at all that she would win. England was approaching her great test of the century, the assault of the Spanish Armada, when the combined sea and land resources of the greatest nation in the world were thrown against the impertinent island race. And it was small thanks to Elizabeth that England survived.

The Queen refused to believe until the last minute that she had a war on her hands. To smoke-screen his invasion plans King Philip of Spain had sent out through the Duke of Parma in the Netherlands suggestions of peace negotiations – and Elizabeth leapt at them eagerly. She might have acted more realistically had she known that Philip was having drawn up in Madrid a black list of 'the principal devils that rule the Court and are leaders of the Council' who would all be executed when the Spanish troops landed by the Armada marched into London. The Queen herself could not expect the same reverence she accorded other sovereigns, no matter what their religion. 'I wish to God,' wrote the compiler of the black list, referring to Elizabeth's imprisonment during the reign of her sister Mary, 'that they had burnt her then, as she deserved, with the rest of the heretics who were justly executed.' Parma, the alleged peace negotiator, was busy marshalling convoys of flat-bottomed boats to ferry his armies across the Channel.

Young nobles like Essex revelled in the prospect of imminent battle, and even old Burghley to whom war – and more particularly its expense – was anathema, thought action the only alternative to annihilation. But as she had wavered when the Netherlands stared disaster in the face, so now Elizabeth found definite commitment abhorrent. She despatched in April 1588 an embassy to negotiate with Parma, secretly instructing it to agree to the surrender of the provinces of Holland and Zealand and all the English garrisons as well if that was what was necessary to save England from invasion. Yet her diversionary tactics proved of no avail, for at the end of May the Armada put out of Lisbon, and, despite storms, was sailing up the Channel by the end of July 1588, a vast crescent of warships seven miles wide.

The Queen's neglect of defence preparations had been as scandalous as the treacherous desertion of her allies she had contemplated as the price of forestalling the attack. The financial allurements of piracy meant that England could count on ships and sailors to defend her shores more nimble and seaworthy than most. But should the enemy's professional soldiers succeed in landing there were few trained troops to meet them. A hastily strung together chain of beacons inspired alarm among the scattered billhook-armed bands that constituted England's national militia system: a Roman camp at Tilbury was refortified by the Earl of Leicester, reappointed to supreme military command with the same royal disregard for battlefield incompetence that was to stand the Earl of Essex in such good stead: and among the motley-equipped men camped there Queen Elizabeth rode on a white charger to make a speech whose empty bombast well matched the hollowness of her preparations for the fight: 'I know I have but the body of a weak, feeble woman, but I have the heart and stomach of a King – and a King of England too – and think foul scorn that Parma, or Spain, or any Prince of Europe should dare to invade the borders of my realm.' It was an incantation as relevant as the strange fairy rites and dances which the people of Devon and Cornwall had been performing to frighten invaders away from their beaches.

For by the time Elizabeth had made her speech, the danger was past. Stormy weather, inconstant winds, Spanish incompetence and English seamanship had ten days earlier scattered the great Armada and driven its unwieldy galleons into the North Sea and up towards the wave-lashed rocks of Scotland. Parma's invasion army that the great fleet was to have escorted from the Netherlands to its English beachhead remained blockaded in Brill, Flushing and Ostend. England was saved, after a fashion.

The great crisis had been more noteworthy for the personal initiatives of ordinary people than for firm leadership from the government. When the Privy Council had hesitantly asked the Lord Mayor of London if he could supply 5,000 men and fifteen ships, he asked them if they would accept twice as much. And the Earl of Essex repeated his Netherlands preparations and raised a personal company of sixty harquebusiers and two hundred light cavalry – the whole company decked out in silk uniforms of tangerine and white – the colours of the Devereux arms.

Elizabeth was so grateful for her escape from catastrophe she had a patent made out to bestow the extraordinary rank of Lieutenant-General of England and Ireland on the Earl of Leicester. It was a virtual vice-regency, and councillors like Burghley and Walsingham rushed to dissuade her from the dangers of such a promotion. But they need not have worried, for the Earl of Leicester was a sick man. The malaria from which few in sixteenth-century England were free had lain him low. On 4 September 1588 on a journey to take the waters at Buxton he died 'of a continual burning fever'. The Queen retired to her chamber at the news and did not reappear for two days, so that Burghley had to order her door to be broken down. But she kept her grief as a private affair, and her public face was set hard as her commissioners pursued the £25,000 the dead Earl owed her at his death. Confessed his will: 'I have always lived above any living I had, (for which I am heartily sorry).'

Elizabeth insisted on a public auction of his goods to meet his debts – which amounted to a further £25,000 to private creditors. She had no intention of letting Lady Leicester enjoy any more of her inheritance than she was entitled to. The will named the Earl of Essex as a major beneficiary from Leicester's scattered lands, but only after the death of his mother. Lettice was to enjoy them freely for the rest of her lifetime which was, in fact, long to outlast her son's. Never one to be cast down for long, she remarried soon after Leicester's death his Master of Horse, Christopher Blount, a man of notorious Popish sympathies. Sentimental legacies were all that Essex received from his stepfather: to 'my good son-in-law [an interesting difference from our use of the term, but a precise description for a stepson] the best armour I have, one my Lord Chancellor gave me, two of my best horses, with a George and Garter, in hope he will wear it shortly.'

The hope was realized almost immediately, for the Queen bestowed the Order of the Garter on Essex for the tangerine soldiers he had paraded at Tilbury. And just as the death of Sir Philip Sidney had seemed to mark the beginning of a new rôle for the young warrior, so on the death of his stepfather he appeared to assume a position of clear dominance at Court. It was somehow symbolic that Leicester's last great public appearance had been as a spectator at a review organized by the Earl of Essex in the tilt yard at Whitehall to celebrate the Armada victory: 'the last time I saw him,' wrote a newsletter writer, 'was at the Earl of Essex's review at the window with the Queen.' And while the great favourite was making his final journey to the waters in hope of a cure, Elizabeth suggested that his attractive stepson should take over his lodgings at St James's Palace.

For the death of Leicester marked more than the conclusion of one lifetime – it heralded the end of an era. It was appropriate that it came so closely on the defeat of the Armada; and it was followed in the next few years by the deaths of all the great figures of the high Elizabethan age. Mildmay went in 1589, Walsingham in 1590, Hatton in 1591, and old Burghley lived on but a shadow of his former self. Gloriana's days were numbered, and she had chosen for a close companion in her declining years just one wild and wayward youth, Robert Devereux, 2nd Earl of Essex.

8

'A Lady whom time hath surprised'

At the age of twenty Robert Devereux was chief favourite of the Queen of England. The relationship between Essex and his Elizabeth became an established and acknowledged 'romance'. But whether it deserved that name is doubtful. And it is still more doubtful whether it was ever consummated. The young lord might stay in the old Queen's apartments playing 'one game or another with her, that he cometh not to his own lodging till birds sing in the morning,' but there is no reason to believe that Elizabeth Tudor did not die the Virgin Queen she always claimed to be. Some said she had a membrane, a solid hymen that made sexual intercourse impossible for her: she might have been malformed.

But the truth lay in her mind not her body: it was simply not in her nature to commit herself physically or emotionally to anyone: what she called love was better classed as romance, what she called romance as flirtation. For there was little of substance between Essex and Elizabeth save temporary infatuation prolonged by mutual exploitation. Their relationship was not important for what it contained in itself, but for what it gave each partner to use in his or her own way. The long elaborate letters they sent to each other liberally larded with that convenient monosyllable, love, fitted exactly the conventions of a courtly *affaire* – but their object was courtly profit: for Essex power, status and wealth; for the ageing Elizabeth the compliment of a handsome young man's attentions. It was in essence a political relationship and the partners were thrown together not so much by personal attraction as by the fact that no one else in the Court circle could provide them with what they required. As such some might say it deserved its tragic end: the impossibly divergent motives involved certainly made tragedy a likely conclusion.

For Essex was seeking the undisputed political power he felt to be the proper concomitant of the emotional primacy he appeared to hold in the Queen's affections. And Elizabeth was seeking something even more unlikely – to forget about death, to blow it away in a childlike infatuation with a boy thirty-four years her junior. It was this desperate refusal to acknowledge her age which made her a different woman from the Elizabeth who had flirted with Hatton and Leicester, and which made her peculiarly Essex's Elizabeth. She was old – 'a Lady whom time hath surprised,' said Sir Walter Raleigh, though others put it less charitably. She well knew, she told the King of Scotland, that her funeral had been long prepared.

She kept a brave front showing to the world – especially with Essex's help – but there were times when the mask collapsed. One occasion was to occur in May 1596 when Essex was away preparing his expedition to sack Cadiz. Sir Thomas Egerton had been sworn in as Lord Keeper of the Great Seal of England, and after the pomp and ceremony of the installation, the processions, the obeisances, the ringing oaths and solemn affirmations, the sixty-three-year-old Queen took her new-sworn servant aside. She harked back to the days when she was the bright rising sun of England, the young maiden whose frail promise embodied the aspirations of her people. She remembered the gloom and misery of life under her sister Mary, when smoke from the fires of Smithfield had hung dark and choking over the country and how she, a gauche young girl, had been called to the throne to make England merrie once more.

She recalled that in those days her Lord Keeper had been Sir Nicholas Bacon, the father of Francis, the young lawyer who was now making such a name for himself as adviser to the Earl of Essex. Sir Nicholas had been her first Lord Keeper, she recalled, and he had guided her well up the path that had led towards the heights of England's greatness. But now she was over the hill – perhaps England was as well – and she feared Egerton was the last man she would ever again swear in as her Lord Keeper.

'God forbid, Madam,' cried Burghley – himself to die two years later. 'I hope you shall bury four or five more yet.'

'No, this is the last,' sobbed the Queen and clapping her hand over her heart, she stumbled weeping from the room.[1] Egerton was indeed her last Lord Keeper – and no recollections of past greatness could disguise from a failing old woman that she was soon to die. 'It is credibly reported,' wrote Burghley's secretary, John Clapham, after Essex's execution, 'that not long before her death she had a great apprehension of her own age and declination by seeing her face, then lean and full of wrinkles, truly represented to her in a glass.'[2] And she wept openly at the sight, as she had never done while the Earl of Essex was still alive. He alone had enabled her to maintain the pretence of youth.

She was sharp with those who saw through the pretence, either in her dealings with other people or in the lengths she went to to preserve the appearance of a young woman. When the Bishop of London preached in the Queen's bejewelled and powdered presence against 'the vanitie of decking the body too finely,' she was heard to remark that Bishops could be deposed and that if Lord London continued to preach so presumptuously 'she would fit him for heaven; but he should walk thither without a staff and leave his mantle [of office] behind him.' Remarked Sir John Harington: 'perchance the Bishop hath never sought her Highness' wardrobe, or he would have chosen another text.'[3]

And when the Bishop of St David's, Anthony Ridd, presumed to say prayers that implored God to give the ailing Queen strength,[4] Elizabeth had him arrested for heresy.

Her temper – never equable – was becoming more and more irascible with old age. 'When she smiled it was a pure sunshine,' said Sir John Harington who was her godson, 'but anon came a storm from a sudden gathering of clouds, and the thunder fell in wondrous manner on all alike.'[5] Mistress Bridges and Mistress Russell, two ladies-in-waiting, were caught secretly passing through the Privy Galleries to see the Earl of Essex taking exercise. The Queen called for them, screamed at them, struck them and then drove them from her presence. Exiled from the Court they had to take refuge with Lady Stafford for three nights. Their offence was partly their attachment to the Earl of Essex, but equally for being overheard 'talking of physic and medicine'. For Elizabeth would tolerate no mention of the bodily ailments that she knew were soon to overwhelm her. Her obstinacy earned her a certain reputation for hardiness – but it could disrupt State business and drive her counsellors to distraction. 'The Queen hath now a desperate ache in the right thumb,' complained Burghley, 'but will not be knowen of it.' She absolutely refused to admit she was in pain – but she refused with equal firmness to sign any papers, for signing would hurt her thumb. She had an inflammation in the chest, but 'her mind is altogether averse from physic'.[6] And she dealt sharply with the doctors who tried to soothe the pains of her declining years. When in 1602 she had the whole court shifted from Richmond to Greenwich 'by reason of an ache in one of her arms,' she summoned to her 'a cunning bone setter'. In the strange medical language of the time this surgeon told her she had 'a wind with a cold rheumatic humour settled' on her arm which could be removed 'by rubbing and applying first oils and ointments'.[7] Her Majesty told him he was mistaken, for her blood and constitution were, of their nature, very hot, and when he presumed to argue she had him banished from her presence.

She tried desperately to hide her age, but her appearance was greeted with quiet ridicule instead of the awesome respect that had once attended the unveiling of each new dress and makeup. Only Essex paid her the compliments she felt she deserved – but after a time even they sounded strained and false. 'It was commonly observed this Christmas,' observed one courtier slyly in 1600, 'that her Majesty, when she came to be seen, was continuously painted not only all over her face, but on her very neck and breast also, and that the same was in some places near half an inch thick.'[8]

The French ambassador, Hurault de Maisse, attempted to confine his description of the sixty-three-year-old woman he met in 1596 to her dress and jewellery: 'She was strangely attired in a dress of silver cloth, white and crimson, or silver "gauze" as they call it. This dress had slashed sleeves lined with red taffeta, and was girt about with other little sleeves that hung down to the ground, which she was for ever twisting and untwisting. She kept the front of her dress open, and one could see the whole of her bosom, and passing low, and often she would open the front of this robe with her hands as if she was too hot.' Strange behaviour for a woman of sixty-three. 'The collar of the robe was very high, and the lining of the inner part all adorned with little pendants of rubies and pearls, very many, but quite small. She had also a chain of rubies and pearls about her neck. On her head she wore a garland of the same material, and beneath it a great reddish-coloured wig, with a great number of spangles of gold and silver, and hanging down over her forehead some pearls, but of no great worth. On either side of her ears hung two great curls of hair, almost down to her shoulders and within the collar of her robe, spangled as the top of her head. Her bosom is somewhat wrinkled.'

He could not avoid mention of the inevitable traces that time had left on the Queen. 'As for her face, it is and appears to be very aged. It is long and thin, and her teeth are very yellow and unequal, compared with what people say they were formerly, and on the left side less than on the right. Many of them are missing so that one cannot understand her easily when she speaks quickly.'[9]

Elizabeth had never been beautiful – but she had always possessed the strength of will forcibly to elicit the compliments that attend on bodily attraction. Gloriana – the radiant, dazzling Virgin Queen – had been a myth created by the monarch's political agility, and justified by the successes of her policy. But as the 1590s wore on and history flowed less kindly for England, the pretence demanded by the tetchy, wrinkled woman became more difficult to sustain. The sham of kneeling before this shrunken, toothless bewigged old harridan and mouthing the platitudes of courtly love was becoming increasingly obvious. It had always been a charade – but as its tenuous connections with reality snapped one by one, the game grew more and more pointless. The clichés of court sycophancy rang even more hollow, for it was difficult to worship the setting sun. Said the Queen sadly to William Lambarde: 'I am Richard II. Know ye that?'[10] And the uncertainties of her policy were becoming dangerously Richard II-like. 'Her Majesty loveth peace,' Francis Bacon reminded Essex. 'Next, she loveth not change.' She loved not decisions either. Her ability to avoid issues or postpone confrontations, which had served England so well in the past, was by the end of the century becoming an increasing liability. When young, her refusal to name an heir had been founded on commonsense. It kept rivals guessing and eager to please her. In her old age it was no more than self-indulgence. The young Protestant James VI of Scotland was the only serious candidate for the English throne, but Elizabeth's refusal to give him a straight answer about the succession tempted him into rash flirtations that could have made the outcome of the Essex conspiracy enormously more disastrous.

Too tired for fresh ideas, the Queen was applying old solutions to new situations – but anxiously aware of her inadequacy she endeavoured more than ever to prevent her decisions becoming reality. She had always been reluctant to commit herself. Now she was positively evasive. 'Her wisest men and best counsellors were often sore troubled to know her will in matters of state, so covertly did she pass her judgement' wrote Harington. 'When the business did turn to better advantage she did most cunningly commit the good issue to her own honour and understanding: but when aught fell out contrary to her will and intent, the Council were in great straits to defend their own acting and not blemish the Queen's good judgement.'[11]

The tired endorsement in the margin of a letter preserved in the State Paper Office explains why the scribe never sent it: 'A letter which her Majesty willed me to write . . . but before I had fully ended the letter, she sent to me to bring it to her before it was closed, which I did upon the point of six o'clock; and then her Majesty having read and scanned it three or four times and sometimes willing me to send it away, and sometimes altering that purpose, commanded me at last to stay both the letter and the post.'[12] Complained the Earl of Essex overwhelmed by similar orders, counter-orders, emendations and alterations: 'The Queen wrangles with our action for no reason but because it is in hand.'

It was mainly her age. But it was also, to do her justice, the intractable nature of the problems that confronted her – and were to confront English monarchs until the Civil War, only half a century away. For she was hopelessly, helplessly poor. She had to scrape together a living and put on an appropriately regal display from a ragbag of odd incomes worth – thanks to a century of inflation – half as much as when she had ascended the throne. And her expenses of government had more than doubled in the same time. She was compelled to live on her capital. One calculation sets the value of land Elizabeth was forced to sell during her reign at the best part of a million pounds.[13] But she still died £400,000 in debt. Sir Robert Naunton was forced to admit that no matter 'how royally and victoriously she lived and died . . . she left more debts unpaid, taken upon the credit of her Privy Seals, than her Progenitors did or could have taken that way in a hundred years before her.' Because no matter how rapidly she raised taxes or sold land her expenses increased more rapidly still. There was the Spanish War – in which the Armada expedition was but one preliminary episode. Between 1580 and 1590 Elizabeth had been forced to spend at least one and a half million pounds on warfare alone, and over the last third of her reign military and naval expenditure ran at an average of a quarter of a million pounds each year.[14] Most of that was spent in Ireland where the rebels involved English troops in fighting that cost the best part of two million pounds in the six years between 1595 and 1601.[15] It was expense totally out of proportion to the machinery of government – and a major reason for the destruction of that machinery in the Civil War.

And the world knew how mean the Queen of England was. She gave no gift where a smile would serve instead. She deigned not to smile where one curt nod would be accounted a favour. 'The Queen was never profuse in delivering out her treasure,' said Sir Robert Naunton with strained admiration, 'but paid many and most of her servants part in money and the rest with grace, which as the case stood, was taken for good payment.'[16]

For her resources were small. She could count on little more than £200,000 a year without the addition of parliamentary taxation, which seldom amounted to half that. When Drake had brought home £600,000 booty – three years' normal income – from his round-the-world voyage in 1580, it was for financial success, not geographical discovery, that the Queen of England knighted him.[17]

Elizabeth was driven to the most undignified extremes to stay solvent. Her father had made over a million pounds from the sale of property he confiscated from the monasteries.[18] That might have been thought sufficient bounty to extract from the body of Christ, but Elizabeth squeezed her ecclesiastics still harder. Every fresh-appointed bishop owed the Crown 'first fruits' – one whole year's income, plus one tenth of a year's income after that. And when a bishopric fell vacant the whole of its revenues during its vacancy went to the monarch – who, after all, was Supreme Governor of the Church. Elizabeth extracted full benefit from both of these provisions. She kept her bishops in a state of brisk circulation, sending them on a musical-chairs-like tour of England as soon as one died. And she kept some sees vacant for years on end to use their revenues for her own purposes. Ely was without a bishop for thirteen years while Don Antonio, the pretender to the Portuguese throne, and the impecunious Earl of Oxford enjoyed the donations of the faithful.[19] Llandaff was similarly exploited, so that the Bishop, when eventually appointed, suggested his title should be changed to 'Aff', because all the land was gone.[20] And Bishop Fletcher 'got into debt solely by her Majesty's favours in his preferments.' Elizabeth moved him twice in two years and demanded first fruits on each occasion – for malicious reasons: he was involved with and later married a beautiful widow. 'We will divide the name of Fletcher,' ran the Court gossip that reflected the Queen's jealousy. 'He my Lord F. . . . ; and she, my Lady Letcher.'[21]

To keep down her living expenses Elizabeth travelled, filling her summers with stately progresses from one offer of free hospitality to the next – though offer is hardly the word to use. Her servants had no choice but to welcome their sovereign with open arms, open house and open purse. In 1578 three days of royal residence cost Lord North £642, and in 1591 Lord Burghley had to foot a bill of nearly £1,000 for the pleasure of Elizabeth's company. It was not just the food and drink and entertainment; the Queen expected gifts – a nosegay of diamonds from Lord Keeper Puckering worth £400 in 1575, a jewel worth £1,000 from his successor, Sir Thomas Egerton, in 1602.

Then there were the royal servants. The Queen's guards considered £100 a poor tip in 1561[22] – and that sum only partly discharged a host's obligations to a whole retinue that included the household officials, the servants of the chamber and stable, not to mention the trumpeters and travelling companions who all expected hospitality and gratuities. In carts commandeered from the farmers whose lands they passed through, the royal caravan moved across England like a swarm of locusts, and it was no wonder fearful householders plotted the Queen's progress like a rogue typhoon. 'Her Majesty threatens a progress and her coming to my house,' quavered Sir Harry Lee.[23] Fearing a similar catastrophe in 1601, the Earl of Lincoln actually took to his heels, so that the Queen arrived to find his Chelsea doors bolted. But not even craven flight could save the Earl from the one fate the Elizabethans considered worse than death. To soothe the Queen's tantrums, Cecil and Nottingham arranged a lavish impromptu meal – and sent the bill to be settled by the wayward Lincoln.[24]

Essex paid out his fair share of progress hospitality, but for a long time he was reaping handsome dividends from his investment in the ageing Queen. It was his good fortune to provide Elizabeth with exactly the company she needed through the problems of her declining years. He was a member of the next generation apparently prepared to play the games of the last – knowing no better, indeed. He was handsome and he was young. His faults were the faults of youth, quick to anger but quick too to dance, bow, flatter and cajole. He had mistresses, and took his flirtations with them to the physical extremes the Queen would not or could not allow herself with any man: he bestowed his favours on Lady Mary Howard, Mistress Russell, Mistress Bridges and Elizabeth Southwell, by whom, some said, he had a son. Yet so long as these liaisons were not flaunted as open challenges but remained implicit confirmations of her suitor's powers, then Elizabeth was reasonably happy. It made it easier for her to sublimate, to transport herself away from the harsh political realities that pressed ever closer about her as she declined towards the grave. But she forgot that the Earl of Essex was not content with such fantasies – or rather that he had fantasies of his own. And they concerned the very matters of war, money and power she was tired of worrying over. He would not rest for ever satisfied with being an old woman's pseudo-paramour. But in 1589 that particular conflict of fantasies still lay in the future. The quarrels between Bess and Robin could still be laughed off as lovers' tiffs.

9

Shepherd of Albion's Arcadia

The delightful thing about Essex was that his faults were so captivating. Had Elizabeth been serious about him, she would have found his arrogance intolerable. As it was, his vanity sent her giggling off into peals of laughter. And she contrived for her own amusement situations in which his hubris was prickled into the most ridiculous displays of bumptiousness.

At one of the tiltyard tournaments which Elizabeth never missed and in which Lord Essex was so proud to shine, a new young courtier, Charles Blount, had put his opponents to rout. Four years older than the twenty-one-year-old Earl of Essex, he had danced closely attendant on the Queen for the same reason. He was impoverished. His father, Lord Mountjoy, had frittered the family fortune away on alchemists working to discover the philosopher's stone, the magic token for turning lead into gold that was a sixteenth-century Holy Grail as elusive as prosperous estates in Ireland. Charles was but a younger brother, so his share of the squandered patrimony was negligible.

Delighted by the elegance of Blount's performance – and well aware of the effect her action would have on the jealous Essex, the Queen sent the young warrior 'a golden queen from her set of chessmen,' which Blount proudly tied to his arm with a crimson ribbon.

'Now I perceive,' gibed Lord Essex, fuming as Elizabeth had intended him to fume, 'that every fool must have a favour.' Furious to find his tiltyard eminence challenged, Essex was yet more annoyed that this young rival's feats of arms should have won the attention and openly bestowed favour of the Queen. He would have snatched the golden queen piece from this upstart's arm had not Court etiquette refined such acts of petulance into a more formal ritual of revenge.

The first stage was his gibe at Blount. The second Blount's inevitable offence and challenge. And the third, a meeting early one morning in Marylebone Park where the two men fought it out with rapiers. In the event it was Blount who triumphed, scratching his opponent on the thigh. And when Elizabeth heard of Essex's humiliation she burst into one of her fits of giggles. 'By God's death,' she cried, 'it was fit that someone or other should take him down and teach him better manners, otherwise there would be no rule with him.' She was in a good humour for days. It did the old woman good to have two young men shed blood over her favours.

She banned them both from Court until they were reconciled – as they were, and genuinely. Charles was learned and civilized, having turned his father's thirst for knowledge into more fruitful paths than the transmogrification of lead, and he had amassed a considerable library of history and exploration. Coming to his senses Essex must have realized that his quarrel with Blount was of external contrivance, for the two were never at odds again. Indeed Essex's sister Penelope who, despite her marriage to Lord Rich, had managed to become Sir Philip Sidney's Stella, was to become Charles Blount's mistress as well – bearing his children to the spineless indifference of her husband. And after Charles had become Lord Mountjoy (his elder brother dying), the army he commanded as Lord Deputy for Ireland was to become one of the key factors in Essex's preparations for revolt.

In the long term, the quarrel of the golden chessman produced more than Elizabeth ever dreamt of – and immediately it certainly did not achieve its most important intended result. For Robert Devereux was neither taken down nor taught better manners by the incident, and within weeks he was quarrelling again, this time with Walter Raleigh. He challenged his enemy to a duel, but this time the Queen let the game go no further. She had the Privy Council intervene to forbid the fight – an interesting example of the fashion in which the highest executive organ of government would be employed in the most trivial personal concerns of the sovereign.[1]

Essex's pugnaciousness was not entirely of Elizabeth's provocation. Robert was getting impatient with the constraints of life at Court. He knew it amused the Queen to see him burst out in fits of temper, lashing out with his sword or tongue, spattering those around him with his fierce Welsh invective. He knew he was her tame jungle beast, that she was proud of having this wild cat at her beck and call. He knew that it paid him to play up to the role she expected.

But he aspired to other things. The Netherlands campaign had been a sorry episode, but he still thirsted for the battlefield. He yearned to blood the sword that Philip Sidney had passed on to him, to put on the armour that had been worn by the Earl of Leicester. And his ambition was for more than personal combat. The death of Leicester had left a void. There was no great noble at Court who could comfortably assume the dead Earl's mantle as *de facto* Commander in Chief of the military nation. It was the role a king would assume *de jure* along with the headship of the Church and control of the government. But, as Queen, Elizabeth had to leave it to her men, and Essex wanted the position for himself.

But to win it he needed more military experience, so he leapt at an opportunity to join an expedition Sir Francis Drake was organizing to raid the coast of Spain in the spring of 1589. To Drake, to Essex, to Burghley, even to Elizabeth, the prospect of the Spanish ports and treasure fleets with only the shattered remnants of the Armada to guard them was a bait too alluring to be ignored. And there was a ready-made excuse to hallow this project of glorified piracy with an aura of respectability. For eight years Don Antonio, the pretender to the throne of Portugal, had been imploring the English government to assist his restoration to the land from which the Spaniards had expelled him in 1581. Now in 1589 was the time chivalrously to take up arms on his behalf and, hopefully, to return home with holds full of loot. So the Queen gave her blessing to the enterprise, contributing £20,000 and six of her ships in return for a major share of the plunder. Her only reservation was that the Earl of Essex should stay at home. She wanted her Robin by her side.

Her Robin was furious, not only because Elizabeth was denying him a glorious opportunity to win honour by striking at the very heart of Catholic Spain, with the prospect of sun and sparkling sea to set flags and swords and shining armour in an irresistibly heroic context: but because Elizabeth was using the situation to demonstrate her own authority over him. Well, he would not stand for it. She might have foiled his attempt to escape to the Low Countries for a second taste of battle. But she would not get the better of him again. And, like a schoolboy playing truant, the Earl of Essex devised a scheme to steal away from her clutches and escape to sea. To help him in his escapade he enlisted the support of Sir Roger Williams, a rough soldier from Monmouthshire.

Williams, the popular Welsh warrior who was probably the model for Shakespeare's Fluellen, was a professional. He had spent most of his life fighting in the Netherlands – and had fought there for both sides. He might have met young Devereux there, or at Court where the Queen delighted in using him as the butt of her more memorably humourless remarks: 'Fah, Williams, pray begone – thy boots stink.'[2] At all events, he took a great liking to the young Earl of Essex.

Possibly the soldier who made the greatest contribution to English military tactics of the century, Williams was responsible for finally phasing out the traditional long bow and arrow, and was to publish in 1590 a *Brief Discourse on War*. The surprising literacy of the *Discourse* makes his friendship with Shakespeare not unlikely – and has even led certain scholars to ascribe to him the authorship of the Marprelate tracts – virulent anti-Anglican publications whose coarseness, eloquence and nonconformity could well have come from a literate professional Welsh soldier.

For ten years he was to act as an agent of Essex, drink and riotous living gradually clouding his mind until he died of a surfeit, leaving all he possessed to his master.

It was with this rough diamond that Essex began to plan his escape to Spain in 1589. The Welshman set off immediately to Falmouth, a safe fifty miles beyond Plymouth where the main expedition was preparing, and there he fitted out in secret a special ship, the *Swiftsure*, so that it was ready to sail at a moment's notice. Essex spent the last days of March 1589 writing in his own hand – he dared not trust a secretary – some forty letters to leave behind him, and then he invited his brother-in-law, the cuckolded Lord Rich, to come for late supper with him on 3 April.

Yet earlier that evening, between five and six o'clock, there waited in St James's Park with fast hunting horses one Reynolds of Lord Essex's retinue, along with a secretary and a groom. Muffled in a plain cloak, the young Earl joined them, leapt on his horse, stuck his spurs in its side and was far away from London by suppertime. After ninety miles' hard riding he changed to fresh mounts that were waiting for him. The tired horses were sent back to London with a groom who carried a letter to Lord Rich and a key to Essex's desk, in which were found the forty epistles 'to the Queen, the Council, and others of his friends in Court, and his servants, with resolution not to be stayed by any commandment excepting death.'[3]

On the morning of 5 April 1589, when all London was buzzing with talk of his exploit, Essex was in Plymouth, having travelled 220 miles in thirty-six hours and far outstripped any posts and messengers that might be sent for his recall. Avoiding the commanders and anyone who might guess at his identity, he managed to discover what the expedition's sailing dates, meeting-points and main objectives were likely to be, then rode hard to Falmouth, where Sir Roger Williams was waiting. The *Swiftsure* put out to sea on the first tide.

Elizabeth was furious. Her jungle beast had escaped her. She threatened instant death to Sir Roger Williams for his insolence, for his treason. She summoned Essex's grandfather, poor old Sir

Francis Knollys, to her presence and ordered that he set off immediately to bring back his grandson. The ageing invalid had to take to the saddle at once to trace without rest on horseback the several hundred miles the young adventurer had ridden. And the Earl of Huntingdon was despatched a few hours later with yet another batch of instructions. The spring-dampened track from London to Plymouth was dotted with the fugitive, his fresh horses, his returned horses, his pursuers and the various mounts they needed themselves – not to mention the normal royal posts tearing backwards and forwards with furious messages.

Old Sir Francis was no sooner in Plymouth than he embarked on a pinnace into the teeth of a raging gale that tossed his vessel back into the harbour. Next morning he tried again but by then further search was pointless. The young Earl had got away. Elizabeth had been foiled.

But Essex must soon have tired of his war game, for the *Swiftsure* spent more than a month wandering aimlessly at sea until it met up with the main expeditionary force on May 13. The capture of a few merchant ships with corn in their holds was all that enlivened the long wait, and when the *Swiftsure* did eventually sight the English flagship there were stern words and sterner letters waiting for him. All the Queen's frustration was knotted up in a stinging epistle ordering the Earl to return home immediately. And a further letter gave orders for Sir Roger Williams to be clapped instantly into irons and to be brought back to London a prisoner.

This chilling reception was made the more galling by the fact that the main force had already enjoyed lively action. Seven thousand men had landed and taken the port of Corunna, destroying a galleon in the harbour and capturing some guns. Drake was now planning a raid on another port and did not want to be worried by the Essex affair: the simplest thing was to send the carpet knight home. But he could see that the *Swiftsure* might lend valuable firepower to his force. And the wind provided a convenient excuse. So to the Queen he wrote: 'as soon as we met with the Earl of Essex we did our endeavours for his lordship's present return, according as we were required: but the wind being east and northerly ever since his Lordship's being in these parts, we doubted whether we might spare out of the fleet a ship of so good service as the *Swiftsure*.'[4] Essex had his way.

And within a few days he saw the action he had risked so much disfavour to enjoy. On 16 May 1589, some sixty miles north of Lisbon, with the guns of the castle of Peniche booming fiercely and the heavy surf booming louder still, the English army stepped from their longboats on to Spanish soil. One boat was capsized and twenty men drowned, but undeterred Essex 'was the first that landed, who, by reason the billows were so great, waded to the shoulders to come ashore.' Close behind him was Sir Roger Williams, staggering soaked and swearing through the surf. The two men split their forces swiftly, one taking the shore, the other heading through the sand dunes. The garrison came out to do battle, left the town undefended, were outflanked and fled. Within hours the cross of St George was flying over the Portuguese fort. The Earl of Essex had won his spurs.

The expedition's next objective was Lisbon itself further down the coast, and the logical strategy was to re-embark the soldiers, sail south and then make another amphibious assault when they were rested. Yet English soldiers seldom had the opportunity of marching through enemy territory – nor of picking up the plunder a Catholic-Church-strewn route offered. It was decided that the main force under Sir John Norris would cover on foot the sixty miles south to Lisbon.

The march took a week. It was not as hot as summer in Portugal can become, but quite hot enough for the armour-laden soldiers trailing their pikes along the dusty tracks. Essex and the other gentlemen captains rode on horseback, cheerfully indifferent to the loads of weapons and supplies drawn by their men, to which were added plate and jewels whenever a Catholic church was passed – sanctified plunder that carried heavenly as well as earthly dividends.

The one disturbing feature of the advance was the obvious lack of response to all proclamations in the name of Don Antonio. The Portuguese might not like Spanish occupation, but their plundering and heretical English 'saviours' were greeted as a very mixed blessing. Don Antonio's paper claims to the throne received little popular endorsement, and of the 3,000 local men secret emissaries had promised would reinforce the English forces, only forty horse actually showed up. Supplies were also difficult to come by. Foraging parties sent out in search of food and fresh water seemed more interested in uncovering caches of last season's wine vintage, and returned to the main force staggering, happy, but empty-handed. And such local food as was brought in had its traditional effect on pudding-reared English stomachs; local water finished off the survivors.

So the English force that arrived outside the gates of Lisbon on 24 May 1589 was far from being in condition to give the best account of itself. At eleven o'clock that night Essex and Sir Roger Williams sent a few men forward in hope of tempting the garrison to the confusions of a night engagement, but the defenders knew better. And the next night, while the English army's watchmen dozed after their week of marching, some Portuguese infiltrated the invaders' camp and wreaked havoc until the Earl of Essex and his bodyguard drove them back to the town.

The most the besiegers achieved was to burn down the huts and storehouses deserted by Portuguese who had fled inside the city walls. When Drake arrived with the fleet he decided to withdraw the entire expedition to Cascais nearer the sea.

The Earl of Essex was disappointed. It was not for strategic withdrawals that he had risked royal displeasure and run away from Court. He had had too little chance to quench his thirst for martial glory. Appointed commander of the rearguard, he rode alone to the city gates and drove his pike deep into their wood. What Spaniard would dare adventure forth to break a lance in dispute over the honour of his mistress Queen Elizabeth? he challenged. But the garrison 'thought it safer to court their ladies with amorous discourses, then to have their loves written on their breasts with the point of his English spear.'[5] What Francis Drake thought of such Round Table irrelevancies is unrecorded.

He was more interested in a convoy of some sixty ships which had just arrived at Cascais with supplies from the north German

Hanse ports.[6] These Baltic traders had sailed right round the north coast of Scotland to avoid the English Channel privateers that waylaid any ships suspected of trading with Spain. It must have been a cruel surprise to discover their eventual haven surrendered to the enemy.

Their cargoes of corn, copper, wax, masts and cables were hardly the Eldorado gold that had lured so many English ships on the expedition, but they were more fruitful rewards than the army could have garnered sitting outside the walls of Lisbon. The expedition was to return home with some £30,000 worth of officially declared plunder – which probably meant that an equivalent amount went straight into the pockets of the various commanders.

But Essex was to return before the official accounts were taken. With some provisioning ships came a peremptory message from the Queen that omitted the courtesy of a preliminary address:

Essex, your sudden and undutiful departure from our presence and your place of attendance [as Master of the Horse] you may easily conceive how offensive it is, and ought to be, unto us. Our great favours bestowed on you without deserts hath drawn you thus to neglect and forget your duty: for other constructions we cannot make of those your strange actions. . . . We do therefore charge and command you forthwith, upon receipt of these our letters, all excuses and delays set apart, to make your present and immediate repair unto us, to understand our further pleasure. Whereof see you fail not, as you will be loth to incur our indignation and will answer for the contrary at your uttermost peril.

Fierce threats – and with the drums and trumpets part of the expedition clearly over, Essex was not unwilling to comply with Elizabeth's instructions. Her furious letter was already six weeks old – and in another three weeks her joy in finding her favourite restored would wipe out any unpleasant memories.

He left Drake and the other captains to continue their licensed piracy – they were to burn and sack the port of Vigo – and was back in England by the end of June 1589. Elizabeth was delighted to have her young man by her side again – as he had expected.

Once her initial rage had cooled, she was tickled by the childishness of his prank. And her renewed affection was not the only dividend of his escapade. England was entranced to discover so dashing a successor to Sir Philip Sidney, and on the streets appeared a printed broadsheet that soon became a best seller. It was 'An Eclogue Gratulatory', addressed: 'To the right honourable and renowned Shepherd of Albion's Arcadia: Robert Earl of Essex and Ewe, for his welcome into England from Portugal.'[7] It showed the beginnings of a new popular source of power for Essex that was to rival his dependence on the Queen. But whether mass acclaim could ever supplant royal favour remained to be seen. To set people against sovereign was a dangerous game in the sixteenth century.

10

'I will adventure to be rich'

The Earl of Essex was the darling of London. Whenever the Court appeared in public he was cheered and fêted. When he crossed the river to the theatres, the audience singled him out for more applause than the players. His well-known willingness to stand up to the Queen, his duel with Blount, his challenges to Raleigh, these things all appealed to the romantic sense of the people. His dramatic escape from England, his thrusting of his spear into the gates of Lisbon and his bold challenge to the gallants of Spain seemed the few exploits worthy of celebrating in the Portugal voyage. And in an age to which warfare still meant individual feats of chivalry rather than mass co-ordination of logistics and tactics it seemed that the Earl of Essex's achievement had been the only one of military significance. The comparisons with the dead shepherd knight, Philip Sidney, were most flattering. Both warriors, sang the balladeers:

> ... served and watched and waited late,
> To keep the grim wolf from Eliza's gate:
> And for their mistress, thoughten these two swains,
> They moughten never take too mickle pains.[1]

Yet had the doggerel-mongers caught a glimpse of the letters their hero had left behind at his secret departure they would have seen that his motives were little less mercenary than those of his companions. Apart from his childish, but temporarily successful ploy to gain a firm restatement of Elizabeth's affection, the Earl of Essex had gone to Portugal in hope of plunder. He had been living way beyond his means: 'What my state now is, I will tell you,' he had written in a series of scribbled notes left for Sir Francis Knollys, the grandfather who had put his old bones to such great pains in attempting to bring back the truant. 'My revenue [is] no greater than when I sued my livery [i.e. ceased to be a ward]; my debts at the least two or three and twenty thousand pounds; her Majesty's goodness hath been so great as I could not ask more of her; [there is] no way left to repair myself but mine own adventure, which I had much rather undertake than to offend her Majesty with suits, as I have done heretofore. If I should speed well, I will adventure to be rich; if not, I will never live to see the end of my poverty.'[2]

Behind the image of romanticism lurked financial necessity – in military matters as in Essex's dealings with the Queen; £22,000 or £23,000 worth of debts was a substantial sum. Some other nobles owed as much or more, but their debts were usually large sums advanced to them on credit against pledged securities. The Earl of Essex had no securities left to pledge. It was true that he now, in 1590, owed less than his father had owed on his death, but his executors had sold some £10,000 worth of unmortgaged property,[3] and Essex had enjoyed the revenues and patronage at the disposal of the Master of Horse since 1587.[4]

The trouble was that the young Earl was extravagant. His steward, Gelli Meyrick, was later to estimate that Essex had spent some £4,000 on his equipment and retinue in the course of the Low Countries expedition, £3,500 outfitting his tangerine soldiers for the Armada invaders that were never landed, and £7,000 on the Lisbon raid[5] with nothing to show for his investments but popular glory and a handful of freebooting captains he could call followers so long as his return to the battlefield seemed likely.

And then there were all the expenses of life at Court. There were rich pickings for those who gathered close about Elizabeth, but to win money you had to spend it. A proper town house was needed, a regular palace staffed by scores of servants, where one could also house one's clients and retainers.

Essex House was an old bishop's palace on the Strand. Just south of the Aldwych and where St Clement Dane now stands it backed on to the River Thames, where Essex Street and Devereux Court commemorate its situation to this day. There was a great line of these rambling mansions with courtyards, high walls and imposing gateways running between Westminster and the City of London. Before the Reformation the great bishops had owned them. Now they housed the new Lords of Creation, the Earls of Bedford, Southampton, Shrewsbury, Pembroke – and Essex. The new owners spent fortunes renovating them and on keeping up the style of life that went with them. They bought themselves coaches, clumsy contraptions with cartwheels and solid braced suspensions that must have been agony to travel in over potholed roads; but at £200 with trappings and horses they were undeniable tokens of status, and the Earl of Essex was not negligent in keeping up appearances.

There were all the clothes which Elizabeth expected her men to sport in her presence. When Essex's stepfather died, seven of his doublets and two of his cloaks were valued at £543. But Essex could not possibly have worn them, even if he had wished to. Elizabeth had the keenest eye for details like that, revelling in the oblique homage to her femininity that she considered a changing male wardrobe to represent. In 1594, after everyone had fitted themselves out for the agreed season's fashions, she was to order the whole Court to change into short cloaks. And taking up long ones was not permitted. To please the Queen in 1599, Roger Manners, Earl of Rutland, who was to attempt to redeem his failing fortunes in the Essex rebellion, spent £64 just having the Manners peacocks embroidered on his tunic.

Clothing was but one of Essex's heavy expenses. Gambling was Elizabeth's great passion. Lord North found it worth his while to lose £40 every month playing cards with the Queen, and Ben Jonson averred she always wagered on loaded dice.[6] Even the careful penny-pinching Lord Burghley had his portrait painted playing a card game for high stakes.[7] Essex loved games of chance both at Court and in his tent when campaigning. He gambled away long hours with the two young Earls who were to be fellow conspirators in his rising – Rutland and Southampton. There is no evidence that he picked up much of the £1,000 to £1,500 that Rutland wagered away every year, in fact Essex's losses were probably similar. And Southampton was even more reckless: he once lost some £5,000 on a single game of tennis in Paris.[8]

The Court of Queen Elizabeth was not only a market place of conspicuous consumption, it was a battleground in which the weapons were dress, wagers, a town house, a well-equipped retinue, and lavish hospitality. To win royal favour and redeem his initial debts the Earl of Essex had to incur thousands more. To earn dividends, he had to invest. And even if he had been a man of system, he would have found it impossible ever to calculate exactly how the great equation was balancing out for him. Was he up or down on the deal? Although he naturally paid out bribes and accepted gratuities of which no record was kept, his recorded income and expenditure were never entered in a fashion that made profit and loss an easy thing to determine.

The fault lay not in his own clerks and stewards but in the sixteenth century's accounting system – or lack of system. Credit and debit columns were simply non-existent; receipts and payments were just entered haphazardly in the same ledgers. Only a careful reading of each entry made it possible to determine whether the money was coming in or going out – and Essex had as many separate ledgers confused in this fashion as he had manor houses and estates. So he treated as day-to-day income revenue that was really long-term – like the fines his tenants paid him. These fines were lump sums paid to renew a lease at a set rent, but for sixteenth-century accounting purposes they were classed as ordinary revenue, not something that should be spread with the rent over the term of the lease. So when Essex had found himself faced with particular financial embarrassments he had simply charged his tenants higher fines – which meant, of course, granting them longer leases. As a means of mortgaging future income

for immediate cash it was as good as any other, but the accounting system did not show it for what it was. And it was a device
Essex had been resorting to through most of the 1580s, raising
some £5,000 by this means at the expense of his future prosperity.[9]

By 1590 he could mortgage no more. And he could not reasonably ask Elizabeth for further assistance, for she had already been
most generous to him. Apart from his appointment as Master of
Horse she had actually lent him £3,000 cash, and had transferred
to him lands attached to the bishopric of Oxford worth some
£300 a year – which left very little for the poor cleric who took
over the see in 1589: one of the bishop's predecessors had complained that he had but one palace to his name 'and that the
Queen's Majesty hath bestowed,' so Essex must have polished off
the last acres.[10] And in 1588 Elizabeth had given her favourite
another grant worth £300 annually from a clutch of parsonages
which some shady dealings had turned into £965 at the defenceless parsons' expense: judicious profit-splitting in the first year
bought the silence of the officials and auditors concerned.[11]

Essex could not have the impudence, the sheer gall to ask for
more, especially as it had been the expense of fitting out the
Swiftsure for his secret escape to Portugal that had dealt the final
blow to his solvency. But he did not hesitate. He told Elizabeth
that his creditors were pressing him hard and that he needed more
money from her.

Elizabeth did not hesitate either. She replied that he should not
expect another penny out of her until he had repaid the £3,000
her kindness had already lent him. For she knew she had no need
to advance further sums to keep the young Earl in her debt.

And Essex knew he was at her mercy. In 1600 he was to react
in blind fury to the bald statement of his financial dependence on
Elizabeth. Now he did as he was told, and cleverly turned his
submission to his own advantage. He offered to the Queen one of
the few unmortgaged manors he possessed – a fine house and
estate at Keyston in Huntingdonshire. To Lord Burghley he
grumbled: 'This manor is of mine ancient inheritance, free from
incumbrance; a great circuit of ground, in very good soil . . . I
am so far in debt and so weary of owing.'[12] But to Elizabeth he

turned a generous smiling face: 'now that your Majesty repents yourself of the favour you thought to do me, I would I could, with the loss of all the land I have, as well repair the breach which your unkind answer hath made in my heart as I can with the sale of one poor manor answer the sum which your Majesty takes of me.'[13]

The gesture paid off handsomely. For so delighted was Elizabeth with Keyston and more especially with the humility Essex had shown in surrendering it, that she decided to bestow upon him one of the late Earl of Leicester's principal sources of income, the so-called 'Farm of Sweet Wines'. Essex would have the right to levy all duties on the sugary wines imported from the Mediterranean – the profitable and popular Malmseys, Muscadels, Muscadines, Bastards, Romeneys and Vernages from Greece and the island of Candy (Crete). It cost Elizabeth nothing to bestow and it brought a significant and constant income to whoever controlled the 'Farm'. All imported wines carried a duty of two or three shillings a tun. Sweet wines carried a further duty that doubled the levy.[14] The 'Farm' represented a substantial corner of the national tax office, and it was to form the basis of the Essex ascendancy that was to be the enduring feature of Elizabethan politics through the 1590s.

The young Welshman's trip to Court had proved well worth the effort. He had won the means to redeem his father's debts and to build a substantial fortune for himself. He could afford to man his palace by the Strand with the retinue appropriate to his station. He could buy all the clothes and carriages and lay all the bets he wished to. He had the resources to build up a secretariat and a network of agents to lend him political weight. And he could find the cash to equip whole armies as his stepfather before him had done. For the 'Farm of Sweet Wines' represented more than simple revenue. It was excellent security for raising yet larger sums on credit.

There was just one little condition that Essex in his euphoria forgot, and which Elizabeth in her generosity certainly did not. The grant was not eternal. There was a ten-year term on it. The Earl could revel in his prosperity all through the 1590s. He could go to war, sit in state, or raise more credit. But on Michaelmas Day 1600 it would all revert to the Faerie Queen. What she gave she could also take away. Lord Essex would have once more to kneel humbly before his Elizabeth.

11

First Command

It was characteristic of Robert Devereux that even as he was fighting for the triumph of his Sweet Wines grant, he should be pushing his good fortune to the limit in other directions. The financial necessity that had forced him to beg the Queen for money had underlined his ultimate dependence upon Elizabeth; but despite that, or perhaps, perversely, because of that, he now proceeded to test her response still further. He got involved in the most dangerous game of all – marriage without the Queen's knowledge or consent.

The Earl of Essex was a handsome man. Now, in 1590, fully grown, he was tall, broad and muscular, with a flaming red beard and piercing eyes. He had the looks to match his impetuous temper and insistent romanticism. And the Queen was far from being the only attractive woman at Court, much though she might wish to think so. There was a whole bevy of beauty a handsome young man could choose from. Apart from wives of the courtiers whose time and energies were consumed by attendance on their royal mistress, there were the ladies-in-waiting, for whom attendance on the Queen could fulfil the same function as dancing in a twentieth-century chorus line. With looks, luck and skilful surrender a maiden could catch herself a title and guarantee herself comfort for the rest of her days.

It would have been surprising if a man so eligible, and

attractive, as the Earl of Essex had not been a prime target of fe-male attention, despite the dangers that any woman attached to one of the Queen's favourites ran. And that the Earl himself was only too ready for venereal dalliance would have seemed likely, even without the rumours of a bastard son and his later attempts to cure himself of syphilis. He was whispered at Court to be habi-tually 'grateful to ladies'[1] – though only whispered. What Essex might do to anyone retailing such rumours was nothing to the reception that sort of gossip would get from Elizabeth.

So when the Earl of Essex went to woo he wooed secretly, and the Court kept his secret for the sake of a quiet life. Yet his choice of lady love was strange – or rather displayed the enthusiastic but erratic logic that inspired the rest of his actions. Having inherited Sir Philip Sidney's sword after the Netherlands expedition, and having been hailed as the successor to the Protestant hero's mantle, Robert Devereux, after the Lisbon raid, paid court to the shep-herd knight's widow, Frances; it was a chivalrous, charmingly medieval conceit fancifully linked to the Old Testament tradition of brothers caring for each other's widows. And what were Sidney and Essex if not brothers-in-arms? Yet there seemed no other good reason for such a match. The lady was not wealthy, for her first husband had left her little but debts, and her father, Sir Francis Walsingham, was very near his end. As a power in high places such a father-in-law was a spent force, and when he died his body was secretly buried at midnight in St Paul's for fear that his creditors should seize it.

So did the Earl of Essex marry for love? If he did, it was an emotion as fleeting as his other enthusiasms, for he was soon to be as conspicuously unfaithful to his Frances as Sir Philip Sidney had been, and he showed no evidence even of the redeeming low-key affection with which the most dissolute of husbands depend on a steady if slighted life-mate. After his trial in 1601 he expressed no farewell to his wife, formal or informal. Though she bore him five children Frances remained in her husband's life, letters and in Elizabethan history generally a 'gracious silence', never cited in anger or affection – placid, faithful and neutral, so colourless as to be strangely significant. For never once in his life did Robert

Devereux manage to construct a relationship that could fairly be described as personal or lasting. All collapsed in the mistrust and misunderstanding that attended his later breach with Elizabeth. Campfire comrades he might have, and useful contacts too, but there was nothing else deeper than briefly intense enthusiasms. And so the most probable explanation of his secret marriage in the spring of 1590 to Frances Sidney (née Walsingham) was just impulse or a wish to find a woman as unlike his demanding, unavoidable mother as possible. Or, of course, that having seduced the widow of a comrade-in-arms the Earl of Essex felt impelled by his antiquarian code of honour finally to play the gentleman.

His marriage must have eased his conscience through the summer of 1590 as Frances' belly swelled. Yet honour's solution to her obviously pregnant plight raised political problems of frightening size. For in concealing the date and place of his marriage from the Queen – as well as from posterity – Essex was sailing dangerously close to the wind. He had seen a decade earlier what fury and disfavour his mother's clandestine marriage to Leicester had provoked. And Elizabeth was not entirely ignorant of Essex's other amatory adventures. To compound those injuries with this final insult was expecting more of providence than one man had a right to hope for.

The Queen stamped and raged and roared when she heard of Essex's marriage. Yet by her own standards her fury was curiously shortlived. After a fortnight of petulance she welcomed the Earl of Essex to her side again, and even went so far as to acknowledge his new wife – a concession Leicester had never wrung from his sovereign. But then Frances, Essex's new spouse, was a very different character from Lettice his mother; and he was only twenty-three, still a boy compared to Leicester when he had slighted his Queen. Whereas marriage between Elizabeth and Leicester had been a possibility worth discussing, the flirtation between Elizabeth and Essex was always acknowledged as just that – flirtation. Its *raison d'être* lay in the escape from reality it granted the Queen; and Essex's domestic arrangements were really irrelevant to the main object of the exercise. Besides, at the end of 1590 the Queen had other things to worry about.

For nearly half a century France had been torn apart by sporadic but savage disorders which the contestants ennobled with the title of 'Religious Wars'. And by the beginning of the 1590s the struggle had resolved itself into a battle between on one side the politically legitimate but religiously unacceptable Protestant, Henri IV, who could call on the wealth and Puritanical determination of the French nonconformists (or *Huguenots*); and on the other the noble Guise family backed by the forces of the Roman Catholic league with valuable subsidies and reinforcements from Spain. Like the anti-Spanish, anti-Popish war in the Netherlands the struggle for survival of Henri IV stirred Protestant valour in English breasts; valour Elizabeth ignored as profitless pugnacity – until in October 1590 an army of Spaniards landed in northwestern France, while the Duke of Parma invaded with another force from the Low Countries.

Elizabeth had no special love for the King of France and certainly no wish to get involved in his domestic affairs, but she had to admit that if this two-pronged Spanish attack snuffed him out it would mean a Catholic France through which Spanish reinforcements could pass unimpeded to the Netherlands – and perhaps produce an entirely Spanish mainland of Europe within a few years. Even if the advance were only to prove temporary it would still give Spain control of the northern French ports just a few dozen miles from the south coast English beaches. Since Drake's Lisbon raid had so singularly failed to tackle such serious Spanish naval strength as had survived the 1588 débâcle, another Armada from immeasurably more practical bases was a distinct possibility. Could England rely on the weather for salvation a second time?

Elizabeth reluctantly decided not. And she saw advantage as well as salvation in sending an English force to France. Just as the Dutch had surrendered 'cautionary towns' to their English allies in return for their help, allowing English troops under an English governor to garrison Brill and Flushing, so the French might be persuaded similarly to hand over Calais, with perhaps other remnants of the old English transmarine empire like le Havre and Rouen. Calais had, after all, been English till 1558.

Through the winter of 1590 and into 1591, as the new Lady Essex grew ever larger eventually to give birth to a son, another Robert who was to become the 3rd Earl, Elizabeth haggled with the French representatives sent across the Channel by Henri IV. They proved as crafty as their master – and craftier than the old woman they had to deal with, for early in 1591 Elizabeth sent to France 600 men under Sir Roger Williams, a 3,000-strong expeditionary force under Sir John Norris, and agreed to send another army later in the same year – without any definite promise of 'cautionary' territory in exchange. The Duke of Turenne, Henri's emissary, had kept Elizabeth very neatly dangling on his master's bait. And in the course of his negotiations he had also cast an appraising eye over the rest of the English Court. Of the Earl of Essex, wild to command an army in France, he wrote: 'the difficult thing is to restrain him, not to push him forward.'[2]

He mistrusted Essex's rashness – of which he had ample evidence. Despite the risk of disfavour which his secret romance, seduction and marriage had run, the young Earl had begun sulking and ostentatiously remained away from Court when Elizabeth declined his suggestions that he should lead the English army to France. Three times the Queen refused him the position, on one occasion after he had spent two hours begging and pleading on his knees before her. Her feminine revenge dragged on through April and May until in June 1591 she abruptly agreed to let Essex take another English force to help Henri IV.

It was his first command – and his enthusiasm was usefully channelled as he prepared for it. He wrote to the steward of his Chartley Estates, Richard Bagot, asking to tell 'my friends in all places, if you know any or can stir up any, that will send either tall men well horsed or good horses or geldings, they shall be very welcome to me.' And he had his secretary write to Bagot with sterner instructions to all the Essex tenants: 'they are bound by their leases, some to furnish a horseman, and most a footman [foot soldier] . . . the tenants in this necessity of service are to make no excuses: if they do, their leases are void, and my Lord is not to use any friendship afterwards to those that will not do their duty in furnishing him in this service, and they that will refuse, my lord will use the extremity of the forfeiture.'

Soldiers compelled by the threat of eviction can have had little enthusiasm for battle in a foreign land – despite the £14,000 the Earl of Essex spent equipping and dressing them in his tangerine and white liveries.[3] The Queen expressed grudging appreciation of their turnout when she inspected them in mid-July at a parade in Covent Garden, yet in her instructions to Sir Henry Unton, the newly appointed English ambassador to Henri IV, she showed how little she was deceived by such appearances. Sir Henry was to keep an especially close eye on the actions of the Earl of Essex – and the royal commission to the Earl laid down the guidelines to those actions.

The commission stressed how ill Elizabeth could afford to send 4,000 more soldiers to join the 3,000 already in France, and that the Earl should sign the agreed terms of alliance with the French ambassador before moving his troops from Dieppe. He was not to commit English troops to action until the French King had promised to fulfil his side of the bargain. And a special clause was added instructing Essex only to bestow knighthoods for valour in battle after careful consideration: titles were not to be debased by casual distribution.

In August 1591 the Earl of Essex landed with his army at Dieppe, to discover that he was completely cut off from his French allies. His orders were not to leave his port of disembarkation until the French King had agreed to the terms of his treaty with Elizabeth; but Essex was separated from Henri IV by one hundred miles of enemy-held territory. Henri was dragging his feet over the siege of Rouen – the ostensible purpose for which the English reinforcements had been sent, for in Catholic hands this town on the River Seine could turn the ports around le Havre into Spanish bases. The King was even declining to promise the payments his ambassadors had hinted at. Three messages from the Earl of Essex received no acknowledgement, until, in the middle of August, Sir Roger Williams rode into the Dieppe camp. He was commanding the English troops that had been with Henri since earlier in the year and, as a professional soldier who had spent most of his career commanding English reinforcements to cautious continentals, he took his allies' reluctance to fight philosophically. The French King had sent him with an invitation for Essex to travel to talks at Compiègne, a hundred miles from Dieppe and the same distance from Rouen. It was hardly the instant action the young Earl had hoped for, but he had no choice – as Roger Williams made clear.

And a hundred-mile sally across enemy territory had attractions of its own for the young Earl who had tasted all too little danger and excitement in the Netherlands. Roving somewhere between the English and King Henri was a force of 2,500 infantry and cavalry commanded by Villars, the Catholic League's governor of Rouen, who had good reason to keep his separated besiegers apart. Until they settled around the walls of his fort he would take full advantage of the open country they left him to harass their routes of communication.

So a sharp dash was called for on Essex's part. Yet he had no wish to ride into Henri's camp without an impressive train of attendants. Nor should they be dressed in soiled travel clothes. So one hundred horsemen were trimmed in the best Devereux tangerine and jogged off proudly across the unguarded fields between Dieppe and Compiègne. The outward journey, at least, was uneventful, and the Earl of Essex's entrée into the muddy camp of Henri's battle-stained army achieved the appropriate effect.

'As to the person of the said Earl of Essex and those of his suite,' wrote one observer, 'nothing more magnificent could possibly be seen: for at his entry into Compiègne he had before him six pages mounted on chargers and dressed in orange velvet all embroidered with gold. And he himself had a military cloak of orange velvet covered all with jewels. His saddle, bridle and the rest of his horse's harness were in like sort. His dress and the furniture on his horse alone were worth sixty thousand crowns. He had twelve tall body-squires and six trumpets sounding before him.'[4]

Whether the cynical Henri IV took an orange velvet saddle and bridle quite as seriously as his young English guest intended is doubtful. But he welcomed Essex warmly and showed every appearance of being eager to reach the agreement that was the precondition to battle. He took Essex straight to his tent for two hours of discussions, then wined and dined his fresh allies as lavishly as his battle supplies would allow.

Then after a day or so of such hospitality and apparent straight talking Henri summoned 300 gentlemen, bade Essex farewell, and rode off eastwards, even further away from Rouen than before. English troops had once again become the pawns of Continental strategy, for Henri knew that with Essex's army at Dieppe, Villars' Catholic forces would not dare to stray far from Rouen. So with one ally, however reluctantly, pinning down one major segment of the enemy, Henri knew he was free to ride off towards Germany and negotiate for still more assistance.

Essex was outflanked – and stranded. For Villars, having heard of the Earl's journey to meet Henri, had put out heavy patrols to stop the English getting back. The tangerine troupe had to take a circuitous and hard-riding route to regain their companions; several soldiers were lost on the return lap of a mission that had achieved less than nothing. For after a month lying idle in the marshes round Dieppe the English army was succumbing to malaria and dysentery. Three thousand men concentrated in one spot through the heat of August were too much for the sanitary and medical facilities of the sixteenth century. And the Earl of Essex's jaunt had given them no hope they might see action, or even fresh countryside.

From England came despatches overflowing with royal choler. Elizabeth had travelled down to Portsmouth, hoping Essex would persuade Henri IV to sail over the Channel for a brief meeting. She had waited for days – to be told that Essex had taken his cavalry on a mad dash across enemy territory while Henri had gone marching off towards Germany. Essex's protestations that he had received no news of her journey to Portsmouth, let alone her reason for it, were discounted in advance.

Then Essex himself collapsed with the fever that was afflicting so many of his troops. And while prostrate on a litter he suffered a personal tragedy that wiped from his mind all his political problems. He had persuaded his younger brother Walter to join him on the expedition to France. On 8 September 1591, Walter was leading 1,200 foot-soldiers and a detachment of cavalry towards Rouen to make a token sally in front of the walls when he fell into a French ambush. In sight of his objective, he was struck through the cheek by a sniper's bullet that pierced up through his skull to kill him within minutes. With difficulty the captains rescued his body and bore it back to his brother.

Already weak, Robert was paralysed by the news of Walter's death. He blamed himself bitterly for it and remained crying in his tent from sorrow and fever, his back wracked by an ague he had caught from the lowland damps. The most furious despatches from the Queen were ignored. Sir Henry Unton, the English ambassador to France, wrote back to the Privy Council that the Earl of Essex was the most 'perplexed and afflicted' man he ever did know. He doubted if he would recover unless the Queen could be persuaded to send some sign of favour that might mitigate her former wrath.

She sent nothing of the sort. Instead on 24 September 1591 she had published 'A Declaration of the Causes that move her Majesty to revoke her Forces in Normandy,' and she informed Essex that ships were coming to bring him back to England. The English army had in two months been systematically exploited and deceived by Henri IV – and Elizabeth would have no more of it. The Earl of Essex's commission was at an end. His troops could come home.

Elizabeth decided to recall her commander at the very moment that Henri's army, left under the command of Marshal Biron, finally started taking definite action. With some 12,000 men Biron marched towards Rouen, pausing only to besiege the fort at Gournay that blocked his advance and would, had he left it occupied by the enemy, have threatened his communications with Henri. It was contrary to Elizabeth's commission, but Essex took the English troops to join the siege, and on 27 September 1591 Gournay fell.

Still unaware of Elizabeth's decision to recall him, he kept up a constant battery of fearful complaints to his mistress: 'I wish to be out of my prison, which I account my life:' 'I live still to curse my birthday and to long for my grave. I have been sick all day and yet write at night till my dim eyes and weak hand do fail me:' 'Unkindness and sorrow have broken both my heart and my wits.'[5] Long rambling paragraphs justified his jaunt to Compiègne – which, in all honesty, he could hardly have avoided. For Elizabeth had been content to send an army abroad before final agreement with the French was reached, and Essex had only been attempting to patch up the work she had left incomplete. His style was open to criticism – but his style was Essex. Flamboyance was the medium of all his actions, as he demonstrated when the news of his recall reached him.

The next morning, 8 October 1591, he mounted his horse and rode up a hill overlooking the city of Rouen. He sat dramatically sunk in thought in his saddle, then turned and rode back down to his army waiting in a final parade. He called his officers around him and made a short emotional speech. Then he, the Earl of Essex, at the tender age of twenty-three, with a few short months of command and not a single major battle or victory to his credit, drew his sword from its sheath and proceeded to knight twenty-four of his officers, bestowing as many new titles in a couple of minutes as the Queen normally awarded in a couple of years. His temerity was breathtaking. Elizabeth, firmly of the opinion there were too many of her subjects swaggering around with titles, had allowed the number of Knights in England to fall from around 600 in 1558 to half that number by 1580.[6] She had been infuriated by the quantities of knighthoods handed out by the Earl of Leicester in the Netherlands in 1587. And she had added a special rider to Essex's French orders that he was only to award titles for valour in battle after the most careful consideration. How would she react to this quite deliberate flouting of her instructions and debasement of the royal prerogative?

Essex found out the moment he arrived back in London. Elizabeth's reception was icy. Her first words were not of welcome but of criticism. She sneered, she complained and when she did not rebuke she ridiculed. The young Earl was hurt. He retired sulking to Essex House and sent a little note of protest: 'I see your

Majesty is constant to ruin me . . . I appeal to all men that saw my parting from France, or the manner of my coming hither, whether I deserved such a welcome or not.'[7] He was seized by the black melancholia that overpowered him at all the difficult stages of his life – as irrational enthusiasm would sweep him away in the good times. After the glorious euphoria of his battlefield knightings, Essex saw his career ended, and ended in disaster and dishonour.

Elizabeth had got what she wanted. Her favourite had begged for the French assignment to make up for his past mistakes and his secret marriage. She had made his foreign expedition a true purgatory. And having proved her point, she promptly sent him back. On 18 October 1591 the Earl of Essex was in Dieppe again with instructions to behave like a general and not some 'soldier or executioner' – a reference to the behind-the-lines dash to Compiègne and the report of how 'you did hazard yourself at Gournay by trailing of a pike, to approach the place like a common soldier, a thing not commendable in you.'[8]

But Essex arrived back in Dieppe to discover that he scarcely possessed an army he could act as general over. There were only 2,000 fit soldiers surviving from the 4,000 who had landed in early August. 'There are divers of our soldiers run away,' wrote Essex to the Privy Council; 'and many of our gentlemen, which were voluntaries, have had passport to go to England.' The gentlemen could be persuaded to return, but 'the soldiers are of the basest sort and cannot be called back, for they disperse themselves everywhere upon all highways: and if they return they will do us more harm than good.'[9] He asked the Privy Council for reinforcements once the siege of Rouen began, but admitted he could hardly expect further help until then.

And by the same post he sent to Elizabeth a letter whose sudden beautiful effusion reveals how this strange, flawed personality could exert an attraction and promise his actions never quite lived up to:

. . . the two windows of your privy chamber shall be the poles of my sphere, where, as long as your Majesty will please to have me, I am fixed and unmoveable. When your Majesty thinks that heaven too good for me, I will not fall like a star, but be consumed like a vapour by the same sun that drew me up to such a height. While your Majesty gives me leave to say I love you, my fortune is as my affection, unmatchable. If ever you deny me that liberty, you may end my life, but never shake my constancy, for were the sweetness of your nature turned into the greatest bitterness that could be, it is not in your power, as great a Queen as you are, to make me love you less.[10]

Yet Elizabeth was less concerned with her favourite's fine words than with the state of his troops – and Henri IV's persistent failure to exert himself as she wished. By the beginning of November Essex's letters were confessing 'we are not 1000, yet we bear the name of 4000', and when he sent Sir Roger Williams to London to ask for reinforcements none of the Privy Council were 'willing to move Her Majesty to choler' over the matter.

Rouen was finally besieged, but the French participation was half-hearted. It was the English army that bore the brunt of the work. Enemy detachments would sally out from the fort, harass a particular position for an hour or so, then withdraw behind the safety of their walls. In all these engagements Essex's men came off best, killing three commanders and several dozen foot soldiers and cavalrymen in a skirmish one afternoon in early November. The enemy sallies became less frequent. Elizabeth wrote to her Earl congratulating him on the valour of his troops and promising to send more – but concluded her letter with a paragraph that must have struck him dumb. Having finally displayed his courage and vindicated his honour he could now in all conscience come home again; it was beneath the dignity of an Earl and general to skirmish around a provincial French town with a handful of troops. And it was beneath the dignity of the Queen of England to commit one of her foremost servants to so menial a task if the King of France would not deign to assist in the enterprise in person.

So for the second time Essex went home. Yet no sooner was he in London than news came that the Duke of Parma was moving Spanish troops from the Netherlands towards Rouen. So the Earl retraced his steps yet again, only to find that the recipe was very much the same as before. Parma got bogged down by the hard winter going in the Somme, and the sudden French decisiveness crumbled. The 600 reinforcements sent from the seasoned

English troops in the Netherlands did most of the real siege work. The French army was obviously saving its strength. Henri IV wrote to Elizabeth that he saw no prospect of paying her for her help. Disease ate away at the English strength: Essex evacuated the sick to try and stop the infection spreading – but to little avail: 'I have sent away with passport as many as were able to creep towards Dieppe on their feet; the others I cannot send for I have no carriage.'[11]

By late December it was obvious there would be no real action until the spring or summer of 1592, and Essex decided to return home for good. If sickness continued to spread he would have no troops left to command. But before his departure he could not resist a final flourish, a gesture similar to the one he had made in Portugal. He sent a personal challenge to Villars, the governor of Rouen: 'If you wish to engage in personal combat, on foot or horse, I will maintain that the cause of King Henri is more just than that of your League, and that my mistress is more beautiful than yours!'

The chivalry was futile – as Villars gently pointed out in declining the challenge on the grounds of his responsibility as governor. And, as the Queen said, it was according a rebel too much status.

Yet Essex felt, as he handed over command to Sir Roger Williams on the 8 January 1592, that he had done his utmost. He had for the first time taken charge of an English army in the field. He had dubbed twenty-four knights despite Elizabeth's disapproval. He had negotiated with another sovereign as his Queen's representative. He had seen some action, and though he had won no notable victories, the north coast of France remained in friendly, Protestant hands. He had done his best and could fairly hope for a greater share of the glory next time. In anticipation of that, as he embarked on his ship for England, he drew his sword dramatically from its sheath and kissed the blade with passion.

12

New Directions, New Friends

The Earl of Essex's return from France at the beginning of 1592 marked a turning point. He was now twenty-four. Until his marriage to Frances Sidney and the birth of their son he had been one of the many scarce-bearded youths that paid suit to Elizabeth: an exceptionally favoured and pampered youth who stood out from his fellows, but a youth just the same. And until he was appointed to command the expedition to France his military status was equally that of an immature and insubstantial *primus inter pares*.

He had achieved little in France to give any reason for altering that judgement, but, just the same, he returned from the abortive siege of Rouen to take up a new place in the constellation of stars that shone around Gloriana. For the nine years until his death he was to wear the military mantle of Leicester, as the Queen's *de facto* chief of staff; whenever foreign warfare was in question it was the Earl of Essex who led the British contingent.

His practical ineptitude might be matched only by the lack of experience that had first qualified him for the job – but he kept the job. The Queen could not pick her servants with her old skill: the range of reliable talent open to her to choose from narrowed with the death of each old companion: and the Earl of Essex had also taken on, after the Rouen trip, a new political role which enabled him to beat off contenders for his scarce-justified military pre-eminence.

For Robert Devereux aspired not only to be a courtier and a warrior but a statesman; and 1592 was the year in which he began building the power base that was to give him nominees in Parliament, a seat on the Privy Council and, eventually, as Lord Lieutenant of Ireland, viceregal powers over one of Her Majesty's dominions. That this final appointment did not lead on to a place as Elizabeth's closest and most powerful adviser, deciding the fate of the kingdom during her lifetime, and who should succeed her after her death, was due to the weaknesses inherent in Essex's own personal makeup.

Yet for all his faults he was an attractive man. Elizabeth's shortcomings were those of age – and they were getting worse. But Essex's failings were the failings of youth, and through most of the 1590s it seemed reasonable to presume that they would vanish with maturity. He had other, such compelling qualities that could prove worthwhile assets if they were allowed to develop. His presence was magnetic. People were drawn to his magnificence and took on themselves some of his warm impulsiveness – despite their more rational judgement. His way with the ladies of the Court was as legendary as the sway he held over their Queen. Somewhat careless of his appearance, a somewhat awkward dancer whose tall frame stooped with his head thrust forward as he moved, silent and contemplative at mealtimes, his behaviour hinted at poetic depths which slicker courtiers lacked. His long brooding sulks, which in later years were to infuriate Elizabeth beyond recall, fitted exactly into the fashionable conventions of pastoral melancholia. His furrowed brow and furious eyes could exert a Byronic attraction. And when he smiled his beauty was irresistible.

He was a thoroughbred: tall and aristocratic, with a schooled charm that set off the proud shortcomings that thoroughbreds are heir to. To be in his company was to be exhilarated with his enthusiasm – or his temper. He aimed high – and made no secret of it. His ambitions embraced war, peace, poetry, wealth, men, women – and his Queen. His genius was the more overwhelming for being so unpredictable. He was a prodigy, a gilded child of the Gods who, while he remained a child, was judged with the affectionate indulgence his better qualities deserved. In a caste-constructed society whose leaders were automatically selected from a limited and pre-determined élite Essex stood out as the man of the future.

Yet he could not remain eternally the youth whose promise would flower tomorrow. And at the age of twenty-four, on his return from France, Robert Devereux evidently realized this. For in the course of the next two years he set about constructing the machine of advisers, assistants and contacts necessary for advancement – and survival – in the upper zones of Elizabethan politics. The Queen's favour could raise up to the heights: yet so long as a favourite's wealth and power depended exclusively on his personal ties with Elizabeth he could be cast down by the same whim that elevated him. She was a capricious woman – but she had a shrewd eye for servants useful to her; and if a favourite could prove himself not only attractive but well-informed and reasonably industrious he could work towards a more solid relationship with his sovereign as a councillor. This is what Robert Devereux proceeded to do in the spring of 1592 – and by good fortune he lighted upon two companions uniquely suited to advise and assist him in his quest – the Bacon brothers, Anthony and Francis.

Francis is the famous one: his 'Essays' were to establish new norms for modern English prose; and though he cannot have been the author of the Shakespeare plays some enthusiasts would credit him with, his work has probably had more influence on everyday writing than has that of his more illustrious literary contemporary. As one of James VI's closest advisers and Lord Chancellor he was to rise to the heights of power and wealth that his early protector, the Earl of Essex, dreamed of but destroyed himself in attempting to achieve. But Francis Bacon was schooled in tough circumstances.

The youngest of eight children, Francis was a quiet, withdrawn individual. In 1578, when he was eighteen years old, his portrait had been painted by Nicholas Hilliard who, having traced the boy's shy, delicate features, left the motto: 'si tabula daretur digna, animum mallem' – 'if one could but paint his mind'. At that age Francis had already passed through the same Cambridge college where Essex was studying and had been to France as an attendant on Sir Amyas Paulet, the English ambassador. The death of his father, Sir Nicholas Bacon, compelled him to cut short that service and he returned to England with a note from the ambassador commending him as one who 'would prove a very able and sufficient subject to do her Highness good and acceptable service.'[1] Referring to Bacon's sickliness the note added the proviso 'if God give him life' – and through the next dozen years as he struggled for economic survival Francis was frequently ill. He chose the law as his profession and painfully established himself as a member of Gray's Inn. In an attempt to win Court attention he circulated a tendentious diatribe – *Observation Upon a Libel* – which defended with excessive length and vehemence the policy of the Queen and Privy Council against a Catholic pamphlet that had appeared blaming the Spanish War on English belligerence. And he composed elaborate eulogies to Gloriana for masquers at Gray's Inn to recite at their Christmas revels. Judicious bribes and flattery had bought him the seat for Melcombe in Dorset for the 1584 Parliament, and in 1586 he represented Taunton. He was a member of one of the committees set to work out the details of a special financial 'benevolence' to help the Queen through the height of the crisis with Spain, and in 1589 he sat on another committee that drew up provisions for a special double subsidy to meet the cost of reorganizing national defences against the possibility of a second Armada. A discreet homosexual, he had no intimate friends save the beautiful boys he seldom kept long, but he everywhere earned respect for his painstaking work and attention to detail. It was a precise reflection of Elizabethan society that in 1592, after over a dozen years of hard work and closely applied intelligence, Francis Bacon's greatest good fortune was to become the hired retainer of an Earl infinitely his inferior in wit and nine years his junior but whom inheritance, good looks, a stepfather and three undistinguished military escapades had made one of the greatest in the land.

And it was the young Earl's good fortune on returning from France to meet not only Francis Bacon but his yet more intelligent and certainly more loyal elder brother, Anthony. Anthony had been at Trinity with Francis in 1573 and had also gone abroad to learn the intricacies of the diplomatic service. But when their father died in 1579 Anthony had opted to stay on the Continent. The two brothers had been entrusted by old Sir Nicholas to the care of the great Lord Burghley whose wife Mildred was their aunt – a sister of their mother's. Yet Burghley greeted all Anthony's requests for help with 'fair words, with no show of real kindness'.[2] So while Francis had to fight for a living at Gray's Inn, Anthony roamed the courts of Europe as a freelance spy cum scholar. He sent back intelligence reports on diplomatic developments to Sir Francis Walsingham in London, and picked up extra money as a secretary and adviser who could command a variety of languages and an ever-widening circle of contacts.

Though troubled by weak eyes, gout and the stone he lived on his wits, and when to the joy of Francis and his mother he decided to return to England early in 1592, he was an accomplished and valuable asset to any courtier with serious political ambitions. How Essex and the Bacon brothers came together at this critical juncture in all their careers is uncertain. Francis and Essex had probably met before. And the whole trio had connections with Lord Burghley which the old man had at various times gently but firmly declined to turn into obligations: two penniless title-less and somewhat over-intelligent brothers had little to offer a man endowed with all the intelligence he needed: and the Earl of Essex had been tied too obviously to the Leicester bandwagon to expect success from his attempts to chum up with Lord Burghley's faction. Besides, Burghley had his own son Robert whom he was grooming for future office.

So in the spring of 1592 Essex and the Bacon brothers found themselves outside the citadel of real political power: but possessing between them the intelligence, the industry, the contacts, the wealth and the pedigree they needed to force an entry. The story of the next six years is the story of how between them they did just that and carved out for themselves a position of potentially overwhelming might: and the story of the three years following – which ended with that private execution in the Tower of London – is the story of how the Earl of Essex threw away all that the three of them had so skilfully achieved.

But in 1592 the disaster was nine years distant. The world was young Robert Devereux's oyster which he had with sword begun to open; and which the Bacons now taught him to exploit with more subtle methods. Anthony Bacon set about gathering intelligence from his European contacts. One was a mysterious Catholic named Anthony Standen, who had been chased out of England to Spain but took advantage of his position as a religious refugee to gather information which he sold back to England. He cast his net wide; he sent lists of the Catholic Irish aristocrats who had visited the Spanish Court with plans to expel the English troops that occupied Ireland; he described the strengths of garrisons in the Spanish coastal provinces and the numbers of warships defending harbours like San Sebastian; he passed on rumours of an invasion to be launched by Spain on Guernsey and Jersey; he posted comforting details of the poor relations between Spain and Turkey and the discontent that war taxes aroused among the ordinary Spanish people: he helped trace the movements of those Englishmen in exile who were Catholics willing to lend themselves to schemes against Elizabeth; he kept his ear to intrigues in the Spanish Court which might betoken new changes of policy; with a hint of special pleading, he suggested there was reason to believe that a relaxing of the anti-Catholic laws in England might incline Philip to act more leniently towards heretics in his own domains; he charted carefully the journeys of diplomats from both sides involved in the French Civil War: the Catholic League was obviously committed to Spain, but there seemed signs as well that Henri IV was willing to betray his Protestant subjects and allies; and the health of King Philip himself was watched and reported upon with the greatest care: the ageing king was compelled to lock his eldest son, Don Carlos, in a lunatic asylum: a disputed succession would play right into English hands.[3]

Some of the information was known already; some of it was out of date. But as Essex was able through 1592 to present reports of this nature to the Queen, so his stock rose. He became quite a plausible alternative Foreign Secretary, corresponding with ambassadors and establishing relationships with English envoys abroad like Thomas Bodley, who grew closer to him than to the

Cecils. Sometimes he tried too hard. He spent £300 sending a Mr Edmonds on an abortive trip to Lyons and spent a further 600 crowns trying to gather the information the journey had failed to locate.[4] The Privy Council's own agents never had such princely sums at their disposal. So when an agent let Anthony Bacon down, Essex ran the risk of royal sarcasm which Burghley, his nose put somewhat out of joint by the success of the Bacon brothers he had once disdained, was only too happy to pass on: 'Her Majesty would have me let you know that she liketh well of your advertisements,' said Burghley to Essex when a report from Spain arrived late, 'if they might come in season: adding thereto that an apple in time were better than an apple of gold out of time.'[5] He also expressed disapproval of Anthony Bacon's willingness to employ Catholic agents.

Yet Elizabeth had no reservations on that score. By the age of twenty-six she had lived through five officially endorsed and inflexibly opposed versions of the Christian religion and was cheerfully cynical towards all of them. If Essex could deliver the goods on time and at his own expense she inquired not too deeply into the methods and men he employed. And just when this decorative but hitherto useless courtier was demonstrating a new seriousness and utility, another of her Court's chief ornaments ruled himself out of the race for undisputed favour.

Sir Walter Raleigh was unfaithful. Not as Essex had been unfaithful, marrying with youthful enthusiasm a noble, if penniless, widow. But by seducing, at the mature age of forty and in full possession of his senses, the eldest and most ugly of Elizabeth's maids of honour – Bess Throgmorton. To marry, after a dozen years of courtly loyalty, his mistress's attendant seemed a calculated insult. And Elizabeth certainly took it as such. She had the new husband and wife clapped instantly behind bars in the Tower of London – in separate cells. Essex must have breathed deeply to think how close he had been to a similar fate, and to see one rival to his eminence so neatly cast aside.

For Raleigh had disgraced himself in more than one respect. Convinced poor organization was to blame for the failure of the Portugal raid of 1589 he had pulled together another privateering band to plunder Spanish convoys in the summer of 1592. The honest avowal of a profit motive ensured, at least, that there would not be the confusion of aims which had bedevilled Drake's riposte to the Armada, but Raleigh had little naval experience. His posthumous reputation as a seaman seems to have been founded largely on a Victorian painting of his fictionalized boyhood. Unlisted on the rolls of 'gentlemen and captains of the sea' who had served on naval expeditions, omitted from the marine activities against the Armada in 1588 and Portugal in 1589, he owed his right to organize the 1592 sortie to his 'bold and plausible tongue'.[6]

Restrained from sailing with his ships by Elizabeth, who had caught hints of his romance with Elizabeth Throgmorton, Raleigh had to yield command to Martin Frobisher and William Burrough. And they captured off the Azores the *Madre de Dios*, a treasure-laden carrack worth about a third of a million pounds, well in excess of Elizabeth's total annual income. But Raleigh's captains immediately set about rifling the galleon of her most precious possessions – and when Raleigh was briefly released from prison to secure for the Queen her rightful share he discovered that his much-vaunted organization had collapsed and that a shameless free-for-all had developed. Sailors staggered drunk through the harbours of the West Country dropping jewels like pennies from their pockets and dripping with perfumes, silks and precious calicoes. Robert Cecil, who was sent down to Exeter to recover the spoils, found he could pick up the looters by their smell of ambergris and musk. One sailor alone had '320 sparks of diamond, a collar of a threefold roll of pearl with six tags of crystal garnished with gold, a small round pearl garnished with gold, two chains of twofold pearl with buttons of gold and two small jewels hanging unto the ends thereof, also three silver hafts for knives and a silver fork.'[7]

That particular pocketful was recovered, but others were not, and the total haul valued in London amounted to only £141,200: a fair sum, but far short of the original capture. The Queen took for herself the lion's share, but made sure Raleigh got less than six per cent return on his original investment. And then he was sent back to prison.

It left the field free for Essex and his new advisers. Their main obstacles were now Lord Burghley and his younger son, Robert, whom the old man was most obviously grooming to be his successor. And the Cecils were in many ways more formidable opponents for Elizabeth's favour in possessing none of the conventional courtly attractions. Their appeal to the Queen was based on their intelligence, their industry and their administrative ability. Burghley had devoted his life to the service of Elizabeth, and Robert Cecil showed every sign of possessing the same persistent bureaucratic dedication. Physically short and hunchbacked, mentally quiet and introverted, his one pleasure seemed to be the political service of his Queen. He was already a member of the Privy Council and had distinguished himself through unremitting toil.

His father made no effort to hide from Elizabeth or the world his opinion that his Robert was infinitely better suited to guide England and Elizabeth through the last decade of the century than that other Robert, Lord Robert, the Earl of Essex. His Robert was temperate, prudent and economical in public matters as in private. Lord Robert went to extremes in everything. His Robert was a man of peace in personal affairs as in political. Lord Robert cared not whom he offended and seemed dedicated to a policy of costly and dangerous war against Spain at every opportunity. His Robert might feather his nest comfortably from favours and gratuities, but the men he patronized were able and deserving. Lord Robert had a disturbing affection for feckless swordsmen whose only aptitude was battlefield bravado, handing out pensions and titles to them with indiscriminate abandon. His Robert looked only to the Queen for service and reward. Lord Robert courted common popularity.

Essex and the Bacons would have to work hard to disprove the justice of these comparisons. And at the end of 1592 an excellent opportunity for proving their effectiveness presented itself. It was announced that a Parliament would be summoned to meet in February 1593. The two Roberts could display their respective abilities to the elected nation – and to the Queen who would be watching closely.

13

The Parliament of 1593

The Parliament in which Robert Devereux and Robert Cecil were to clash in the spring of 1593 was far from resembling the modern institution which bears that name: or even the body which less than fifty years later was to raise an army against the King. Yet it was certainly not the acquiescent collection of men who had voted through the religious changes involved in Henry VIII's break from Rome. It was some 120 members larger, for at the request of borough corporations and nobles who wanted their own nominees to represent them at Westminster Elizabeth had agreed to the creation of large numbers of new seats. It showed the growing power of the merchant classes – and the anxiety of aristocrats to have connections among them. And the House of Lords was no longer the unquestionably dominant chamber, for the Commons had a mind – and a power – of its own. Elizabeth called Parliament only when she wanted money and when her Council had a sheaf of measures that could be administered more smoothly with the stamp of popular approval; but the sanctioning of that stamp was becoming less and less of a foregone conclusion. What was said in the debates at Westminster mattered. A voice in the Commons was a voice in the land – in a real sense. And Essex and the Bacons determined to get such a voice for themselves.

At the end of December 1592 Essex wrote to his steward Richard

Bagot a letter that would be the subject of incredulity – not to say legal action – today:

I have written several letters to Lichfield, Stafford, Tamworth and Newcastle for the nomination and election of certain burgesses for the parliament to be holden very shortly; having named unto them:
for Lichfield, Sir John Wingfield and Mr. Broughton; for Stafford, my kinsman Henry Bourchier, and my servant Edward Reynolds; for Tamworth, my servant Thomas Smith; for Newcastle, Dr. James; whom, because I do greatly desire to be preferred to the said places, I do earnestly pray your furtherance, by the credit which you have in those towns.[1]

When the Earl of Essex wanted soldiers to fight for him in France he wrote to his steward and told him to levy and organize support: when he wanted men to represent him in Parliament, he did the same.

He had estates around Lichfield, Stafford, Tamworth and Newcastle: voters did not indicate their preferences by secret ballot but had to stand on the hustings and proclaim it to the world – and Essex's agents: and the right to vote was restricted to a defined group of men of reasonable substance – whose substance depended not a little upon the largest landowner. So all Essex's nominees were elected without incident – except his secretary, Edward Reynolds, who was replaced by another member in the Devereux interest, Francis Cradock. It was a normal enough way for Members of Parliament to be selected before the Civil War – indeed for long after the Civil War until the nineteenth-century Reform Act. And a letter to Essex from the Mayor of Carmarthen, Thomas Davies, also represented standard electoral practice: 'Although it pleased the Lord Keeper [who summoned Parliament] . . . to request the nomination of our burgess of Parliament, yet we have, according to our duties, transmitted the blank herein enclosed, leaving the appointment of the person to your lordship's best liking.'

Along with his Welsh MPs and his nominees in Lichfield, Stafford, Tamworth and Newcastle the Earl of Essex could also count on the voice of Francis Bacon, chosen to represent Middlesex, and Sir Christopher Blount, the Earl of Leicester's former Master of Horse who had become Lettice's third husband and who was nominated in the Devereux interest for the seat of Staffordshire county. It represented a not inconsiderable little party that could rival the Cecil faction – and formed the core of the Essex group who were to rise, strengthen and increase around their patron until the disaster of 1601. Sir John Wingfield, sitting for Lichfield, had distinguished himself in the skirmishes around Rouen and had been employed by Essex as one of his message bearers to and from the Queen. He was to sail with Essex to Cadiz in 1596 and die valiantly in the assault on that town. Richard Broughton, the other Lichfield member, was the old Welshman who had been Essex's tutor and trustee on the death of Walter, the first Earl. And Sir Christopher Blount was to pay for his rôle in the 1601 rising with his life.

In recognition of the obvious influence that her favourite wielded in the new Parliament – and also, doubtless, in acknowledgement of the intelligence reports Anthony Bacon had organized in the last twelve months, the Queen on 25 February 1593 had the Earl of Essex sworn in as a full Privy Councillor. He became officially a member of the institution that in an uninstitutional age most closely approximated to the description of a government. And it was a sign of the times that the Crown should feel the need to add strength to its support at the opening of a Parliament.

'His lordship is become a new man,' reported Anthony Bagot a week later, 'clean forsaking all his former youthful tricks, carrying himself with honourable gravity, and singularly liked of both in Parliament and Council-table for his speeches and judgement.' Responsibility became the latest enthusiasm and he worked hard at his new duties: 'Every forenoon, between seven and eight, his lordship is in the higher Parliament House, and in the afternoon upon committees, for the better hearing and amendment of matter in bills of importance.'[2]

Elizabeth had come in person to hear the opening speech made by the Lord Keeper explaining to members why Parliament had been summoned. Apart from the Queen's perpetual insolvency, which was well known, understood and therefore only hinted at, there had been intelligence reports of a two-pronged Spanish attack being prepared through another Armada and through bribing disaffected Scottish nobles to organize a war party against England. Her Majesty had summoned Parliament, said the Lord Keeper, 'that she might consult with her subjects for the better understanding of these intended invasions which were now greater than were ever heretofore heard of.'[3]

That warning had come at the opening of Parliament, on 19 February 1593. Just a week later Robert Cecil rose in the Commons to table a motion offering Elizabeth a double subsidy and a double one-tenth and one-fifteenth tax: one-tenth and one-fifteenth were theoretically exactly what they said: levies amounting to one-tenth or one-fifteenth of a taxpayer's property. So two-tenths and fifteenths together should have amounted to a sizeable proportion of the national income. In fact, assessment was so defective that the yield from Cecil's combined package of subsidies totalled at most £300,000 gathered over a period of time.

Cecil had risen ostensibly to make his offer as an ordinary member. In fact, of course, he was one of the group of Privy Councillors who sat in the House of Commons roughly playing the rôle of a government front bench. Francis Bacon, a would-be member of the same charmed circle and representing Essex who sat in the House of Lords, rose to speak in support of the subsidy suggestion, and that afternoon a committee met to discuss the full implications of raising such a large sum of money. Subsidies and tenths and fifteenths were usually granted separately: to add them together and double them was to ask a lot of the taxpayer. On a Tuesday the committee reported that it was agreeable to such a large package being levied, but insisted that a clause be inserted into the subsidy bill making clear that this combined and multiple exaction should not become a precedent for others.

The bill was to be drawn up on the following Saturday, but suddenly, on the intervening Thursday, the House of Lords sent a messenger to the Commons suggesting a conference between representatives of the two Houses. The suggestion was a government-inspired move and Robert Cecil responded with alacrity.

He would go to find out, he said, what their lordships wanted to confer about. Next morning he reported, with apparent surprise, that the Lords wanted to offer Elizabeth three whole subsidies paid over the next three years. The Queen's Lord Treasurer had reported that the last double subsidy with double tenths and fifteenths had raised only £280,000 and their lordships felt merely to offer the same again was inadequate: 'their lordships would not in anywise give their assent to pass any act in their own House of less than three entire subsidies.'[4]

The transparency of the stratagem was unashamed. Discovering the Commons more amenable to the double subsidy than they had expected, the Privy Councillors were trying to up the levy through their representatives in the Lords. Francis Bacon was on his feet instantly. It was the Commons' prerogative to offer money to the sovereign, he pointed out. If the Lower House met the Lords and accepted their suggestion 'the thanks will be theirs and the blame ours, they being the first movers.' In a rapid vote in which the Essex party were prominent lobbyists, the idea of a conference with the Upper House was rejected by 217 voices to 183.

Essex's protégé had shown his teeth – and his patron's power. Next week Robert Cecil had to step down and when referring to his plea for a conference with the Lords made it clear that the Lords would make no subsidy suggestions. When the meeting finally took place, their lordships simply informed the Commons that Spain was preparing 'divers dangers not heard of before' – and left it to the Lower House of their own accord to suggest a triple subsidy in the light of these new dangers.

It was an academic but definite victory for the privileges of the Commons – and an illustration of the way in which the importance of the two Houses of Parliament had been reversed in the course of the sixteenth century. It was also a definite victory for Francis Bacon and the Essex faction. But they had achieved it at the expense of Robert Cecil and the Privy Councillors who had worked out their strategy for extracting money from Parliament before Essex had become one of their number: he had been sworn in as a Privy Councillor only on 26 February. It was not the most tactful way for a new arrival to demonstrate his strength to his colleagues – and he paid for it, through the instrument he had chosen to make the demonstration.

Francis Bacon had delivered a further speech urging that the collection of the triple subsidy be spread over six instead of four years. Otherwise gentlemen would have to sell their plate and farmers their brass pots, he pleaded. But his picture of the various social classes hocking their respective types of hardware did not meet with the success of his earlier intervention, and at the closing of Parliament on 9 April 1593, the Lord Keeper, as the mouthpiece of the Queen, referred testily to 'some persons . . . who had seemed to regard their countries, and made their necessity more than it was, forgetting the necessity of the time.'[5]

The displeasure was more than simply verbal. When, in the course of the next few months, Bacon attempted to secure for himself a government office of prominence and profit – and when Essex backed his bid – both were sharply rebuffed.

The post was that of Attorney General. The previous occupant, Sir Thomas Egerton, was moving on to become Master of the Rolls. And Essex set his heart on securing the attorneyship for Francis. Also vacant was the lesser, but not inconsiderable post of Solicitor General. As a lawyer whose career had been relatively obscure until the Parliament of 1593 Francis Bacon could have counted the solicitorship as a valuable and, indeed, a fortunate acquisition. It was just about within his grasp. But Essex would not hear of his protégé accepting less than the best. He would scale the heights or fail completely. Francis should have the attorneyship or nothing. It would be a test of the Queen's devotion to her Essex. It was inconceivable she would demonstrate a second-rate affection.

Yet Essex had miscalculated. The speech that had been intended simply to discomfort the Cecils had discomforted the Queen as well. The 1593 Parliament had been awkward enough without supposed government supporters like Francis Bacon obstructing the passage of an increased subsidy bill. Peter Wentworth, the Member who in 1576 had asserted 'none is without fault, no, not our noble Queen,' and had asked in 1587 'whether the prince and state can be maintained without this Court of Parliament?' had had in 1593 the further temerity to suggest that the Commons should draw up for Elizabeth a bill to decide on her successor. And a few days later James Morice, a Puritan, had presented bills to diminish the power of the bishops – whose maintenance of religious orthodoxy was a cornerstone of the status quo. Both trouble-makers had been squashed, Wentworth being locked in the Tower until his death four years later, but their agitation had ill-disposed Elizabeth to look with favour on obstructionists like Francis Bacon. It was made known that not only were his hopes of the attorneyship futile, but he should not expect to have access to inner Court circles until Her Majesty's displeasure had cooled. Creditors who had stood off while his hopes of high office seemed bright now moved in quickly.

It was a sharp and sudden reverse. Yet Essex was confident he could overcome it. He spoke twice to the Queen defending Francis's speeches and intentions as 'being well grounded and directed to good ends'.[6] And he made sure Elizabeth saw a letter from Francis explaining his motives: 'It might please her sacred Majesty to think what my end should be in those speeches, if it were not duty and duty alone. I am not so simple but I know the common beaten way to please.'[7] The fact that the rest of Bacon's career abjectly pursued this common beaten way to official favour would indicate that he – and Essex – were suffering the penalties of a miscalculation rather than paying the price of the principled stand some historians have taken the anti-subsidy speeches to represent. Over eager to cast a dart at Robert Cecil, they had also wounded the Queen.

Essex badgered Elizabeth time and time again on Francis's behalf. He launched into a long dissertation on Bacon's virtues. Why would Elizabeth not take her Essex at his word? He knew what was best for her and the kingdom too. She should show proof of her affection towards him by granting this simple request that would redound to the profit of all concerned.

No, said the Queen. Lord Burghley thought Bacon suitable only for a lower position – and she trusted Burghley's opinion in such matters more than Essex's. Besides there was Sir Edward

Coke, the Speaker in the previous Parliament, who was older and more experienced than Francis.

Essex grew heated, as Elizabeth intended him to. It was Burghley's habit, cried the young Earl, to prefer men like Coke who were dependent on Burghley's favours and subservient to Burghley's will. And age was irrelevant to the appointment. If Sir Edward Coke's beard were to grow grey with antiquity he would still be no match for Francis.

Elizabeth cut him short and swept off to her apartments, disdaining to point out that Bacon was even more dependent on Essex than Coke on Burghley – and that no matter what the young Earl might think, youth did have certain lessons to learn from age.

But when he pestered her again later that day she threw off all restraint. She would be advised, she cried, by men whose judgement and experience had been proved. He should not presume too much on her affections. She would not be badgered into yielding to a brash young man's every whim.

It was Essex's first real setback, the first indication that his position of high favour with the Queen did not give him the automatic right to have his own way. He was forced to report back to Francis that their hopes of the attorneyship would have to be placed in abeyance: access to the royal presence at some later date was the best Bacon could hope for. And Elizabeth had reminded Essex that 'if it had been in the King, her father's time, a less offence than that would have made a man be banished from his presence for ever.'[8] It was disheartening and Francis made desperate – and secret – approaches to see if the Cecils could not do more for him. He was sent packing in no uncertain terms: he should stay close to the Earl of Essex, said Robert Cecil, for it was the Earl 'who hath both true love towards you and the truest and greatest means to win it [the attorneyship] of her Majesty.'[9] Francis was playing a dangerous game. If the Earl of Essex had heard of such attempts to switch allegiance, his true love would have been shortlived. The Bacons' star was now hitched to the Devereux destiny – and Francis would just have to make sure neither his master nor himself made similar miscalculations in the future. They were playing for high stakes.

14

The First Setback

Robert Cecil had come off best in his first duel with Lord Essex, and Essex's champion had suffered for it. So the Earl decided to drop his pleadings on Francis Bacon's behalf until the events of the 1593 Parliament had faded somewhat from Elizabeth's memory. He would promote a more promising protégé, Francis's brother, Anthony. And the Queen seemed anxious to meet the enigmatic little man whose contacts so shrewdly charted the dark labyrinths of continental diplomacy. She made it known that whatever cloud of displeasure Francis might be under his brother would be made welcome in the royal presence.

The trouble was that Anthony Bacon was sick. His failing eyes that needed almost constant medical attention had been one reason for his return to England in 1592. And he had other ailments. Like so many Elizabethans whose predilections for foods like liver, brains, sweet-breads, spinach, rhubarb and asparagus built up solid material in the kidney he suffered from 'the stone'. Sharp pains would shoot through his back and side and blood flow in his urine as the deposit grew into a little crystalline marble that could kill a man. Seizures of gout made it almost impossible for him to hold a pen. A sudden cold snap in July 1593 meant that Anthony Standen, the spy, back in England, had to write to Essex on his behalf: 'Mr. Bacon, by this change of weather, is assaulted with his familiar infirmity . . . for it seized his left elbow and hand, likewise the right thumb, in such sort as he hath not been able to write to your lordship.'¹ On several occasions through that changeable summer plans were laid for Anthony to meet the Queen, but illness frustrated them. On 8 October 1593 the invalid set off from Twickenham towards Windsor for an audience, but never reached his destination. This time it was a sharp attack of the stone that laid him low, and he had to be content with a message of sympathy from Elizabeth. If this elder Mr Bacon had 'but half as much health as honesty,' she declared, then she could not hope to find 'a better servant and more to her liking.'²

Anthony was by now working full time for the Earl of Essex, and he moved into Essex House. As spies and agents went to and fro, Essex House came to resemble an embryo foreign office or Chancellery. Working with Anthony were four secretaries – three of whose qualifications and abilities implied far more responsibility than that title carries today. There was Temple – a run-of-the-mill transcriber of letters. But Reynolds was one of the candidates Essex had nominated for the 1593 Parliament; Henry Wotton who, like Anthony Bacon, had travelled all over Europe and had got as far as Transylvania and Poland, was later to be knighted and to be appointed Provost of Eton by Charles 1; and Henry Cuffe was to exert an influence that made him a Mephistopheles to Essex's Faust. He was an ambitious man whose conspiratorial career was grafted strangely on to yeoman origins among the cider orchards of Donyatt, Combe St Nicholas and Hinton St George in Somerset. By 1586 he was a fellow of Merton, professor of Greek and a proctor at Oxford University – yet by no means an academic: 'Mr Cuffe's brain can be wonderfully shaken by the importunity, or rather sauciness, of the undiscreet martial sort.'³ How he came into Essex's service is uncertain – but he must have been drawn towards the rising star of the Court as Thomas Cromwell was drawn towards Wolsey over half a century before. The Machiavellian mystery surrounding both Cromwell and Cuffe is similar – and both ended their convoluted careers on the scaffold. Cuffe played an even more significant role in Essex's career as the 1590s wore on; he travelled to the Continent on his behalf and became one of his closest confidants as Anthony Bacon grew more infirm and as Francis took fright at the apparently insatiable ambitions of his patron.

Yet in 1593 Essex House was by no means the dark centre of intrigue and treachery it was to become seven years later. The agents who used its side entrances were doing business on the Queen's behalf – though they used Essex's name. And the callers who paid social visits did not yet bear the worried look of men who realize they have become embarrassingly more valuable to their most useful contact than he is to them. Essex House in 1593 was the centre of a glittering social circle whose members seemed to hold all the promise and brilliance of a generation about to come into its own.

Chief among the Essex circle was Henry Wriothesley, the profligate young Earl of Southampton, who had just become the patron of a promising dramatist and poet, William Shakespeare. Whether patron and poet were lovers is one of literature's longest-standing and most inconclusive controversies. Certainly the Earl of Southampton enjoyed the company of homosexual friends. He was a handsome man with piercingly brilliant eyes. Unstable, slapdash, petulant and hot-tempered he was curiously similar to Essex in his shortcomings. And in his generosity, enthusiasm and warm loyalty to his friends he shared the qualities that gave both men compensating charm and attractiveness.

Essex and Southampton were kindred spirits, with linked histories and intertwined destinies. They probably met for the first time when both were wards of Lord Burghley. And when in 1592 and 1593 they set systematically about establishing their imprint upon the social scene they worked in conscious harmony, pursuing together the ideal which, like some wraith from a former age of gold, exerted so strong and nostalgic an influence upon their generation: the model of *homo universalis*, Sir Philip Sidney.

There were ties of kinship: Sidney's widow who had married Essex; Sidney's 'Stella' who was Essex's sister Penelope; Charles Blount of the golden chessman who also became Penelope's lover; Sidney's younger brother Robert who was a friend of Southampton's; Sidney's daughter who married the extravagant

young Earl of Rutland, another member of the Essex circle; Sir
Henry Danvers, knighted by Essex at Rouen, who had been
Sidney's page and then became a client of Southampton's. And
there were the ties of imitation, of which Southampton's patronage
of Shakespeare is the most memorable example. They were all
martial young men, talking and dreaming of foreign glory –
which they were, indeed, later to organize, but blending their
militarism with talk of poetry, scholarship and music:

> The height of armes and artes in one aspiring,
> Valor with grace, with valor grace attiring,

wrote John Florio in a dedicatory sonnet to Southampton.

They enjoyed the badinage of drinking companions like Roger
Williams. Yet they went to plays, dined with poets and composed
ballads of their own. In 1588 one critic said Essex was then
'accounted one of the best poets among the nobility of England'.[4]
If that were so, then such few examples of his verse that have
survived say little for the versifying abilities of the rest of the
nobility. Yet aristocrats have seldom been noted for their poetry
and, as in other fields, Essex's significance lay not in achieving but
in aspiring to the rôle he sought – and in the ease with which he
got others to accept the face value he set on himself.

So the dilettante circle at Essex House played its way through
the rest of 1593. And while Anthony Bacon kept up the hard
work on which their hopes of serious advancement were pinned
Essex himself performed at Court the rôle of favourite which was
the other cornerstone of his ambitions. He flirted, squabbled and
laughed with his Elizabeth, and on Twelfth Night at the beginning of 1594 appeared as her attendant at the Court celebrations.
There was masquing and dancing at the palace in Whitehall, and
as Robert led his sovereign through her graceful steps, one long-
serving courtier was compelled to acknowledge 'she was so
beautiful to my old sight as ever I saw her'.[5] Gloriana nodded and
smiled in all her glory, radiating her pride in herself and the tall,
handsome young knight at her side. 'She often devised in sweet
and favourable manner' with Essex, giggling intimacies into his
ear more like a girl at her first dance than a head of state who had

passed her sixtieth birthday. Essex too was in good humour, and since the post of Attorney still remained vacant, he decided shortly afterwards to renew his petition on Francis Bacon's behalf.

He was bumping in a coach back from the Tower of London with Robert Cecil who, a few months earlier, had told Francis firmly to expect no help from the Cecil faction. Not only had he hampered their parliamentary tactics, but they had protégés of their own. Yet the Cecils had also made clear that they would offer no objection to Francis taking the solicitor-generalship. It accorded far more suitably with his legal experience and stature, and did not preclude later promotion to the attorneyship. The profits of office were not insignificant.

The two young Roberts, Devereux and Cecil, whose struggle for power was the theme of Elizabeth's declining years, fought in that coach clattering noisily along the river's edge the second of their battles over this typically trivial but crucial matter of preference.

'My lord,' said Cecil, showing proper deference to his superior in title. 'The Queen hath resolved, ere five days pass, without any further delay to make an Attorney-General. I pray your lordship to let me know whom you will favour.'

Essex 'wondered Sir Robert should ask him that question, since he must know that, resolutely against all the world, he stood for Francis Bacon.'

'Good lord,' replied Cecil, 'I wonder your lordship should go about to spend your strength in so unlikely and impossible a manner. Can you name one precedent for the promotion of so raw a youth to so great a place?'

It was a rash retort to make, for Cecil, much younger than Bacon, was angling at that time for the much grander office of Secretary of State. Yet the rashness was deliberate, for it raised Essex's ire.

'I have made no search for precedents of young men who have filled the office of Attorney-General,' he shot back angrily; 'but I could name to you, Sir Robert, a man younger than Francis, less learned and equally inexperienced, who is suing and striving with all his might for an office of far greater weight.'

Robert refused to be drawn and coolly goaded Essex further. Did his lordship not consider, he asked, that promoting Bacon for the lesser rank of Solicitor-General might be easier digestion for the Queen?

'Digest me no digestions,' cried Essex, his temper now lost beyond recall; 'the Attorneyship for Francis is that I must have; and in that I will spend all my power, might, authority and amity, and with tooth and nail defend and procure the same for him against whomsoever: and whosoever getteth this office out of my hands for any other, before he have it, it shall cost him the coming by.'[6]

They were fierce threats but proved empty. A few days later Elizabeth gave the attorneyship to the Cecils' Sir Edward Coke, who had worked so hard on the Queen's behalf in the very Parliament in which Bacon had been so obstructive. And it was a logical choice, for as well as his services to the Crown Coke was indeed a more eminent and experienced lawyer than Francis. Seven years later Essex's threats of destruction rebounded nastily, for it was Coke who led the prosecution at the Essex trial.

And there was to be one further hangover of the battle for the attorneyship. The solicitorship later also eluded Essex's nominee and the Earl, dejected not only by his own failure but by the fact that he had failed a friend, insisted that Francis should accept a piece of land as some sort of compensation. And it was generous compensation – Twickenham Park and Garden, worth the best part of £2,000. Yet when, in 1601, Francis played Judas and joined with the prosecution of Essex, his former patron, the gift of land was recalled as a particularly damning example of Bacon's faithlessness. And Francis felt impelled then to publish an *Apology* in justification of his conduct.

The Earl of Essex, he claimed later, was heartbroken by this failure to secure a position for a friend: ' "you have spent your time and thoughts in my matters: I die" – these were his very words – "if I do not somewhat towards your fortune; you shall not deny to accept a piece of land, which I shall bestow on you." ' So Francis, with great reluctance according to his later account, accepted the present to avoid grieving his patron. And made it clear that such a gift could not purchase his allegiance away from the monarch. A likely story, since no disloyalty was in question at that time and the gift was offered – by Bacon's own account – as a reward for past services and not as a pledge of future allegiance: 'if I grow to be a rich man,' Francis unctuously recalled himself saying, 'you will give me leave to give it back to some of your unrewarded followers.' Francis did grow to be a rich man, and disloyalty to his former protector was not the least reason for his riches; but the Earl of Essex's 'unrewarded followers' never derived any benefit from Twickenham Park.

15

The Sad Case of Doctor Lopez

The beginning of 1594 saw the Earl of Essex achieve a spectacular, if to modern eyes dubious, success in domestic affairs. And it was a success born of the network of intelligence contacts that Anthony Bacon had established for the Earl.

Several of his agents were in touch with Spain, and through them Anthony was occasionally able to pick up news of the spies that King Philip was financing in England. He heard from one of these counter-espionage sources that a certain Esteban Ferrera da Gama, a Portuguese gentleman, was in touch with Madrid. The interesting fact was that this Ferrera was staying in Holborn in the house of Doctor Roderigo Lopez, the personal physician to the Queen. Might it be, wondered Bacon, that the great Doctor Lopez himself was also in contact with Spain? And if so did he simply deal in information on King Philip's behalf, or was he plotting in a fashion both more sinister and more obvious for one who frequently administered drugs and medicaments to the monarch?

Had Doctor Lopez's contact with the Queen not contained such perilous implications, Anthony Bacon might have kept his suspicions to himself and placed a watch on Ferrera to see how justified the accusation against him was – and what other contacts he might reveal. But in the century of the Borgias, and only a few years after a Catholic plot to kill that other Protestant hero, William of Orange, had succeeded, Anthony could take no chances.

He passed on the facts he knew about Ferrera and his contact with the Queen's doctor to Essex, who took the obvious action. He had Ferrera arrested and once he had the Portuguese behind bars proceeded to cross-question him fiercely. There was no need to place any formal charge. And orders were sent to the ports of Rye, Sandwich and Dover instructing that all letters from Portugal be opened and examined. The sixteenth century was not troubled by the legal niceties that theoretically prevent such intrusions on personal liberty today.

The letter opening worked. One Gomez d'Avila was arrested at Sandwich. He had mysterious epistles on him that talked ambiguously of pearl, musk and amber purchases. He suspiciously refused to attempt an explanation even of their ostensible purpose. The letters were addressed to the imprisoned Ferrera. And once arrested d'Avila asked that news of his arrest be carried to Doctor Lopez, the Queen's physician.

The plot thickened. Neither Ferrera nor Doctor Lopez himself had heard of the arrest when Ferrera sent a note to the doctor from prison through an Essex agent who pretended to betray the Earl's trust. Both the note and the reply that Lopez sent back were examined by Anthony Bacon. As Bacon subsequently reported, Ferrera urged Lopez 'for God's sake' to prevent Gomez d'Avila from coming to England, 'for if he should be taken the Doctor would be undone without remedy.' And Lopez replied that 'he had already sent twice or thrice to Flanders to prevent the arrival of Gomez, and would spare no expense, if it cost him £300.'

This reply never reached Ferrera. Instead, the prisoner was confronted with the contents of his note to Lopez and told that the doctor had betrayed him. Anxious to get his own back and to clear himself, Ferrera did his best to incriminate Lopez. He confessed that he and the Doctor were indeed involved in a plot and that the plot involved poison. But he insisted that the object of the conspiracy was not Queen Elizabeth but Don Antonio, the exiled Pretender to the Portuguese throne, on whose behalf Francis Drake had launched the miserable raid of 1589.

Gomez d'Avila, the arrested courier, was taken to the Tower and shown the rack. He also freely confessed all he knew. There was a plot, he said, to subvert the son of Don Antonio to the Spanish cause. The references to pearl, musk and amber in the letters he carried referred to the bribes to be offered to the young man to persuade him to disown his father's anti-Spanish policy. Gomez d'Avila said that the letters had been written by one Tinoco, in Brussels, who was in the pay of the Spanish government.

So far the entire investigation had been conducted by Anthony Bacon, the Earl of Essex and friends of Don Antonio whom Essex had known since the 1589 voyage. The mention by Gomez d'Avila of Tinoco, the Spanish agent in Brussels, brought the Cecils into the enquiry. For through one of his own contacts Lord Burghley was, in fact, in touch with Tinoco. Tinoco claimed to have valuable secrets to reveal to Burghley, and had asked for a safe-conduct to come to England and communicate them personally. Burghley readily sent the safe-conduct – and had Tinoco arrested the moment he set foot in Dover.

Brought to London, Tinoco was discovered to be carrying an extremely large sum of bills of exchange, and two more letters to Ferrera from leading Spaniards couched in mysterious terms similar to the despatches that Gomez d'Avila had tried to smuggle into England.

Elizabeth, kept in ignorance by Essex of the full ramifications of the plot, suggested that Robert Cecil examine Tinoco. Which he did with little success, since he was as ignorant as the Queen of the facts Essex had discovered. Then Tinoco was examined by Cecil and Essex together – and the Earl got the prisoner to admit that he had been sent to England 'to try and win Doctor Lopez' to do 'service for the King of Spain.'

It was all Essex had been waiting for. He triumphantly ordered the arrest of Doctor Lopez, principal physician to the Queen. The doctor was whisked off to Essex House, interrogated closely, and his house in Holborn was searched from top to bottom.

But the search revealed nothing, and, when Lopez was examined by Burghley and his son as well as Essex, the doctor's account of his actions seemed respectable enough. Had Essex blundered? Young Robert Cecil certainly thought so, and he rode off rapidly to Hampton Court to tell Queen Elizabeth exactly what he thought of her favourite's suspicions and the jealous way in which the Earl had handled the previous information he had received from the other Portuguese involved in the case. It was seldom that a Cecil allowed himself such a display of open irritation – and it had its effect. When Essex, who had discovered Robert's design, came fast riding down the road from London and dismounted at Hampton Court, he found Elizabeth in a high fury. How dare he arrest her personal physician? He was 'a rash and temerarious youth.' He had brought vile accusations against her own doctor, yet produced no real evidence to substantiate his charges. His strange and jealous behaviour in keeping to himself such facts as he had amassed betrayed his motives – malice and nothing else.

Furious, Essex opened his mouth to expostulate, but the Queen cut him short. With a wave of her hand she ordered him from her presence, and he stalked out of Hampton Court seething. He jumped on his still sweating horse and rode madly to London back along the same route he had pursued only a few hours earlier. Arrived at Essex House, he angrily brushed aside the attendants waiting to greet him and without a word or a look strode to his room and locked his door.

He was indignant. Worse, he was humiliated. After working for months on the coup that he hoped would finally establish his reputation as a man of affairs, he had been brushed aside by the Queen with a wordless gesture. The hurt might have been easier to bear if it were not justified. But Essex was compelled to admit that all he had in fact discovered was a plot amongst Portuguese against Portuguese. Doctor Lopez might well have a guilty secret, but it concerned the incestuous politics of frustrated exiles. The Queen was not threatened by it, and might, indeed, have been very glad to have had the embarrassing and expensive pesterings of Don Antonio dealt with. She had long ago tired of the Pretender's repetitious petitions for assistance. And the 1589 expedition had proved how little affection the Portuguese people had for him. She liked her Doctor Lopez for the strange Latin lore and dangerous aura of mystery that drew her to that other man of science, Doctor Dee, the alchemist.

For two days Essex wrestled with the problem alone, and then suddenly he came bursting from his chamber with a new radiance. He sat down at once to write to Anthony Bacon: 'I have discovered a most dangerous and desperate treason. The point of conspiracy was her Majesty's death. The executioner should have been Doctor Lopez; the manner poison.'

The rest of the tale is sordid. On 18 February 1594 Ferrera was 'pressed more straitly' – the Elizabethan euphemism for being tortured or threatened with torture. Under fear of the rack he said that 'he had some inclining . . . that the Doctor would poison the Queen's Majesty.' Then Tinoco was 'brought to the manacles', and he too confessed what his examiners wanted to hear. Essex, who had supervised the investigation, made sure that the confessions were given wide circulation. So it was in a climate of popular anti-Spanish and anti-Semitic hysteria that Robert Cecil and the Lord Admiral, Charles Howard, came to interview Doctor Lopez on 26 February 1594. With London whipped into a frenzy by nightly performances of Christopher Marlowe's *The Jew of Malta* there was no longer any profit to be gained from defending Lopez, innocent though he might be. The old Jewish physician was bombarded with a barrage of hostile questions and, knowing how Tinoco and Ferrera had been induced to 'confess', and after weeks of confinement and interrogation, he collapsed. Whatever their lordships asserted was true.

No time was lost. Within forty-eight hours Doctor Roderigo Lopez, principal physician to the Queen of England, was being tried for conspiring to murder her. His assertions in court that his so-called confession had been extorted under threat of the rack were ignored. When he was found guilty and condemned the spectators burst into enthusiastic applause. He was the archetype of the foreign villain England needed to hate in a testing time of war. His villainy was hissed in ballads, and his execution was an occasion for the most riotous celebration.

His attempt to speak from the scaffold was drowned in howls of laughter when he asserted that he loved his mistress better than Jesus. A tired old man, he was strung up, cut down while still living, castrated, disembowelled and cut in four. Ferrera suffered the same fate and then Tinoco, who had watched the agonies and heard the screams of the other two, was third for the ordeal. But he recovered his feet when cut down after the hanging and caught his would-be castrator a sharp blow. Suddenly on the side of the foreigner, the crowd cried with delight and broke through the guards to form a ring and watch the scuffle. But Tinoco had no chance. Felled by two soldiers, he was held down screaming while the executioner's knife went through the grisly process that the law prescribed.

It was an unsavoury end to an unsavoury triumph for the Earl of Essex. For he was the hero of those execution crowds, and he proudly took the credit for bringing the vile Jew to justice. The way in which the Cecils had acquiesced in the condemning of Lopez when they knew that his conspiracy, such as it was, did not threaten the Queen was unpleasant. And Elizabeth's politic silence after her initial outburst was also discreditable. But the real villain of the piece was Essex himself. After his original suspicions had proved misplaced, he had determined to shed Lopez's blood to redeem his reputation and he had cynically hounded the old Jew and his pathetic companions until he got what he wanted. Francis Bacon could be proud of his patron's fierce new Machiavellism, except, of course, that Essex had triumphed over no one except the three men he sent to the gallows. The Cecils and Elizabeth knew the facts of the case, and were no more impressed with the Earl's handling of affairs than they were before he started. Indeed, Essex's willingness to resort to popular hysteria as a weapon of policy against those who crossed him was disquieting.[1] Where would he turn to for support if his paranoic theories of malevolence were directed against more powerful victims - say, the Cecils: especially if Elizabeth supported them?

16

Violent Courses

The hounding of Doctor Lopez added little lustre to Robert Devereux's good name. And then in the autumn of 1594 the Earl of Southampton, who had become Essex's main companion and ally at Court, got involved in an escapade whose scandal reflected equally poorly on the whole *jeunesse dorée* that centred on Essex House. Southampton was still very young, his twenty-first birthday was not until 6 October 1594, and two days before the celebrations two of his drinking companions committed a murder. They were the brothers Sir Charles and Sir Henry Danvers who held lands near Southampton's main estates at Titchfield, just north of the Solent and almost half way between the towns of Southampton and Portsmouth. The elder brother, Sir Charles Danvers, was some five years older than Southampton and after touring the courts and battlefields of the Continent had developed literary interests similar to those of Shakespeare's patron. The younger brother, Sir Henry Danvers, had been a page to Sir Philip Sidney in the Netherlands and had taken part in the seige of Rouen in 1591. He had received one of the twenty-four knighthoods that Essex had over-liberally dispensed there, and he could be counted, with his brother, as one of the ever-growing swarm of clients who made up the Essex 'party'.

The Danvers family had a long-standing feud with another Hampshire dynasty – the Longs. Such vendettas were a common and violent feature of sixteenth-century life. Only a century earlier they had formed the basis of the quarrels that post-Walter Scott romantics dubbed the 'Wars of the Roses'. And the pattern of allegiance in the Civil War – nominally a constitutional struggle between King and Parliament – was also shaped by such local and personal animosities. They were crude and vicious: the only significant difference between the way in which social disharmony expressed itself in sixteenth-century England and the American Wild West was the relative efficiency of the instruments of destruction available.

Sir Henry Danvers' shooting of Henry Long on 4 October 1594 in the sight of several witnesses was an unusually efficient and daring action, for sixteenth-century disputants did not often employ pistols: they were so cumbersome, unreliable and inaccurate that the firer had to approach to a point at which a fatal swordthrust from his opponent was the penalty for damp powder, a poor flint or a crooked barrel – not to mention a simple backfire or explosion. And the danger was compounded by the need for both hands to hold the heavy instrument steady while the elaborately packed and solitary shot was let off.

Yet admiration for the technical competence of Sir Henry Danvers' action could not disguise the sad lack of justification for it. Some Long retainers had on a previous occasion thrown a glass of beer in the face of a Danvers retainer, 'saying in derision they had nowe doubbed him a knight allsoe': a jibe at the title bestowed by Essex on Henry Danvers. And Henry Long had informed Sir Charles Danvers that 'wheresoever he mett him he would untye his points and whip his etc. [sic] with a Rodd: calling him Asse, Puppie, foole and Boy.' It had been in the course of the affray consequent on this remark that Sir Henry Danvers' incredibly accurate and fatal pistol shot had pierced Henry Long through the heart. Yet this was no defence for the murder – and the Danvers brothers wisely fled.

They went straight to Titchfield, the seat of their patron, where Southampton was preparing for his twenty-first birthday celebrations. He hid them in one of his lodges, a couple of miles from his main house, and two days after his birthday party rode down with them and a small bodyguard to the Solent. The plan was for the Danvers to take refuge in Calshot Castle on the other side of Southampton Water, but the garrison commander, Captain Perkinson, a client of Southampton, was on holiday. Since his deputy could not be trusted to put his allegiance to the Earl of Southampton before his oath to the Queen to uphold the laws of her land, the Danvers had to spend a day and a night in a small open boat drifting in the chill October winds of the Solent. So eager were they to land that when they were signalled the news that the vacationing Captain Perkinson had sent orders to his deputy to welcome the two outlaws, they allowed no time for the message to reach the castle. So they disembarked at Calshot, to be promptly arrested by the master gunner.

That confusion was sorted out. But a week after the original offence the authorities finally stirred themselves. The local Justice of the Peace, Sir Thomas West – as anxious as Captain Perkinson not to offend the Earl of Southampton – was prodded into action by a letter from the Privy Council in London. He passed it on reluctantly to Captain Perkinson, who sent an urgent warning to Calshot and to Southampton himself, waited to hear definitely that the fugitives had flown, and then despatched the official summons slowly on to Calshot. The Captain stayed resolutely on holiday throughout the emergency and went nowhere near his castle.

The Danvers brothers almost swamped their boat in their anxiety to get out of Calshot and back across Southampton Water. They returned to the lodge which had originally hidden them and sent one of their servants to London with secret letters stitched in the lining of his cap. Essex must have been the great man they begged to intercede on their behalf. Meanwhile, on a ferry crossing the Solent, Southampton's explosive Italian language tutor, John Florio, found on board Laurence Grose, the sheriff who had raised the original hue and cry – and 'threatened to cast him the saide Grose overboorde and said they would teache him to meddle with his fellowes, with many other threatening wordes.'

A few days later the Danvers were safely in France at the Court of Henri IV; and in England the commission investigating their offence was mysteriously cut short before any of the crucial witnesses – the Earl of Southampton's servants – were called. The letters to London stitched in the lining of a hat must have taken effect. Enquiries stopped before the complicity of Southampton was too closely established. The Danvers brothers were back at Court in less than four years.

What Essex had to do with hushing up the scandal in London is much less certain than the evidence relating to the subversion of justice in Southampton's own local area of influence. Essex most probably hammered out a financial bargain with Lord Burghley: for when Southampton declined to marry the lady whom Burghley, as his legal guardian all through the young Earl's minority, was entitled to nominate, the enormous fine levied was far above what was customary in such cases. And Southampton paid his influential guardian with a haste and grace that was equally far from normal.[1] But it was not simply money and Essex influence that had caused the scandalous Danvers' murder to be so rapidly forgotten and forgiven. The Elizabethan age was a violent one. There can have been few courtiers who had not been involved in affrays similar to that in which the Longs and the Danvers fought, and the fact that their particular conflict ended in death was considered unfortunate rather than criminal. In the *fin de siècle* malaise that hung over Elizabeth's Court such vicious little incidents seemed to be becoming more, not less, common: newsletters retailing London gossip to the provinces listed twenty duels in the 1590s compared to just five in the previous decade.[2] In 1593 they had told the story of the brawl in Fleet Street when a band of Talbot and Cavendish men lay by the *Three Tuns* in ambush for John Stanhope and his servants: Stanhope got away, but one of his oldest retainers was cut down and hacked at viciously where he lay. Lord Cromwell, one of the participants in the Essex rising, was involved in a similar pitched battle nearby in 1596. In 1598 a feud between the Markhams and the Holles erupted in an ambush and skirmish in which a Markham was wounded. In the same year the Earl of Sussex nearly killed one of his serving men trying to break up a quarrel between them: and Hentzner, a German traveller, noted as one of the sights of London the thirty heads impaled on poles the length of London Bridge. The hideous death suffered by Lopez and his two Portuguese companions on the scaffold was the normal execution process which crowds gathered to cheer.

In such an age of naked brutality and casual bloodshed it was no coincidence that Shakespeare's plays should centre on personally inflicted acts of justice and revenge: the feud between the Montagus and Capulets came from life in London of the 1590s where 'cutters' and 'hacksters' could make a good living selling their villainous services. The Earl of Oxford had a whole crew of them in his personal service, and when he asked them if they did not think their likely death on a gibbet to be a painful experience, was told by one: 'Marry, that shall your lordship presently know, seeing the experience.' The man then proceeded to take off his garters, tie a noose and hang himself, swinging until he 'waxed very black in the face, strangling and labouring for life.' Cut down, he told his master he would not again endure such pain for all the world – and his comment was endorsed by a sceptical friend who insisted on trying the same test for himself.

The splenetic violence of the Earl of Essex, both in speech and action, reflected a sixteenth-century norm. The rich and well born – who were idle almost by definition – had the time and resources to indulge the short tempers that were attendant on an existence of malnutrition punctuated by bouts of chronic over-indulgence. And the way in which Essex's acts of boorishness were accepted or applauded by his contemporaries should put into perspective any attempts to pretend that the Elizabethan era represented some golden age of English civilization. It was a crude, vicious, half-formed epoch, exciting for the steps towards true culture, not for the achievement of the goal. By their aristo-crats ye shall know them. Henry, Earl of Lincoln, quarrelled with a neighbour in Chelsea – so he had a load of nightsoil dumped on a nearby wharf to annoy his enemy. But he met his match when he started feuding with Sir Edward Dymock. The knight paid for a play to be performed in which the Earl of Lincoln was carried off by the devil, while notorious prostitutes from London, Lincoln and Boston sang over his dead body. When Ambrose

Willoughby quarrelled over cards with the Earl of Southampton he pulled out several tufts of the good Earl's hair. And when Thomas Hutchinson was assaulted by Sir Germaine Poole 'he bit off a good part of his nose and carried it away in his pocket.'

As peers were to muster their retainers to fight in the Civil War – and even when Napoleon's armies seemed about to cross the Channel – so they used them under Elizabeth in pursuit of their private grievances. In 1589 the ever-quarrelsome Earl of Lincoln had attacked Weston Manor with scaling ladders, sixteen armed followers and twenty-four reinforcements hired for the occasion. In the same year Sir Thomas Langton killed Thomas Houghton at Lea Hall after a battle in which the defenders had thirty men and the attackers eighty. In true Wild West style Edward Lord Dudley rounded up 140 followers to drive Sir John Lyttleton's cattle out of Prestwood in 1592. And, of course, the Earl of Essex brought his tempestuous relationship with his Queen to a tempestuous close by parading his followers – many of them tenants from his estates – through the streets of London in 1601 in an attempt violently to right the wrongs he imagined to have been inflicted upon him.

His was not a sudden, inconsistent action but an act of aggression implicit in the violence of his speech and attitudes all through his career. In the sixteenth century, expressions of pugnacity were not figures of speech. Elizabethans who spoke of getting their own back were talking in physical terms. Rare were spirits like the Cecils and the Queen herself with the intelligence to derive satisfaction from abstract revenge.

A fine example of that refined sense of torture and the skill with which it could provoke Essex's bull-like outbursts of fury occurred in the course of 1595, when the Queen appointed Sergeant Fleming to the solicitor-generalship which Francis had wanted as consolation prize for his failure to secure the attorney-ship. Essex ranted and raged and uttered all manner of threats. Elizabeth smiled demurely, happy to have caused so much pain without lifting a finger. It was one consolation for being a woman in a man's world.

It was bad news for the Earl, and it came at a bad time. For in

1595 a book reached England whose implications for Essex were dangerous in the extreme. It was entitled *A Conference on the Next Succession to the Crown of England*, and it was prefaced with a fulsome dedication to Essex himself, as though the Earl in some fashion endorsed the contents. It speculated on the subject Elizabeth had forbidden all to meddle with – who should succeed on her death. Its initial arguments demonstrated that blood alone was not a sufficient claim to the throne. And it went on to survey the claims of everyone who might consider themselves to be Elizabeth's successor: James, the King of Scotland; the daughter of Philip II of Spain; the Earls of Beauchamp, Derby or Huntingdon who all had ties of blood with Elizabeth; and a child of the Earl of Hertford or the Countess of Derby – also relations. Had the writer come down in favour of any one candidate it might have been possible to shift responsibility for the tract on to that particular claimant. Yet the argument ranged evenly between – with the clear implication that there would be disputes between the rivals and possibly civil war on Elizabeth's death. The author was not content in his preface with thanking the Earl of Essex for past favours to friends of his: he also suggested that on Elizabeth's death no other man was likely 'to have a greater part or sway in deciding of this great affair' – the succession – than Essex himself. The Earl could be King – or kingmaker, at least.

Some might have whispered that suggestion. None had dared voice it openly, for it was treason. The preface was signed R. Doleman 'from my chamber in Amsterdam'. Yet the Protestant address was a blind, for it had come into England by secret routes, and appeared in London in the hands of those connected with Roman Catholic spies and missionaries on the Continent. And since the style was reminiscent of tracts from the pen of Robert Parsons, one of the most determined English Jesuits working for the overthrow of Elizabeth, the whole thing could be represented as a Popish attempt to stir up trouble between the Queen and one of her most loyal followers.

But any hint of discussions that involved her death threw Elizabeth into a panic which overcame such rational explanations.

And there had already been quite enough gossip that compared the Earl of Essex to Bolingbroke, the usurper in Shakespeare's *Richard II*. It infuriated her that the possibility of Essex holding king-making power after her death was so difficult to deny with conviction.

The favourite was under a cloud. But he made a gallant attempt to regain royal favour at the November celebrations to mark the 1595 anniversary of Elizabeth's succession. In one of the mumming shows that were staged to entertain the Court on such occasions – and from which writers like Shakespeare were painfully quarrying the dramatic structures we now recognize as plays – the Earl of Essex attempted to portray his plight. Though intended as a conceit, an amusing diversion, it struck strangely close to his schizophrenia. Actors representing a hermit, a secretary of state and a soldier made elaborate speeches to persuade the Earl to follow their own particular course of life. Then a chorus explained that the Earl felt himself torn between these three separate modes of existence – to be a recluse penning poems away from Court, to be a man of affairs, or to be a man of war – but that he was resolved to devote his poetic, administrative and military abilities all to the service of his mistress, the Queen.

It sounds a crude performance – but was certainly no less sophisticated than the normal entertainments the Court staged for its own amusement. Yet Elizabeth chose not to join in the general applause and rose the moment the charade was completed. Had she known so much would be said of her, she remarked, she would have gone straight to bed without bothering with the performances. And she stalked out haughtily.

The year ended gloomily. On 13 December at 3 o'clock in the morning Sir Roger Williams died. He had been Essex's most trusted and experienced military adviser – and his worth was acknowledged nationally. He was buried in St Paul's Cathedral on 16 December with full military honours – at the Earl of Essex's expense. He had left all his worldly goods, a little over £2,000,[3] to his young patron, and after a coarse and lusty camp-fire life had met his end religiously. His last words were words of thanks to his Lord of Essex 'who, indeed, saved his soul, for none but he could make him take a feeling of his end; but he died well, and very repentant.'⁴

Whether or not Essex felt like celebrating the Christmas of 1595, he was to have little opportunity. Lord Huntingdon, the President of the Council in the still wild north of England and Scottish borderlands, had fallen dangerously ill. There was no news of crisis in the north: but no news either that there was none – and that was not reassuring. North of the river Trent was as another land – more foreign to most Elizabethan courtiers than France. The Queen herself never strayed from the south. The only method she had of keeping the northern regions quiet was to persuade as many of its barons as she could to stay close to her in London, and to send a semi-military, virtually autonomous governor to exercise over their chiefless lands and followers a tough dictatorship in her name. For all she knew the Earl of Huntingdon's illness might be the very occasion the uncouth hotspurs of those cold and savage parts were waiting for to raise a riot. And it was a marvellous pretext ostentatiously to parade through the Court's Christmas festivities without her favourite. She would not be really happy without him by her side; in his absence she might be drawn, as the old are, into harking back to previous, more joyous Christmasses, which friends, now departed, had celebrated with her; but proving a point always gave her greater satisfaction than being happy.

So Lord Essex spent Christmas exiled from his mistress, riding north. And fortunately for him, his temporary fiefdom decided to celebrate the season of good will in a festive fashion. Perhaps, as he returned to London at the beginning of 1596, he took advantage of the comparatively trouble-free ride to reflect on the state of his relationship with the Queen. Since the Parliament of 1593 he had stood still. His protégé Francis Bacon had been twice defeated in his attempts to gain office. And he himself had gained no promotion. He was listened to on the Privy Council, Anthony Bacon's agents were turning in useful reports, and gossip assured him of a powerful future. Despite his disagreements with Elizabeth, he was still the Queen's constant companion. But the honeymoon was over.

17

Winters of Discontent

As Robert Devereux rode south through the dead winter countryside at the beginning of 1596, he must have been shocked by the scenes of want and desolation in every village that he passed through. For England had just endured two of the worst harvests in living memory – and, though she did not know it, had two even more terrible harvests to come. Shakespeare painted the catastrophe graphically.

> The ox hath therefore stretch'd his yoke in vain,
> The ploughman lost his sweat, and the green corn
> Hath rotted 'ere his youth attain'd a beard:
> The fold stands empty in the drowned field,
> And crows are fatted with the murrion flock . . .
> No night is now with hymn or carol blest . . .
> The seasons alter: hoary-headed frosts
> Fall in the fresh lap of the crimson rose . . .
> . . . the spring, the summer,
> The childing autumn, angry winter, change
> Their wonted liveries, and che mazed world,
> By their increase, now knows not which is which.[1]

As the London theatre audiences listened to Titania's grim description they knew exactly what it meant to have a harvest washed away. It was a national disaster, far eclipsing the worst havoc that enemies like the Spaniards could possibly wreak. For nine tenths of Englishmen lived on the land, and the remaining tenth retained a close connection with it. Very few Londoners were entirely urban people: like Shakespeare – and Essex – they had been raised in the country. Even the great dynasties of the City of London had their country estates in Wandsworth or Highgate or Hammersmith.

The heavy rains of the years 1594, 1595, 1596 and 1597 brought famine, disease and rebellion to the land. The catastrophe struck the Earl of Essex no harder than anyone else; in fact, as a nobleman, he was cushioned from the worst personal impact of the disaster. But it made a significant difference to the political context in which his ambitions were shaping. For if Merrie England had not been dead when the Armada sailed, it was certainly washed away with the harvests of 1594 and the succeeding years.

Children died of starvation. Men, through no fault of their own, were thrown out of work. Some were hanged as vagabonds. One Hugh Platt published a book of remedies against the famine recommending that bread be baked of the roots of aaron, called cockoospit, or of parsnip roots; since inns could not afford to brew beer, travellers should prepare for their journey concoctions of water, aniseed and a branch of rosemary.[2] In 1597 the purchasing power of the average weekly wage fell to a point lower than at any time between the thirteenth century and the present day.[3] Money had been becoming more and more worthless as prices rose all through the century. Now men found they literally could not afford to live, and their despair and resentment were focused, inevitably, against the government and the Queen. In the last twelve years of Elizabeth's reign, between 1591 and 1603, Englishmen had to pay, when they could least afford it, four times as much taxation as had been levied in all the thirty-three years before.[4]

These were the twilight years, when England was no longer dazzled by the brilliance of Gloriana. The government seemed bankrupt not only of funds but of ideas, and its demands on its people's loyalties were running rapidly into the red. To salve the hurts of the rural population it could only suggest old cures already tried and found wanting: proclamations against consuming meat on Wednesdays or Fridays, prohibitions on the export of corn, an Act against Enclosures, a Statute against the decay of husbandry.[5]

Voices were raised in Parliament. The forces of misunderstanding and resentment that were to explode in the Civil War of 1642 were beginning to build up. The fact that the whole situation, particularly the catastrophic price rise, was completely outside any government's control only bred a new scepticism, a questioning of authority that spread from economics, through politics, literature, art and science to philosophy and religion itself. The growing violence in London was part of this. The Crown was 'losing the initiative' in the House of Commons to subversive elements. 'Now the wit of the fox is everywhere on foot, so as hardly a faithful or virtuous man may be found,'[6] complained Elizabeth herself, acknowledging that the patronage system was degenerating into a cynical exercise in bribery and corruption. England was locked in the most costly and perilous war in her history – and still had her main efforts to make. Things were falling apart. 'Rust was eating into the shackles of the great Chain of Being.'[7]

Men wondered whether the outrageous Peter Wentworth had really been so far off the mark: 'none is without fault,' he had claimed, 'no, not our noble Queen, since then Her Majesty has committed great fault, yea dangerous faults to herself.' He had been imprisoned for his declamation in 1576. But in 1590 the Somerset Commissioners of Muster were equally defiant and resorted to tactics of resistance that were to become standard antimonarchical ploys in the years leading up to the Civil War. Asked by the Privy Council to levy troops for foreign service they had their lawyers prepare an opinion to show that the commission to levy was invalid except in time of rebellion or invasion.[8] And in 1596 Sir John Smythe took a similar line when he addressed the Colchester Musters. He said that parliamentary consent was necessary before troops could be levied for service abroad – and swept away by the momentum of his speech he called the Lord Treasurer a traitor for maintaining anything to the contrary.[9]

Afterwards he pleaded drunkenness – but the worried Privy Council discovered that he had consulted lawyers, had compared English law to Spanish law, and had discovered old statutes stating that only volunteers who came forward freely at the sound of the drum could be enlisted for foreign service.

The tactics of this sixteenth-century Hampden were ominous, for similar searches of precedent and identical legal ammunition primed the muskets that were to be levelled at English monarchs in the seventeenth century. And the disintegration that was to be the one constant factor of that century had begun:

> And new Philosophie calls all in doubt,
> The element of fire is quite put out;
> The sun is lost, and the earth, and no man's wit,
> Can well direct him where to look for it . . .
> 'Tis all in pieces, all coherence gone.[10]

The implications of all this for the Earl of Essex were both dramatic and dangerous. As England became more and more disillusioned with the concepts and figures of the past she looked to the future, and there the bold inspiring figure of Robert Devereux seemed to stand out as one clear certainty that could be clung on to. He embodied all the promise of a new generation, a new century. And although in many ways his ideas and values were legacies of a former age, there was a very real sense in which he was hastening the destruction of the old order.

Behind his quaint feudal concepts of honour and chivalry, and behind his material battle for financial survival, Lord Essex was an ambitious man. He wanted power. And he wanted it in such a compulsive, unconditional, unselfconscious fashion that he was to destroy the very system he was seeking to dominate. For Elizabeth had always based her government on a form of consensus. She was a dictator, an absolute monarch and proud of it. But she relied inevitably upon advisers, and she had always been most careful to balance them precisely. Never would she allow one faction to dominate her Council. It was an axiom of her government that no single man or group of men should have exclusive control over office, patronage or access to her presence.

'She never chose nor cherished favourite,' wrote Fulke Greville,[11] 'how worthy soever, to monopolize over all the spirits and business of her Kingdom.' She would have but 'one mistress at court and no master,' she told Leicester. So to offset that Earl's influence she had smiled kindly on Sussex. And she raised up William Cecil to be Lord Burghley. Against him she had set Knollys and Hatton and Wilson and Walsingham. Her system was based on an equilibrium of which she was the point of balance – and the deciding weight.

But Essex refused to accept the basis of this system – though hardly in any philosophical sense. In the 1580s he had been comparatively satisfied as one of the many suitors for royal favour. But as the older generation died off and Robert Cecil emerged as the other main rival for power and patronage it simply was not in Essex's nature to rest content with a position of balance or equality. It was impossible for him to live and let live, and it was Elizabeth's great failure not to realize this until it was too late. Then she got the better of Essex, but only at the cost of surrendering to Cecil and establishing the pattern of a single chief minister which she had fought so hard to avoid, and which was to be, through Cecil himself, Buckingham and Strafford, one of the most prominent and hated characteristics of the early Stuart autocracy.

Theirs was the very same monopolistic position that the Earl of Essex was aiming at and, ironically, his efforts to achieve it earned him great popularity through the difficult years that brought the Tudor century to a close. For Robert Cecil was unpopular. Even more than his father, he lacked the public graces. He was deformed and easily ridiculed. Men scrawled 'toad' on his palace walls. He bore the brunt of the growing dislike of the Court's financial privileges and the patronage system – and indeed, he was as responsible as anyone for turning the Tudor method of getting things done into the vicious Stuart machine of bribery. His rôle in securing the notorious Toby Matthews' appointment to the bishopric of Durham in 1595 was particularly devious and disreputable. Episodes like that overshadowed in the public mind his very real qualities and the very close identification between his own self-interest and that of the State. He might be working to end a war that was straining royal government to its foundations, from which, indeed, the Crown never quite recovered, but that only made him the more unpopular in a jingoistic and bellicose society.

And Elizabeth too was unfairly treated by public opinion. The economic disasters of the century's end were due to a variety of factors: the staggeringly expensive war, a rise in population, an artificial injection of precious metals into the monetary system, the bad weather, a readjustment of England's traditional cloth trade – all of them factors outside her control. But she suffered for them. Her people were as bored with the myth of the Virgin Queen as her Court was. Some of her subjects even refused to keep the anniversary of her Accession as a holiday.[12] Our knowledge that James I soon lost England's affection should not obscure the fact that in 1603 people were glad to see him come: that the crowds who welcomed him to London were very much larger and more emotional than those who had mourned the death of Queen Elizabeth. She had outstayed her usefulness and her people's tolerance.

So Essex's well known willingness to stand up to the capriciousness of her difficult years earned the Earl an admiration he would not have received in the earlier part of her reign. Essex polarized a very real national emotion as the heavens opened on the harvests of the mid-1590s. He met a very real national need. He stood for hope, pride, confidence – and the enigmatic flaws in his personality were forgotten. How did the poet Spenser describe him? 'Great England's glory and the world's wide wonder.'

The trouble was that this public encouragement, almost incitement, inveigled the Earl fatally to extend his own wilfulness beyond the boundaries that royal tolerance would permit. And in the end, unpopular though she might be, Elizabeth was still Queen. Public opinion might interest the historian of the sixteenth century, but in its own time it counted for little. It did not bring about the Civil War. It was certainly no basis on which the Earl of Essex could build. He himself would have laughed off the idea that the people possessed any importance. But he liked to listen to their cheers and in due course they seduced him into losing touch with where realities lay.

In 1596, as he rode south through the devastated winter countryside, Lord Essex had four years left before his Farm of Sweet Wines expired, and five years before his rising and execution in 1601. It was his tragedy to forget in his sixty surviving months that he owed his wealth, his power and even his popularity to the wrinkled old woman who, in these hard times, had lost her people's love.

18

The Fall of Calais

Something had to be done about Spain. The defeat of the great Armada still rankled with Philip II – and he had learned the lessons of his past failures. His treasure fleets no longer drifted across the Atlantic unprotected. The flotillas sailing for Spain with South American gold and silver were organized into convoys systematically protected by man-o'-war squadrons. English pirates were lucky to pick up spoils like the *Madre de Dios* whose jewels had rolled through the streets of Plymouth in 1592. They more usually met the sustained firepower that had blasted Sir Richard Grenville's *Revenge* into splinters – and into English legend.

> Let us bang those dogs of Seville, the children of the devil,
> For I never turn'd my back upon Don or devil yet,

was how Tennyson immortalized Grenville's decision to pick a fight against hopeless odds. Yet the importance of the action was not one English pirate's act of pointless braggadocio, but the new skill with which Spain organized her warships and her treasure fleets.

Sir Francis Drake and Sir John Hawkins, with Grenville and Frobisher the great captains of England's age of sea heroes, ran into similar difficulties. In 1595 they attempted an old-style raid on the South American treasure fleets, and were met with the new-style Spanish resistance. They expected to fall upon lumbering galleons, but were, in fact, outstripped by five fast frigates who got the treasure to Puerto Rico and warned Spanish squadrons throughout the Caribbean. The two old heroes, Drake in his mid-fifties, Hawkins in his sixties, had lost touch with modern developments. Hawkins died as the squadron neared Puerto Rico, overcome by remorse at having urged the Queen to support a venture he could now see to be doomed: in a sad effort to make amends he left his worldly wealth, some £2,000, to his sovereign. And after the puny English attack was beaten off by the far superior Spanish guns, Drake too died, of dysentery. His final gesture – an attempt to land a few troops to cut the isthmus of Panama – showed how far the old sea dog had lost contact with reality. Three centuries later, Sir Henry Newbolt's poem captured the exact spirit of nostalgic anachronism that characterized Drake's last voyage:

> Take my drum to England, hang et by the shore,
>   Strike et when your powder's running low;
> If the Dons sight Devon, I'll quit the port o' Heaven,
>   An' drum them up the Channel as we drummed them long ago!

Encouraged by his enemies' sudden loss of touch, Philip II was preparing a new, more streamlined and altogether more formidable Armada to invade either England or Ireland before the end of the century. Anthony Bacon's spies were not the only agents to report systematic activity in the Spanish seaports. If England did not want to be taken by surprise she would have to act quickly. There could be no more of these pinprick raids – 'half-doings' as Walsingham had scornfully described them. 'Her Majesty did all things by halves,' said Sir Walter Raleigh with rare insight, 'and by petty invasions taught the Spaniard how to defend himself... which, till our attempts taught him, was hardly known to himself.'[1]

The obvious answer was an invasion like the Portugal expedition of 1589 on which Essex had played truant, but an invasion that avoided the mistakes of that sad enterprise. And who better to command such a venture than the Earl of Essex himself who had seen all the mistakes at first hand but who seemed young enough to learn from them? Rightly or wrongly, popular opinion had already hailed the dashing redhead as Drake's successor, and this corresponded exactly to the young Earl's image of himself. His attempt to play the Court statesman had, after a promising start, somewhat misfired. He had had enough of backstairs intrigue, half statements and misleading face values. He could never bring himself to admit he was constitutionally incapable of adjusting his blunt enthusiasms to that world; but he could see he needed a new field in which to display his temporarily over-shadowed talents, and he became the vociferous champion of a fierce, direct offensive against Spain.

He had strange and rare allies in high places. Old Burghley, only two years away from death, and never one for enterprises in which violence or expense was involved, seemed to feel that an immediate attack would be cheaper and safer than sitting back and waiting on events. His arguments in favour of an offensive were set out in a long and detailed paper entitled 'To the Queen's Majesty's only most fair hands, from a simple weak hand.' Sir Francis Vere, on Roger Williams' death England's most experienced land soldier and schooled in the gritty caution of Continental warfare, also backed the project: even setting aside all concern with national reputation and honour, he argued, such an enterprise was vital to 'the main proceeding of this war, which cannot prosper with us if in time we bring it not nearer to them'.

So the Privy Council agreed to launch an offensive: a vast combined military and naval assault on Cadiz, the main Spanish port. In conditions of great secrecy plans were laid for a spring campaign – 12,000 men with supplies sufficient for five months. The Lord Mayor and aldermen of the City of London were instructed to provide fifteen of their largest and soundest ships: England's other ports were ordered to have their best vessels ready for Her Majesty's service by Easter: Lord Charles Howard of Effingham, the Lord Admiral, went down to Chatham to oversee the preparations of the Queen's own ships.

Through the early months of 1596 the whole enterprise swept along with unwonted efficiency: detailed estimates of costs were prepared: the intricate organization of victuals and munitions was set out in complex memoranda: it was decided that the fleet itself should be divided into four squadrons commanded by the Earl of Essex, the Lord Admiral, his brother Lord Thomas Howard, and Sir Walter Raleigh, who had been fighting his way back into favour ever since Elizabeth's anger had cooled sufficiently to allow him and his secretly wedded wife out of the Tower. The land sector of the attack would be under the command of Sir Francis Vere who, to match his own experience, would bring a strong body of hardened campaigners from the Netherlands. The only unresolved question was who would exercise overall control over this clutch of energetic and self-willed commanders. None would take kindly to orders coming from any of the others – and their bristly *amours propres* made joint military decisions an even more unlikely prospect than usual.

The difficulty was temporarily shelved in the flurry of activity that marked the preparations through January, February and March 1596 – and by the unexpected crisis that occurred just as the plans for the expedition were nearing fruition.

In 1593 Henri IV of France had tried to come to terms with the Catholic League against whom Essex had briefly and unsuccessfully helped him fight at Rouen in 1591. Henri became a Roman Catholic – and from the date of his conversion his campaigns grew more and more successful. Paris proved well worth saying a Mass for. Yet Spain refused to accept the validity of his conversion, especially as it was not, unsurprisingly, accompanied by persecution of the Protestants who had for so many years been the backbone of Henri's cause. So Spanish troops continued to fight in France, and in the spring of 1596, just as England was secretly preparing for her assault on Cadiz, Spanish troops thrust towards the north French coast. Their objective was Calais – the French port nearest, indeed in sight of, the white cliffs of Dover. At the beginning of April the Spanish forces began besieging Calais and the boomings of their cannon were heard in Dover. On still days the sharp-eared claimed they could hear sounds of the battle from London.

The prospect of Calais falling into Spanish hands obviously set an immediate halt on the launching of an expedition bound further afield. And it seemed obvious that at least some of the ships and soldiers gathered to attack Cadiz could usefully be turned towards this objective closer to home. The Earl of Essex and the Lord Admiral were ordered immediately to organize a relief expedition. Essex set out at once for Dover while the Lord Admiral collected together ships in Chatham and London.

On 3 April 1596 Essex sent out a small man-o'-war to spy out how close the Spaniards were to capturing Calais, and was told that they were still outside the walls. The harbour was open and English reinforcements could be landed without difficulty. It only remained for Elizabeth to give definite orders for a relief force to sail.

Yet the orders did not come. Henri IV had, of course, sent an urgent appeal to Elizabeth the moment he heard that the Calais garrison was threatened. And he had begged Essex, as a former comrade in arms, to lend weight to his suit. The Privy Council were unanimous in urging immediate action. Yet Elizabeth did not forget she had lent the French King the best part of £350,000 – and had received no repayment or reciprocal assistance. There was obvious interest in establishing English troops once more in Calais, but Elizabeth wanted an assurance that once there, they would be allowed to stay. She kept negotiating fiercely with the French King's representatives – and in the meantime told Essex to go ahead with his preparations.

He decided that Sir Francis Vere would take over the troops as soon as sufficient were mustered and equipped. On 9 April, Good Friday, orders went out to the Commissioners of Musters in the south east to have 6,000 men with arms in Dover by Sunday night at the latest. The Mayor and aldermen of London were listening to the Good Friday sermon at St Paul's Cross when they got the order to raise a thousand men. By eight o'clock that evening they had assembled that number.

But next morning Elizabeth promptly cancelled all her previous instructions. The French King had refused to offer any reasonable securities or accept that English troops could remain in Calais.

As he said to a friend, if he had to lose Calais he would rather lose it to the Spanish than the English; at least when peace came Spain would give it back. It looked, in any case, as though the Spaniards were so close to capturing the port that any relieving expedition would be a waste of money. Elizabeth's Privy Councillors were amazed and indignant at her cancellation: 'these so many changes breed hard opinions of counsel,' sniffed Burghley, irritated that his own advice had been ignored. It had not been easy for him to lend his weight to the Earl of Essex's eagerness for a fight.

But on Easter Sunday fresh despatches arrived from Calais. It seemed the Spanish were not doing so well as earlier reports had indicated. There was still time to save the port – and if an English army did relieve and strengthen the town then possession would be nine tenths of the law.

Elizabeth cancelled her previous cancellation and the expedition was on again. When the news reached the Lord Mayor and aldermen of London those worthy burgesses were once again at worship: yet they responded immediately. Each went to his own parish church and ordered their constables to keep the congregations shut inside until the full quota of men was collected. By noon 1,000 Londoners were again under arms – and by sunset most were marching towards Dover.

The Earl of Essex had been riding from Dover to London and back again ceaselessly in the course of the Queen's vacillations. On Easter Monday, 12 April, he was back in Dover working once more on the assault arrangements. On 13 April the Queen and Privy Council drew up his commission to lead the relief of Calais expedition. But the Queen's decision was still not unconditional. Essex could not sail until the French King agreed definitely to English troops remaining in Calais – or repaid the considerable debts he owed Elizabeth.

Apart from the inevitable frustration this further delay caused Essex, the Lord Admiral, Lord Charles Howard of Effingham, flew into a rage at the fact that Essex alone had been appointed to command the relief expedition. He wrote furiously to Robert Cecil that he would never enter the Queen's service again, 'and if her Majesty lay me in the Tower it shall be welcome to me.' He wrote indignantly to the Queen as well, and with the same messengers went despatches from Essex urging any action rather than the humiliating confusion of orders and counter-orders.

The Queen changed her mind once more and on 14 April – two weeks after the first news of the Spanish attack reached England – she gave what proved to be the final go-ahead: 'as distant as I am from your abode, yet my ears serve me too well to hear that terrible battery that, methinks, sounds for relief at my hands; wherefore, rather than for lack of timely aid it should be wholly lost, go you on, in God's blessed name.'

Yet the 'timely aid' was too late. Essex spent the whole of 15 April embarking his troops, but there was an ominous silence from across the water. And he was snatching supper on board the *Rainbow* that evening when news came that Calais had fallen. Elizabeth had dragged out her waiting game one day too long and in trying to win more had lost all. The fault was hers entirely – for attempting to recapture Calais now was out of the question. By the time the English troops had been equipped for a proper siege the citadel would have been rendered impregnable. There was nothing for it but to launch the originally planned attack on Cadiz as rapidly as possible and to eliminate the Spanish ships which might sail up to take advantage of Spain's new foothold in the English Channel.

Yet the Calais fiasco had delayed by a month at least the preparation for the Cadiz attack. Ships, supplies and men shifted up from Plymouth would have laboriously to be moved back. And Elizabeth had to deal with the problems that the Lord Admiral's hurt pride had raised. She ordered him simply and curtly to get on with the job.

Essex and the Lord Admiral sailed down from Dover to Plymouth at the end of April and set immediately about imposing order on the chaos they discovered there. Stores, ships, munitions and men had been flowing into the town for a month with no one to receive them systematically. Confronted with the need for hard work and action, Essex excelled himself. He compiled long lists of the officers at his disposition, assigned them to separate companies and regiments and furnished each with a detailed disposition of his duties. He sprinkled the soldiers he knew to be experienced into companies of recruits to help stiffen their discipline. And he himself bore much of the expense the preparations involved.

He struck back angrily when a letter from the Queen carped at the postponement of the expedition's originally agreed date of sailing. After all, it had been Elizabeth who was primarily to blame for the month which the Calais scare had wasted:

Here I have our full number and here I keep them without spending our sea victuals or asking allowance or means from her Majesty [he wrote to Robert Cecil on 7 May 1596]. I am myself, I protest, engaged more than my state is worth . . . yet I am so far from receiving thanks as her Majesty keepeth the same form with me as she would do with him that through his fault or misfortune had lost her troops. I receive not one word of comfort or favour by letter, message, or any means whatsoever.

The difficulties involved in mustering English troops for foreign war were formidable at the best of times. For the confusion between public and private duty which gave such a special character to the politics of the Elizabethan Court haunted military affairs as well. Men mustered to serve in the armies of the Queen did not regard their recruitment in any fashion remotely similar to the way in which we, grudgingly, talk of 'national service'.

In theory all Englishmen between the ages of sixteen and sixty were liable to be mustered once a year for a rudimentary drilling at which arms were issued and checked. With a crude disregard for legal niceties, and ruthless treatment of those who attempted to preserve them, the government decided that the men thus mustered for the domestic defence of the realm were also liable for service abroad: and service abroad was something that any man with commitments would pay to avoid. So some of the men who went to the Earl of Essex's Plymouth camp in 1596 were paid substitutes for more substantial citizens. Many were vagrants who preferred the prospect of foreign plunder to being beaten from parish to parish in England. And many, of course, had been forcibly pressed.

Shakespeare used Falstaff in *Henry IV Part I* to describe some of the abuses military service could involve:

I press me none but good householders, yeomen's sons: inquire me out contracted bachelors, such as had been asked twice on the banns . . . and they have bought out their services: and now my whole charge consists of . . . slaves as ragged as Lazarus in the painted cloth, where the glutton's dog licked his sores: and such as, indeed, were never soldiers, but discarded unjust serving-men, younger sons to younger brothers, revolted tapsters and ostlers trade fallen.

It was the commanding officers – captains like Falstaff – who reaped the real dividends of the war game. They welcomed the payments of men wishing to avoid service – or wishing to desert once enlisted. They were paid by the authorities for one hundred men but, in recognition of an abuse the government acknowledged, were only required to show the presence of ninety men on their roll. The remaining ten were 'dead pays' whose 'wages' they could pocket themselves. With skill they could double or treble that number by borrowing men from other companies or from outside the levy when the roll was called – and then sending them off afterwards with a few pennies for their pains. Back in 1560 the Privy Council had foolishly believed the nominal troop strength of the English force besieging the town of Leith and had insisted on an assault; the fiasco which followed revealed that the real size of the army was scarcely half the numbers on the rolls.

Yet so many people stood to prosper from such abuses that they were difficult to eradicate. There were the suppliers – men on whom the whole feasibility of Essex's Cadiz expedition depended. Ordinary soldiers had to pay for their own food out of their wage of 8*d* a day, and they were entirely at the mercy of the freelance caterers who, for a consideration paid to the captains, were allowed to become part of an army's retinue. The staple of a soldier's diet was a loaf of bread or biscuits, butter, cheese and beer. Meat or fish, either fresh or salted, were rare and expensive delicacies; oatmeal, peas or beans were more usual variations. A soldier's daily budget was:

1 lb. of bread or biscuit	$\frac{1}{2}d$.
3 oz. butter	$\frac{3}{4}d$.
6 oz. cheese	1d.
$\frac{3}{4}$ pint oatmeal	$\frac{3}{4}d$.
Transport and general compulsory expenses	1$\frac{1}{2}d$.
	$4\frac{1}{2}d$.

This left $3\frac{1}{2}d$ to pay for drink.[2]

'General compulsory expenses' included items like uniform and gunpowder – none of which were provided free: they too were sold to soldiers by contractors who took a handsome profit. Uniforms were not considered an essential part of warfare in the sixteenth century – nor were they for centuries to come: in the eighteenth century the lack of identifying costume still meant that when regiments approached each other they might be uncertain whether they were friend or foe. Essex's tangerine troops were glittering and much remarked-on exceptions – and even his liveries were confined to his personal retinue. The lack of a national army uniform, in fact, symbolized the lack of a national army spirit: the levy was a collection of individuals whose interests were primarily personal.

The fact that musketeers had to purchase their own powder underlined the free enterprise character of the whole undertaking. It meant they had little interest in practising to improve their marksmanship or to cut down the inordinate length of time it took to reload their weapons: and it meant that, quite apart from the dangers involved, they had the most powerful economic motives for staying out of the thick of battle. Not that musketeers were hard to come by: it was well worth possessing a weapon that could be resold for anything between 18s and 40s – or that could be used for hunting and poaching in time of peace. Conscripts were obviously not supposed to take home the weapons issued to them, but there was no administrative system clever enough – and no officer zealous enough – to pursue those who did. Seven companies of one hundred men each had been levied and equipped in the City of London in 1593, but were disbanded a few days later when the alarm that inspired their levy proved to be false. Officials checking the equipment returned to the store recorded as lost without trace: 55 firearms, 49 pieces of armour, 32 pikes, 14 halberds (combined spears and battleaxes) and 495 swords.[3]

The whole rickety structure of Elizabethan warfare hung together on the prospect of perquisites like filched weapons. Even the chaplains depended on dead pays for their stipends: there was no official provision for paying them. Barber-surgeons were as ready to buy themselves out as ordinary soldiers and leave their crude responsibilities and tools to placemen even less qualified for the job. For a soldier to be wounded was to be as good as dead: the rough-and-ready battlefield medicine that barber-surgeons or their ignorant substitutes employed included cauterizing gunshot wounds with boiling oil. The white stripe round the red of the modern barber's pole describes all too precisely the incompetent fashion in which the medically pretentious predecessors of today's hairdressers placed an open bandage on a wounded limb.

It was into unashamed chaos of this sort that the Earl of Essex plunged in the spring of 1596 at Plymouth. And, to his credit, he succeeded in salvaging more order from it than would have most of his contemporary commanders. In relative terms his project constituted one of England's largest military adventures abroad before the twentieth century. Few others matched the manpower and distance involved when compared to the population size and resources available. For a population of five millions at the most to send 6,500 men to Cadiz in cockleshell wooden sailing vessels was easily the equivalent of the Boer War campaigns when the inhabitants of the British Isles numbered forty millions and had almost modern methods of administration and transport at their disposal.

The 6,500-strong army was divided into six regiments of 750 men each and two of 1,000. Incredibly there were to be no dead pays: the perquisites for the captains would be the spoils of conquest: so reward depended directly on performance.[4] Discipline was strict: a lieutenant who accepted bribes to substitute inferior men for pressed soldiers was cashiered and his name, crime and punishment were proclaimed through the streets of Plymouth by the sound of a drum: a soldier who tried to stir up mutiny was executed on the spot: another who murdered one of the reinforcements from Holland was tied to the butchered corpse and thrown into the sea.

With money only dribbling in from the Exchequer Essex decided to meet as many current expenses as he could from his own pocket: delays of pay or victualling dislocations due to suppliers being reluctant to work on credit would have been fatal to morale: 'I pay lendings to above 5,000 soldiers,' he wrote to Cecil on 12 May 1596. 'I maintain all the poor captains and their officers, I have a little world eating upon me in my house.'

It came as a bolt from the blue when a few days later the Queen decided to recall Essex and the Lord Admiral. She resented their rôle in the Calais fiasco that had shown up her own indecisiveness, and she had sudden cold feet about the expense and risk the Cadiz expedition involved. When the pointlessness of replacing Essex and the Lord Admiral with other commanders was made clear to her, she decided to call the whole thing off – or just send the fleet.

Essex exploded. He had spent nearly six months planning and organizing the expedition – most of it away from Court and in the face of perpetual harassment from Elizabeth. The more successfully he worked, the more she seemed to resent it and threw obstacles in his way. He wrote fiercely to the Privy Council. The Queen was being ridiculous. And his case was unanswerable. Having ventured in so far it would cost as much to stop as to continue: 'What shall be done with £30,000 worth of victuals of Her Majesty already provided, since it cannot be sold to London or to the ports?' The amount the cities had given in taxes meant they had no spare cash to buy up perishable surplus food. And they would hardly respond as generously to demands in the future 'since they shall see that our alarms are but false and our journeys but dreams.'

The same could be asked of the Low Countries, which had been unstinting in their assistance. They would not be so helpful again. 'What shall be done to keep France from making peace with Spain; when we neither assist them against invasion there, nor prevent invasions of our own countries?' Was not one of the expedition's objects to prevent Spain assisting Catholic rebellion in Ireland? What would the rebels there think when they 'see all our preparations but smoke, and our threatenings prove but wind?'

So far as the Privy Council was concerned Essex was preaching to the converted; and faced with their solid arguments the Queen was compelled to accept their point of view. Her caprice was revealed. Having got so far with the expedition it was sheer folly to abandon the project. Yet the sudden crisis showed how unpredictable and wayward Elizabeth was becoming with age, and how her critical faculties were disintegrating: spending tens of thousand of pounds on preparing such an expedition and then recalling its chief commanders was a very different matter from quibbling over which one of her courtiers wore the most pleasing costume: yet she approached both situations with the same fickle fancy. Her indecisiveness was not so much comical as positively dangerous.

It was with relief that on 24 May 1596 the Earl of Essex finally received the packet of letters that contained the Queen's definite orders for departure. As well as her Commission the Queen had included a special prayer of her own composition: 'I make this humble bill of requests to Him that all makes and does, that with His benign Hand He will shadow you so as all harm may light beside you, and all that may be best hap to your share; that your return may make you better and me gladder.' For the moment the Earl of Essex was not thinking of his return. He was heartily glad to be gone.

19

The Capture of Cadiz

On 1 June 1596 the wind blew fair for Spain. A breeze from the north-west wafted down the Channel, and when the *Ark Royal* fired its signal gun the English Armada drifted gently out of Plymouth. It made an imposing sight: well over one hundred ships, of which nearly fifty were men-o'-war, seventeen of them the Queen's own galleons: and they were surrounded by a swarm of transports, victuallers, flyboats and pinnaces. The armed might of England had taken to the high seas: this vast fleet was manned by some 5,000 sailors, and the army was 6,500 strong.

The commanders were the cream of English leadership then available. There was the Lord Admiral, Lord Charles Howard of Effingham, who, though old and tetchy, had to his credit command of the English squadrons that had shattered the Armada. He led the fleet in the *Ark Royal*. Behind him came the Earl of Essex in the *Due Repulse*, a spanking new ship for the man in whose career this expedition was to mark a high spot. Lord Thomas Howard, the Lord Admiral's brother, commanded the third squadron in *Mere Honour*. Sir Walter Raleigh in the *Warspite* hoped his command of the fourth squadron would in some measure redeem the Queen's close favour, lost since his secret marriage and mishandling of the *Madre de Dios* plunder. And the fifth squadron was composed of Dutch ships under their own Admiral, Jan van Duyvenvoord, who sailed in the *Neptune*. These Dutch allies whom Elizabeth, ten years earlier, had sent the Earl of Leicester to rescue from annihilation, were now strong enough to make their own independent contribution to this anti-Spanish enterprise; and their sea-power was growing so rapidly that only a few years after the Queen's death it was to outstrip England's. Indeed, England's great seventeenth-century conflicts were to be the commercial wars against these co-religionists and former allies.

Yet in 1596 the Dutch ships and soldiers, together with the 2,000 English troops brought out of the Netherlands under the seasoned command of Sir Francis Vere, Sir Matthew Morgan, Sir Conyers Clifford and Lord Burgh, were to lend the most crucial stiffening to the expedition.

The Dutch proved loyal allies – rather it was the English commanders who fought amongst themselves. Raleigh had squabbled at an early stage with Vere and Clifford over their relative seniorities, and Essex – joint commander with the Lord Admiral – had had to settle the matter by giving Raleigh seniority at sea and Vere on land. Then the Lord Admiral had objected to one of Essex's favourite tricks: the Earl had signed his name on a letter to the Queen so high and close to the text that there was no room for Howard to sign above him. It was a childish game which Essex had frequently played with Privy Council documents and which his elders usually tolerated with quiet amusement.[1] Yet the Lord Admiral could not accept the habit with the same good humour. In a fit of pique he took a penknife and cut out Essex's signature.

The sudden switching of the wind as the fleet reached Dodman's Head in Cornwall was a more serious matter. Sixteenth-century sails were not sophisticated enough for ships to be able to tack into a head breeze and, as the great Armada of 1588 had shown, sixteenth-century naval operations were a frighteningly haphazard procedure. The various fleets were blown, almost at random, across the surface of the waters. A hundred years later William and Mary were to owe their throne to the 'Protestant wind' from the north-east that blew their ships down the

Channel but kept James Stuart's fleet bottled up in the Thames and Medway.

Now there was nothing for it but to be blown back the thirty-odd miles to Plymouth Sound. It was not until 3 June that the expedition could finally get off to a proper start: and not before proclamations had been issued promising certain death to any who attempted to dive off the anchored ships and swim for the shore and freedom. The Lord Admiral called a council meeting of the squadron leaders and it was agreed that not until the fleet lay off Cadiz would it sail within sight of land, and that the target of the expedition be kept secret from all the ship's captains and crews.

They were to sail with sealed orders bearing the warning: 'if you be separated from the fleet by foul weather or otherwise, you shall herein find to what place you shall repair, till when you shall not open the enclosed upon pain of death.' Inside the sealed package were directions for reaching Cape St Vincent (then known as the South Cape) some one hundred miles south of Lisbon and some 150 miles west of Cadiz.

In the ships following Essex's *Due Repulse* were a selection of men whose talents were more than just military. There were courtiers – like Thomas Egerton and Sir Edward Hoby; scholars who had turned their hands to political affairs like Henry Wotton and Henry Cuffe; and poets like William Alabaster and, almost certainly, John Donne. His series of five poems, 'Fall of a Wall', 'A Burnt Ship', 'A Lame Beggar', 'Cales and Guiana', and 'Sir John Wingfield' were all most probably written on the Cadiz expedition.[2]

At dusk each day the ships would move together into their squadrons, greet each other with trumpet calls and cheers, and, having set the watch, follow through the night the lamp of their squadron leader. With dawn they would swing apart and sweep the sea before them, picking up vessels that could betray their presence and carry the alarm back to Spain. The *Swan* engaged a suspicious-looking flyboat that managed to escape towards the coast, and it was only after a long chase that the *John* and the *Francis* succeeded in capturing it. It was worth the trouble. They learned that the bulk of shipping in Cadiz harbour was mercantile and that no warships were expected.[3]

The wind blew steadily behind the English fleet – but on 11 June a select council of the squadron commanders was called. No one was sure exactly where the fleet lay in relation to land, so all the ships' masters and captains were summoned to the *Ark Royal* to give their opinions: 42° southward, about the level of Oporto, and a hundred miles or so from the coast, seemed the general consensus.[4] Another council meeting on 15 June drew up the plans for an orderly landing in Cadiz: regiments were to be split and landed in several parties, the commanders ensuring that equal detachments of the best men in each regiment should hit the beach simultaneously. The first ashore would cover the landings of those behind them.

There was a brief scare on the night of 18–19 June when a foreign ship was suddenly caught sailing into the fleet, and tried to make off into the darkness once it had discovered what hostile company it had fallen into. Yet forced to surrender it turned out to be an Irish merchantman bound for Waterford and two days out of Cadiz: and the captain had the most welcome news. Cadiz was weakly garrisoned and had not the slightest idea that such an Armada was bearing down on it; while outside the port lay a convoy of merchant ships preparing to sail for the Indies.

Should this booty-rich fleet or the town be attacked first? A hastily summoned council meeting debated the choice fiercely – and inconclusively. Eventually it was agreed that Essex should make full use of the advantage of surprise the expedition appeared to possess and that he should assault the town's citadel immediately. The Lord Admiral would worry about the merchant fleet and either capture it or bottle it up inside the bay. The wind freshened, and just after dawn on Sunday, 29 June 1596 Cadiz came in sight.

The surprise was total. Spain had received vague intelligence reports of a warfleet being prepared in Plymouth, but had believed 'leaks' carefully contrived by Burghley to the effect that Brittany, Ireland or perhaps even the West Indies, were the objects of the exercise. The vast arc of English sails rising over the horizon was the first warning the Cadiz garrison had that their port and shipping were threatened. The assault force led by Howard and Essex was many times larger than the small fleet with which Drake had wrought such havoc and 'singed the King of Spain's beard' in the year before the great Armada.

Church bells jangled in the town and the garrison spread its meagre strength around the decrepit walls of the fort. A programme of rebuilding was only half completed and workmen's tools lay in breaches scattered right through the fortifications. Most of the warships assigned to protect the merchant fleet that bobbed in the harbour were away in San Lucar refitting. There were only four galleons and a squadron of galleys to protect cargoes that were among the richest in the world. The galleys – Mediterranean, not Atlantic vessels – were rowed by slaves.

Cadiz itself, Spain's largest oceanic port, a few score miles north of Cape Trafalgar and Gibraltar, lies at the head of the spit of land that juts up like a huge crooked finger for some six miles parallel to the coast. To the west of the town lies the open sea, but to the east the protected waters of a huge bay. The English fleet dropped anchor in the sea to the west of Cadiz and, pursuing the plan of an immediate landing and assault, Essex ordered the soldiers to transfer to the long-boats and barges. The men were armed and powder was issued. The first assault craft were lowered. Yet the wind was rising, and, as the waves grew higher, two boats capsized. Fifteen soldiers weighed down with armour and weapons drowned screaming in the sight of their helpless comrades.

Surf was foaming on the beaches. A detachment of Spanish cavalry and infantry had appeared and had taken up positions behind wine barrels filled with sand. Some war galleys which could not tackle English men-o'-war, but could wreak havoc with open landing craft, were hovering in the middle distance. And the four great galleons which were the rump of the warfleet refitting in San Lucar were anchoring under cover of the fort's guns to the east of the town in an attempt to defend the merchant ships.

To land the troops in good order was obviously out of the

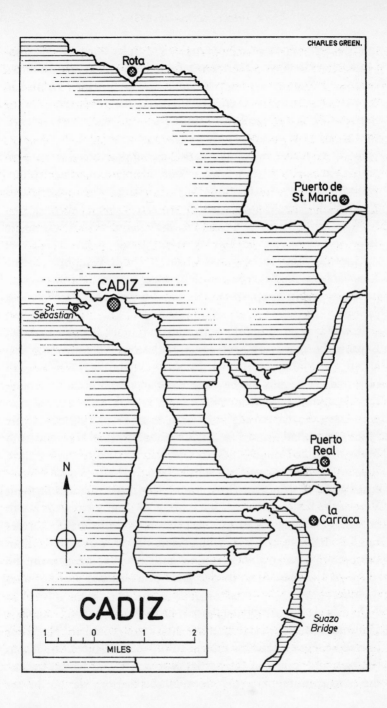

CHARLES GREEN.

Rota

Puerto de
St. Maria

CADIZ

St.
Sebastian

Puerto
Real

la
Carraca

Suazo
Bridge

N

CADIZ

1   0   1   2

MILES

F*

question. But Essex was unwilling to surrender the glory of spear-heading the first assault. He insisted that his soldiers remain in the landing craft bobbing dangerously on the roughening swell, and it was only after Walter Raleigh had made several journeys between Essex and the Lord Admiral that a decision was reached to attack first by sea.

It was not until the afternoon that the English soldiers were re-embarked safely on their own ships, and then the Lord Admiral was unwilling to risk his three flagships – the *Ark Royal*, the *Due Repulse* and *Mere Honour* – in a direct attack. He ordered that his brother Lord Thomas Howard in the *Nonpareil*, Raleigh in the *Warspite*, and Vere in the *Rainbow* should lead an advance squadron against the galleons while Sir John Wingfield in the *Vanguard* attacked the galleys. The bulk of the fleet was to stay in reserve with the flagships. Essex, on the *Due Repulse*, was furious.

It was not till next morning that the attack got under way. During the night the four Spanish galleons – named after the apostles St Philip, St Thomas, St Matthew and St Andrew – had retreated closer into the bay and were anchored broadside on to the oncoming English attackers. Yet the English ships had also been busy during the night, though to more petty purpose. Sir Francis Vere had slipped his anchor in an effort to be at the head of the combined assault, and when he was overtaken by Sir Walter Raleigh he had a rope fastened to Raleigh's ship to pull himself equal again. Raleigh was busy getting this rope cut and reproving Vere as the battle began and the guns of the four great ships began booming. Such ridiculous incompetence was, fortunately for the English attackers, not totally one-sided. Two huge cannon on the shore attempted to join in the defence, but exploded from the strain of the extra gunpowder their firers packed in to extend their range.

As soon as the cannonade started, Essex grew restless. Frustrated that his initial assault had been called off, he chafed at being kept in reserve. He ordered his captain to slip anchor, crept down into the bay, and joined in the battle. Not wishing to be left behind the Lord Admiral made to follow, but his flagship was bottled up in the mass of the fleet. So he had a barge take him to the *Mere Honour* and then he thrust into the fray.

The Spaniards were weakening. Their powder was poor and their cannonballs only bruised and bounced off the English ships they struck. By contrast the English cannon drove their shot hard into the sides of the galleons: the enemy wood started splintering, soldiers and gunners were struck down by the onslaught, and blood began to dribble from the scuppers. After three hours Essex ordered Raleigh to take the *Warspite* right to the galleons and to board with his soldiers. As the *Warspite* upped anchor the Spaniards panicked. The 'Apostles' cut their cables to drift across the bay, but the tide caught them and swept them aground on the sand bars off the mainland beaches. The *St Matthew* and the *St Andrew* were captured. The *St Philip* and *St Thomas* were fired before their English pursuers could reach them, and their sailors tumbled out of the flaming hulks 'so thick as if coals had been poured out of a sack in many ports at once, some drowned, some sticking in the mud'. Wounded, blackened and charred they clung to ropes and spars until their strength failed them and they drowned only a few yards out of their depth. If 'any man had a desire to see Hell itself,' wrote Raleigh later, 'it was then most lively figured.' The Dutch sailors added to the carnage by butchering all the survivors who approached their ships for help. John Donne was to remember the terror in verse:

> Out of a fired ship, which by no way
> But drowning could be rescued from the flame,
> Some men leaped forth, and ever as they came
> Near the foe's ships, did by their shot decay;
> So all were lost which in the ship were found:
> They in the sea being burnt, they in the burnt ship drowned.[5]

Essex had not been prominent in this victory – indeed his orders had made it possible for Raleigh to take the credit for the triumph. Yet that was through no reticence on the fiery Earl's part. He had seen that once inside the calm waters of the bay he could disembark his troops, and, without pausing to consult the Lord Admiral, he gave orders for the landing to begin before the sea battle had finished. With Sir Francis Vere and a handpicked bodyguard he led 2,000 men in barges and flyboats towards the beach. A drum in his boat beat a rhythm that the whole flotilla kept as they rowed towards Cadiz.

They beached in the middle of the afternoon, and there were no defenders to hinder their landing some three miles south of Cadiz. One thousand men under Conyers Clifford and Christopher Blount were sent further south to cut off reinforcements which might march up the narrow isthmus to relieve the town. That left Essex with a force 1,000 strong, and without hesitation he turned towards the citadel. The defenders were amazed at the order with which the little company kept ranks across the hot soft sand through which they advanced almost at the double.

They reached the town gates to discover a cavalry detachment five hundred strong waiting for them. There was no turning back. Essex ordered Sir John Wingfield to launch an open attack with an advance guard while the main body of the column moved concealed behind dead ground. It was a stratagem Francis Vere had learned in the Netherlands. The Spanish cavalry moved imperiously against Wingfield and his impertinent little band of attackers, and Wingfield fell back. The Spaniards came on faster and more carelessly. When Wingfield turned and the hidden bulk of the English column charged in behind him the Spaniards were shattered. They fled in panic through the town gates, which were shut so rapidly by the first to reach safety that some forty horsemen were locked outside. It was lucky for them that their fortifications were being repaired – for they jumped off their mounts and scrabbled through the holes still strewn with workmen's tools.

Essex was among the first to follow them through the walls. Sword in hand, he hacked down all who stood in his way and with a handful of men pushed pell mell to the centre of the town. More prudently, Francis Vere collected the stragglers together, opened the town gates and swept methodically to the market place where Essex's little band of heroes had been checked by a last-ditch stand of defenders in the main Town House. It was a moment fraught with danger. A powerful counter-attack by the

Spaniards could have swept the triumphant but exhausted English advance guard out to the beach again. Yet at that moment the Lord Admiral was marching through the gates of Cadiz with the bulk of the remaining English troops. He had ignored a message from Essex advising him to capture the merchant fleet, and had decided to make sure of the citadel first. As the sun rose next morning the whole of Cadiz lay in English hands.

It was a magnificent victory and, for all his rashness, Essex could justly claim the major credit for it. On sea and land a hundred English lives had been lost at most. The most serious loss was Sir John Wingfield, whose cool strategem in front of the Spanish cavalry had paved the way for Essex's advance. He was buried with full military honours in the captured cathedral, and of his death his friend John Donne wrote:

> Beyond the old Pillars many have travelled
> Towards the Sun's cradle, and his throne, and bed.
> A fitter Pillar our Earl did bestow
> In that late Island; for he well did know
> Farther than Wingfield no man dares to go.[6]

The sack that followed the victory was both chaotic and strangely humane. The Spaniards were amazed by the restraint with which the English left the churches unharmed and evacuated 1,500 monks, friars and women. For this again Essex could take the credit, and he intervened fiercely to prevent the Dutch taking advantage of this opportunity to continue on Spanish soil the savage reprisals and counter-reprisals of the Netherlands War. Yet plunder was what the English troops had travelled and fought for – and plunder they got. In no time the streets were cluttered with chairs, tables, broken bottles of wine and oil, almonds, raisins and spices, all tossed through the windows as the conquerors searched for more permanent and portable wealth. Prudent Spaniards had hidden their jewels in tombs and benefited from Essex's prohibition on the sacking of churches. Yet few of the booty-seekers plundered fruitlessly. Day and night the riot continued and the English army filled its pockets and packs with the spoils of victory.

Yet the richest spoil was to elude their grasp. The Military Commandant of the Cadiz area was the Duke of Medina Sidonia, who had commanded the Armada of 1588 with such conspicuous incompetence. Safely ensconced on the far side of the bay he had watched the whole battle – and had promptly offered his old opponent, Lord Howard of Effingham, two million ducats if the Spanish merchant fleet, defenceless since the capture and destruction of the four great Apostles, were allowed to go free. With thirty or forty heavily laden ships at his mercy Howard did not consider this ransom offer high enough. He demanded four million ducats. Yet he made little effort to secure the vessels he was asking this huge price for. His sailors were too busy sacking Cadiz to arrest the more valuable quarry that lay anchored in the bay.

The Duke of Medina Sidonia acted with rare decisiveness. He could not save the fleet, and the English would not accept his ransom offer. As the sun rose on the morning of Wednesday, 23 June 1596, three days after the English fleet had first appeared over the horizon and two days after they had captured Cadiz, flaming black columns of smoke were seen to be rising from the thirty-six ships anchored in the bay. The fleet had been scuttled. By the time any English boats could reach the scene there were only a few cannon to be salvaged. Twelve million ducats' worth of goods had gone up in flames or lay on the sea bottom. The squadron of galleys took advantage of the confusion to make good their escape.

This terrible act of self-destruction set the seal on a catalogue of Spanish catastrophe: the four Apostles lost, a group of Cadiz's most prosperous citizens held to ransom, a ransom of 120,000 ducats paid for the city itself, Cadiz sacked – and thirty-six of the world's richest ships forfeited. Yet Spanish loss was not English gain. The English could not tally up this same impressive list to their credit. There was the honour of capturing a Spanish port and the slight profit of its incidental pickings. Yet they could not hold Cadiz for ever and the main, incredible, overwhelming prize had eluded their grasp. The expedition could return home covered with honour and the ordinary soldiers and sailors were happy enough with their individual pickings: but the overall expense of the enterprise had barely been covered.

The only hope of redeeming this colossal error of omission was to wait in Cadiz for the return of the Spanish fleet carrying the year's consignment of South American treasure. Essex was for staying. There were enough supplies on the English ships and around Cadiz to keep three or four thousand men healthily alive for four months – by which time a proper system of convoys could have established a most efficient line of communication with England and the Netherlands. The Earl had for some months been nursing the idea of setting up a permanent base on Spanish soil: it would enable English ships to establish a permanent blockade – the very tactic the British navy was to employ in the eighteenth century, and it would also call into being the permanent and professional expeditionary force that the chaotic Plymouth muster had convinced the Earl was so necessary – a small English standing army. Now he had landed with a large and comparatively fresh body of troops it seemed logical to stay. He nominated himself Governor of Cadiz and adamantly refused to listen to any suggestion that some of the fleet should go home or lie in wait off the Azores for the treasure galleons. He threw himself into becoming a governor of occupied territory and, with the Lord Admiral on the Sunday after the landing, knighted some sixty-eight gentlemen who had distinguished themselves in the assault. Among the new knights were Gelli Meyrick, Essex's steward and Charles Blount of the golden chessman, the future Lord Mountjoy.

Yet the Nemesis that cancelled out all the Earl of Essex's more successful achievements was beginning to take effect. For second only to his Elizabeth's wrath when she heard of the scuttling of the merchant fleet, was her fury at the openhanded way in which the Earl had dispensed the honour of knighthood to all and sundry. As she had reminded him after the French campaign, Queen Elizabeth dubbed men knights but rarely. To earn a 'Sir' before one's name a man had to serve Elizabeth long and hard. Now the Earl of Essex was dishing out titles like pennies to the poor. Not only was he debasing the honour: he was setting himself up as a rival to the monarch's divine authority. He had displayed the same indiscriminate largesse outside Rouen – and had been reproved for it. Would he ever learn?

The more immediate problem was whether to go or stay. Feasible though the Earl of Essex's plan to set up a permanent base might seem, it was not allowed for in the royal letters that had commissioned the expedition. It would have to be approved by the Privy Council, and there was little chance of either Burghley or Elizabeth agreeing to such a permanent and potentially expensive military commitment. Much more important, there was even less chance of the ordinary soldiers and sailors agreeing to remain. They still had their lives and, miraculously in the context of sixteenth-century military organization, their health. They each had comfortable quantities of personal plunder and the weather looked ideally suited for a calm cruise home. Most of the captains shared their men's feelings. There was little prospect of immediate further gain if they stayed and the not inconceivable possibility of losing everything – health, plunder and lives – as a result of a Spanish counter-attack. The individual joint-stock character of the enterprise that had brought and held the expedition together during the preparations and outward journey now made for dissolution.

At a series of council meetings Essex raged fiercely against the steady evaporation of the fleet's and army's will to fight. With more and less sincerity his fellow generals agreed it was deplorable, but what were they to do? If desertions began it would undermine the morale of such troops and ships as remained. Rather than stay put and wait for this erosion of will it was better to make the most of such lingering desire for battle as remained, put out to sea, ravage a few more ports and possibly capture the great treasure fleet that was due to come through the Azores in the next week or so. Essex reluctantly allowed himself to be overruled. He could not deny that the treasure fleet was a prize well worth winning and that, given the attitude of the men, the best way to win it was by lying in wait on the high seas.

On 1 July 1596 he began supervising the systematic destruction of Cadiz. The town's cannon were gathered and stowed on board the English fleet. The walls, towers and fortifications were demolished by the pioneers who had had no need to use their skills and equipment in the original assault. And on 4 July 1596, two weeks after the first church bells had jangled out alarm at the sight of the English fleet, the town of Cadiz was consigned to the flames. Only the churches and religious houses were not deliberately fired – and few of them escaped the general conflagration. Essex was the last man to embark on the last boat that left the burning town.

The remaining weeks of the expedition were a mere apology for action while an excuse was sought to go home. The fleet drifted back north as its commanders debated in a desultory fashion the alternative courses open to them. Only Essex came out strongly and clearly in favour of waiting near Cadiz or sailing out to the Azores to waylay the Spanish treasure fleet. His fellow commanders doubted whether the men would be prepared to alter their present Plymouth-bound course. Yet they had to agree that awkward questions would be asked in London if they dashed straight for home. They were passing southern Portugal, the Algarve, and since Portugal was still in Spanish hands it seemed logical to make a rapid raid on one of the Portuguese harbours along the coast. They could perhaps pick up some extra booty at little risk.

Since Essex had spearheaded the capture of Cadiz, the Lord Admiral had been anxious to chalk up a land assault to his credit, so when the fleet anchored off Cape St Mary on 13 July he claimed it was his turn to lead the army. But leading involved a ten-mile march to the town of Faro, and in the blazing heat the Lord Admiral thought better of his gallantry. He would shadow the troops with his ships and Essex could command the land sector after all. On 14 July the march began, Sir Christopher Blount leading an advance guard of the Cadiz heroes and a cluster of gentlemen adventurers hopeful of winning their own knighthoods in Faro. Essex could not resist leaving the main body of the army in order to march with them.

Yet there were to be no heroics – and no knighthoods – in Faro. The inhabitants had got wind of the English attack and had taken to the mountains with their goods. A chasing party of 800 caught only a few oxen and sheep. Essex loaded on to his ship the impressive library of books owned by the local bishop, but Faro's pickings were small and the gentlemen adventurers had to return to the fleet, their swords unbloodied. The town was fired – more in frustration at the lack of sport it had afforded than for any other reason.

As the English ships resumed their northward drift and the commanders resumed their debates on suitable towns to raid, the wind changed. It blew fair for a dash to the Azores where the treasure fleet should by this time have arrived, and Essex argued fiercely in favour of this course. Sir Francis Vere supported him – but the Lord Admiral and other commanders would have none of it. Essex suggested he take just a small raiding party – but again he was overruled. The idea of attacking or waiting off Lisbon was also rejected. The fleet, it was decided by the majority of the Lord Admiral's war council, was unfit for further campaigning. They would sail for Plymouth and just pause at Cape Finisterre in the topmost corner of Spain to see if there were any plunderable ships in the harbour of Corunna. It would not be much out of their way home.

So the captains could set a direct north, north-east course with a clear conscience, speeding past Lisbon, and when they got to Corunna on 1 August discovered, hardly to their surprise, since warnings of their presence had had over a month to reach the furthest corners of Spain, that the port was empty. Without more ado they set sail for Plymouth which the fastest ship reached on 6 August.

But a week earlier, the Spanish treasure fleet laden with gold, silver and jewels worth 20,000,000 ducats, had lumbered up the River Tagus into Lisbon harbour virtually unprotected – and completely unharmed. There the Spanish captains learned to their amazement that an English warfleet had sailed past Lisbon less than forty-eight hours earlier. They would have been still more amazed to learn that the English commanders had been arguing as they passed Lisbon by – and that the Earl of Essex's suggestion to attack the town or lie in wait in the roads outside had been rejected by his comrades out of hand.

20

'A dangerous image'

The intoxication of the Cadiz triumph had been exhilarating: the long hangover after it was painful. No one yet knew of the hair's-breadth escape which the treasure fleet from the West Indies had been allowed. But other omissions were already glaringly obvious.

There was the booty, for a start. Elizabeth had invested heavily in the expedition and after the glowing reports of success that the commanders had despatched home she expected her money back and a substantial dividend on top. Knowing well the inefficiencies – and dishonesties – to which such enterprises were liable she had taken the precaution of appointing a special agent, Sir Anthony Ashley, to make sure she got her fair share of the plunder; she had royal commissioners in Plymouth – Sir Ferdinando Gorges, William Killigrew and William Stallenge – waiting to check in all the returning ships and to make a proper inventory of their contents; and the Lord Admiral and Essex had from the start been under the strictest instructions to organize all the swag so that the costs of the voyage were met before individual rewards were distributed.

Yet all these most carefully laid arrangements went awry: Elizabethan government simply was not mature enough to cope with the strains of administration when state and private interest collided. William Killigrew, specially sent down from London, reported back panic-stricken that the ships returning from Cadiz were checking in only briefly at Plymouth before making rapid tracks for their own particular home port, presumably with plenty of loot on board: and that such booty as they did leave in Plymouth was 'in huxter's handling'.[1] Sir Ferdinando Gorges predicted candidly that 'very much goods will be embezzled'.[2] And William Stallenge, who unlike his honestly helpless colleagues had the presence of mind to shift the blame, alleged that 'all or most of the goods landed in this place was given by the Generals to men of desert and is by them sold to others, and the money received, which will hardly be gotten from them.'[3]

Killigrew, Gorges and Stallenge were incompetent but could justifiably plead that, through no fault of their own, they had been set to work hopelessly late in the game. Sir Anthony Ashley, commissioned to keep an eye on affairs from the very beginning, could offer no such excuses. He was not only incompetent but dishonest to boot. Chests of goods were taken into his own London house; a huge diamond that should have gone straight to the Queen was broken up among London jewellers and neither the pieces – nor the profits – were ever seen again.[4] In fury Elizabeth disgraced Ashley for good: he was sent to the Fleet prison.

And it was not only the Queen's trust that Ashley had betrayed. The Earl of Essex had despatched him home ahead of the main body of the fleet to take care of some private errands, for by 1596 Essex knew his Elizabeth well enough to anticipate trouble. She would want to discover, he could predict, exactly what had gone wrong, so she should know on whom she could pour the full weight of her scathing condemnation. And every single other commander would be busy shifting the blame and organizing support for his own particular version of events. Essex prepared a document setting out his own account of what had happened, how he personally had distinguished himself and how his own good advice had been overruled, and entrusted it to Ashley. The plan was to get it printed and distributed in London before anyone else had a chance to tell their own particular story. With Ashley sailed Henry Cuffe, the former professor of Greek who was Essex's secretary, but after landing in England Cuffe unfortunately fell ill on the hard ride up to London.

So Sir Anthony Ashley carried in his saddle-bag *A true relation of the action at Cadiz the 21st June, under the Earl of Essex and Lord Admiral, sent to a gentleman in Court from one that served there in good place.* Yet on arriving in London, in a vain effort to save himself from the consequences of his own dishonesty over the booty, Ashley told both the Queen and the Council of the existence of the document. At once an order was published strictly prohibiting the printing of this or any other account of what had happened on the expedition, and though *A true relation of the action at Cadiz* got to the printers, it got no further. Anthony Bacon had to get written copies distributed to Essex's friends. And when the Earl himself arrived at Court at noon on 12 August 1596 he was greeted bitterly by the Queen.

There was no private audience for the conquering hero. Instead Elizabeth received him where the whole Court could hear her scalding words of criticism. She had paid out £50,000 of her own hard-gathered revenues to finance the expedition, and she had got nothing as dividend from her investment. It was, she declared, exactly what she had expected: she had forseen it all and should have known better: everyone had made a fortune except her. Well, Essex should pay for his incompetence, and no manner of excuses or protestations could convince her he had not failed her grievously. The conquering hero was dismissed in disgrace.

I see [the Earl wrote to Anthony Bacon] the fruits of these kinds of employments, and I assure you I am as much distasted with the glorious greatness of a favourite as I was before with the supposed happiness of a courtier, and call to mind the words of the wisest man that ever lived, who, speaking of man's works crieth out 'Vanity of vanities, all is vanity'.

The lines of a poem the Earl is reputed to have written on his ship returning from Cadiz rang prophetically:

> Happy were he could finish forth his fate
> In some unhaunted desert, where, obscure
> From all society, from love and hate

Of worldly folk, there should he sleep secure;
Then wake again, and yield God ever praise,
Content with hip, with haws, and brambleberry;
In contemplation passing still his days,
And change of holy thoughts to keep him merry:
Who, when he dies, his tomb might be the bush
Where harmless Robin resteth with the thrush:
– Happy were he![5]

Robin might be the name those close to Essex used for Robert, but the Queen had greeted him formally by his titles as though Bess and Robin had never giggled away dark winter nights or balmy summer afternoons. And Elizabeth's displeasure had not been confined simply to modes of address, for in Essex's absence she had helped the Cecils take an enormous step forward in establishing their influence against him. On 5 July 1596, the very day on which the English fleet had upped anchor and of its own accord sailed away from the first – and last – real foothold Elizabethan troops established on the mainland of Europe, Robert Cecil had been sworn in as Principal Secretary to the Queen. After waiting patiently for five years, old Burghley had achieved his last great ambition: to see his quiet, crippled, brilliant son take over the reins of effective power. The old man could die content. His boy Robert would still have to struggle with that other Robert, Earl of Essex, so much nobler born and so generously endowed with the superficial attractions that counted for so much at the Elizabethan Court. Yet as Principal Secretary to the Queen young Cecil was undeniably established – he could hold his own alone against Essex; and given time he could do more than that. Wrote old Lady Bacon, Burghley's sister-in-law, to her son Anthony: 'Sir Robert is fully stalled in his long-longed-for secretary's place . . . you had need now to be more circumspect . . . walk more warily . . . The father and son are affectionate joined in power and policy.'[6]

Essex had nominated his own candidate for the secretaryship – Thomas Bodley – a worthy man who had been an ambassador to the Netherlands: but even Essex's supporters acknowledged he was not up to the efforts and initiative such an office demanded.[7]

Bodley had to be content with what seemed at the time a poor *faute de mieux*, the books plundered by Essex from the library of the Bishop of Faro: though generations of Oxford students who have profited from the Bodleian library, part of whose nucleus these plundered books formed, have since made good use of the consolation prize.

It was a sour empty homecoming for a man who had imagined himself the hero of the hour and who had grown a full square beard that he hoped would set a new fashion – 'Cadiz-style'. His Queen was angry at his inability to organize the plunder on her behalf, and ostentatiously lent her ear to those who maintained that Raleigh and the Lord Admiral should take most of the credit for such successes as the expedition had achieved. She was angry too at Essex's knighting of soldiers by the score: it hit directly at her prerogative if one of her subjects could so freely dispense an honour whose value lay in coming from the Crown. It underlined cruelly the fact which was obvious but which, in being obvious, was all the more difficult for her to come to terms with, that she was not a male warrior king like her father who could dispense knighthoods personally on the battlefield. She was a woman dependent on the services of men like Essex, and her own impotence increased her fury when men let her down.

Only the Archbishop of Canterbury, John Whitgift, the master of Essex's old college, responded to Cadiz as the conquering hero had hoped. He ordered a general thanksgiving for the victory throughout the kingdom. But the Queen intervened to restrict the celebrations to London, and made her displeasure obvious when Dr William Barlow, the Archbishop's chaplain who preached the sermon at St Paul's Cross on the thanksgiving day, praised Essex, criticized his detractors, and was tumultuously applauded by a large crowd. For a disfavoured favourite to be so warmly favoured by the people was a dangerous sign.

When in the first week of September 1596 news reached London of the narrow escape of the West Indies treasure fleet at Lisbon Elizabeth refused to admit that Essex was vindicated. She broadened her anger to include the other commanders – particularly Raleigh – but made no apology to Essex for her former displeasure. Indeed, she declared that since the Earl had so grossly mishandled the spoils of the expedition she would confiscate the ransoms of such prisoners as had fallen to his share. When Burghley intervened on Essex's behalf to hint at the injustice of her continuing displeasure, she turned on him too. 'My Lord Treasurer,' she roared, 'either for fear or favour you regard my Lord of Essex more than myself. You are a miscreant! You are a coward!' Essex's popularity in the country was obviously worrying her.

Burghley wrote to Essex explaining his difficulties with the Queen, and Essex thanked him for his pains. Anthony Bacon seized on the old man's letter and circulated copies of it with Essex's reply among his friends. He wrote to Dr Hawkins, his agent in Italy:

Our Earl, God be thanked, hath with the bright beams of his valour and virtue scattered the clouds and cleared the mists that malicious envy had stirred against his matchless merit: which hath made the old Fox [Burghley] to crouch and whine, and to insinuate himself by a very submissive letter to my lord of Essex, subscribed in these terms: 'Your lordship's, if you will, at commandment.'[8]

Anthony Bacon, immersed in a world of intrigue and diplomacy where deep meanings were read into notes like Burghley's, was jubilant at the temporary triumph. But his brother Francis was not dazzled by such ephemeral victories. He had for some time been worried by the direction in which his patron's ambitions had been tending. He and his brother had nailed their colours to the Essex mast because they thought they had found in the young Earl a man of influence whom they could guide to yet higher greatness. Francis may have checked their mutual progress by his ill-judged opposition in the 1593 Parliament, but that mistake had been paid for. It explained why Francis himself had not been promoted to the offices he sought. It did not explain why the Earl's own progress seemed to fluctuate so wildly – and particularly why Robert Cecil had been given the secretaryship. There were other reasons for that, and Francis Bacon was beginning to ponder them seriously. Perhaps he was backing the wrong horse. The more he attempted to guess the future of Essex and of those associated with him the less hopeful he became. He would not desert the Earl yet, but he would try to explain to him what was on his mind. He could hardly warn or threaten, but he would try to set out the dangers he could foresee: and by studying Essex's reactions to these home truths he might better chart his own future path.

In October 1596 Francis Bacon set down in writing his analysis of his patron's faults and virtues, particularly his faults; and his analysis was perhaps the most penetrating contemporary assessment set down on paper. He began by explaining the four main reasons why the Queen was so frequently displeased with Essex: she found his nature unruly; he displayed little evidence of the abilities or wealth that were needed to justify the great eminence he aspired to; he appealed too directly to the affections of the people; and he was a soldier. 'I demand,' asked Bacon, 'whether there can be a more dangerous image than this represented to any monarch living, much more to a lady, and of her Majesty's apprehension?' It is not only his use of the word 'image' that conjures up the impression of a twentieth-century political agent grooming his candidate. He put forward some practical suggestions about how the campaign should be organized in the future: but, unlike a twentieth-century campaign, the whole show was organized for the benefit of an audience of one – the Queen.

Essex should drop his habit of complaining about past injustices – deserved or imagined. The secretaryship had been bestowed and nothing could be gained by carping on about it. The Earl should try to recapture the earnestness and sincerity with which he had once courted the Queen. His compliments were becoming dangerously offhand. He should enter more into the ploys and games of the Court – suggesting, perhaps, that he had to visit his estates in Wales and then calling the journey off to please the Queen. Or suggesting someone for a vacant office and withdrawing the candidature gracefully the moment Elizabeth expressed a preference elsewhere.

His obvious hankering for military greatness was bound to offend a Queen who had neither the stomach nor means for warfare. It was less than a century since her grandfather was struggling for his life against the military power of over-mighty earls and barons. The Queen was understandably suspicious of anyone who seemed tending towards that same sort of over-mightiness. The Earl of Essex should relinquish his ambition to be appointed Earl Marshal of England or to gain control of the country's artillery by becoming Master of the Ordnance. He would gain more profit and more favour as Lord Privy Seal.

The way in which these military ambitions were coupled with a deliberate and direct appeal to the affections of the people also conjured up understandable fears in the Queen. She was jealous when her favourite earned more cheers than she did: and she knew all about the dangers which such popularity contained for the monarchy. The Earl should eschew his publicity-seeking ways.

How could he lay claim to manage the Queen's affairs when he could not manage his own, and came constantly to her asking for help with the debts his own improvidence had caused?

The Earl should realize what apprehensions his faults could inspire in a woman like Queen Elizabeth, and should act to calm them accordingly. He should go so far as to step down in deference to another: it had strengthened Leicester's position to offer his stepson to the Queen's favour. By showing similar unconcern and generosity, the Earl of Essex could strengthen his own position enormously.

It was all good advice – and showed Bacon had seen to the heart of the dilemma that was Essex's relationship with Elizabeth. But he was inciting the wrong man to play the Machiavel. The Earl was incapable of the subtlety Francis was urging. As Henry Cuffe said of his master: 'He can conceal nothing; he carries his love and his hatred on his forehead.' And, of course, by setting his fears firmly on record Bacon showed that he also had little confidence that Essex could play the part the drama required of him, that it was too late for whispered advice or consultations. His letter was by way of an ultimatum, though he was too subtle, and Essex too obtuse, for that to become obvious. If the patron would not act as his adviser advised, then the adviser would take his advice elsewhere.

But events moved too quickly for Essex seriously to consider the words of wisdom Francis Bacon had set down for him. The news of a sudden Spanish invasion set by the board any prospect of Essex forswearing military greatness – distant though the prospect of such forswearing ever was. For Philip of Spain had been planning to attack England in another Armada in 1597. And now, smarting under the humiliation of Cadiz, he decided to accelerate his plans. Ignoring the protests of his admirals, he drove his fleet to sea in the last week of October 1596. Portuguese prisoners on two ships that reached England in November gave warning of a Spanish fleet they had seen sailing down the Tagus from Lisbon. At once alarm beacons were made ready along the south coast, three light craft were sent down the Channel to spy out for the approaching enemy and give warning, and some 70,000 local militia were placed under arms. The Earl of Essex was appointed head of a special Council of War to advise the Queen, and rough plans were laid for a scorched-earth retreat and multiple harassing actions if the enemy landed. There was no time to assemble the sort of marine force that had defeated the Armada of 1588. Troops were concentrated in the four most likely landing places along the Channel and in London itself.

Yet after the first alarms and feverish preparations, into which the Earl of Essex threw himself with his customary lack of restraint, no more was heard of the Spanish fleet. And it was not until after Christmas 1596 that it was learned reliably that the invasion flotilla had been struck by a storm in the Bay of Biscay. Some twenty or thirty of the warships had foundered and untold numbers of smaller craft had been destroyed. At least 3,000 men had perished. To the pious Englishman the disaster seemed proof of some divine intervention. Although the defence preparations had not been put to the test, the Earl of Essex emerged from the crisis with his reputation enhanced: and his reputation was now inescapably a military one. Francis Bacon began quietly preparing an escape route from the entourage of this dangerous and headstrong patron. The Earl seemed more and more turning towards the company and counsel of the gentleman adventurers whose swords had won knighthoods at Cadiz. Francis could see little future for himself among a crowd of such boorish featherheads. They were already talking in terms of next year's sport and urging the Earl to advocate a raid on another Spanish port – or on the Spanish bases in the Azores.

And besides, as 1596 drew to an end, Francis Bacon had other concerns to occupy his talents. January 1597 saw the publication of the most revolutionary little book to leave the English printing press until then. The first twenty-five of its sixty pages bore a description previously unknown in England; they called themselves 'Essays' and they explored in a graceful, lucid prose themes like 'Ceremonies and Respects', 'Followers and Friends', 'Negotiating' and 'Expense'. As Francis himself wrote, 'some books are to be tasted, others to be swallowed and some few to be chewed and digested.' As one of the chewable minority, Bacon's *Essays* were consummate art, significant not simply in their own right but in the context of English literature as a whole. For modern English prose was born with their publication.

'Mean men must adhere,' he wrote in his essay on 'Faction', 'but great men that have strength in themselves were better to maintain themselves indifferent and neutral.' Considering himself a mean man he now began to take steps to attach himself to a great man more indifferent and neutral than Essex. For his patron was continuing to ignore his advice. In February 1597 Queen and favourite had a flaming disagreement and the Earl retired disconsolate to his bed. Elizabeth went to visit him and he recovered. Then there were rumours of promotion for Raleigh or Thomas Howard, and the invalid's sickness overwhelmed him again. Furious, Elizabeth cried for all her Court to hear: 'I shall break him of his will and pull down his great heart' – and strangely Essex recovered again.

Bacon was wasting his time with such a master. He wrote to Lord Burghley a long, circumspect, flattering letter. 'My singular good Lord, *ex abundantia cordis*, I must acknowledge how greatly and diversely your Lordship hath vouchsafed to tie me unto you by many your benefits.' He gently hinted that he was prepared to switch his allegiance and he apologized for work he had carried out in the past on Essex's behalf that might have thwarted

Burghley's designs: 'In like humble manner I pray your Lordship to pardon mine errors, and not to impute unto me the errors of any other . . . but to conceive of me to be a man that daily profiteth in duty.'

Old Burghley's reply has not survived. But he certainly did not rebuff Francis's wary advance. And as winter turned to spring a dispute blew up over an office in the gift of the Queen which showed how far apart the policy of Essex and the advice of Bacon had drifted. On 5 March 1597 Lord Cobham, who had been both Lord Chamberlain and Warden of the Cinque Ports, died. If Essex had been pursuing the policy suggested by his counsellor he would have directed his efforts towards securing, or securing an interest in, the civil position of Lord Chamberlain which Cobham's death left vacant. But instead he launched a campaign for the military wardenship of the five ports which protected and controlled south-east England. His nominee was Sir Robert Sidney, the young and inexperienced brother of Philip, a choice that aroused little enthusiasm or general support at Court, and which Robert Sidney himself found it difficult to take seriously.

Elizabeth made clear from the start that she considered the dead man's son, the new Lord Cobham, to be the most appropriate choice for the job. Robert Sidney, she told Essex, was too young and already had quite enough to do as governor of the Netherlands port of Flushing. It would be an insult to the Cobham title to offer the post to any man of lesser rank.

This was the point at which to follow Francis Bacon's advice and withdraw gracefully from the campaign. But Essex rose to the bait Elizabeth had mischievously dangled before him. If Sidney's rank were too low, he declared, then the Earl of Essex would offer himself. That was on Monday, 7 March. On 9 March Elizabeth called him to her side and told him definitely that the new Lord Cobham was to have the Cinque Ports. And she had a messenger lying in wait next morning to intercept the Earl when he rode out of London in a huff; when he heeded her summons and returned to her presence, she told him she would make him Master of the Ordnance instead.

Essex was delighted; but he did not realize this was the very military position Bacon had warned him not to accept: nor that the whole pantomime of the Queen hinting that Essex should perhaps try for the Cinque Ports himself, then goading him into a stormy exit which ended in the inevitable and prepared recall and reconciliation, was just a game of cat and mouse in which he was certainly not the cat. Lord Cobham, who now inherited the Cinque Ports' wardenship from his father, was definitely one of the Cecil faction. And behind the smoke screen caused by all these arguments, Cecil himself was quietly manoeuvring for the valuable and important chancellorship of the Duchy of Lancaster.

Bacon could see all this; Robert Devereux could not. He had won for himself the mastership of Ordnance, control of the royal munitions, and he was happy with that promotion. Preparations were now going ahead for a large military and naval expedition to the Azores which he and he alone would lead. There was to be no Lord Admiral to ignore his advice and thwart his plans. If he had pushed his relationship with the Queen to breaking point yet again, he had got his way yet again, and if their meetings were liable to be tempestuous because of that, well, he was not afraid to stand up to his Elizabeth. Besides he was not tied to the old woman's apron strings; he was not bound to sue and scrape day after day at her door. He had important work to do. All through April and May 1597 he immersed himself in preparing the ships and soldiers with which he hoped yet again to vanquish the military might and honour of Spain. He came but seldom to Court. There was a definite coolness between Queen and favourite.

In later years Sir Robert Naunton attempted to explain the strange way in which Elizabeth and Essex swung from hot to cold, from passion to hatred, and he blamed both of them, citing two main reasons:

The first [reason] was a violent indulgency of the Queen which is incident to old age where it encounters with a pleasing and suitable object. . . . The second was a fault in the object of her grace, my Lord himself, who drew in too fast like a child sucking on an over-uberous nurse: and had there been a more decent decorum observed in both or either of these, without doubt the unity of their affections had been more permanent, and not so in and out as they were, like an instrument ill tuned and lapsing to discord.[9]

The expedition to the Azores was to increase the discord between Elizabeth and Essex. The Queen had agreed to its expense against her better judgement, and she intended to make the Earl suffer if anything went wrong. She had little time for his military pretensions and she prevaricated before she finally agreed to sign his commission of command on 15 June 1597. Lord Essex, on the other hand, had no reservations about his likely success. Before the end of the month he was on board his old flagship, the *Due Repulse*, and ready to sail off to the wars again. Robert Devereux saw himself once more set fair for glory.

21

The Islands Voyage

But the glory did not happen. The expedition to the Azores in the summer of 1597 proved to be a decisive turning point in the fortunes of the Earl of Essex – and a turning in the wrong direction. He had to struggle with an array of adversities, poor weather, poor equipment, poor advisers, poor soldiers and poor sailors, but his reactions under stress did not indicate that his own mettle was any better than that of his incompetent fighting companions.

He had emerged from the Cadiz expedition with some credit. His desire to sail up the Tagus to Lisbon had been prompted by motives little more subtle than belligerence and greed for glory, but he had been startlingly vindicated by the arrival of the Spanish treasure fleet a few days later. No such happy coincidence marked his trip to the Azores, and under the stress of misfortune he certainly did not display the coolness and judgement required of the commander of such an ambitious naval enterprise.

A thousand miles off the Spanish coast, three thousand miles from South America, the nominally Portuguese but effectively Spanish islands of the Azores were the crucial staging post in the treasure route that led from the silver mines of Peru to Madrid. The cockleshell craft that bobbed hopefully but, with their primitive steering and sailing gear, almost helplessly across the wild grey reaches of the Atlantic relied on the islands to rest, refit

Robert Devereux, 2nd Earl of Essex, by an unknown artist. This likeness corresponds most closely to verbal descriptions of the Earl – the long, uneven nose, the broad, pallid face. To judge from both his age and the cut of his beard, this portrait was painted after Essex's return from Cadiz.

Queen Elizabeth standing on Saxton's map of England in 1592. Her feet rest at Ditchley in Oxfordshire which she visited as a guest of Sir Henry Lee, the cousin of Captain Thomas Lee who was executed in 1601 for attempting to rescue Essex from the Tower. The fact that Elizabeth was in her sixtieth year is not apparent from the picture which was painted not as a portrait but in the tradition of Gloriana, the mythical Faerie Queen. The sonnet in the cartouche makes this clear, beginning with the lines: 'The Prince of Light, the Sun by whom things live, Of heaven the glory, and of earth the grace.' In her youth Elizabeth had no need of this stylized, almost caricatured form of portaiture which belongs to the later years of her reign.

(*Below*) Robert Dudley, Earl of Leicester. This portrait by an unknown artist shows Leicester when he first established himself as Queen Elizabeth's favourite. By the time he became Essex's stepfather he was a portly, middle-aged man with a white beard and red veined cheeks. He hoped that the good looks of his stepson would re-kindle on his own behalf the attraction he had exercised over the Queen at the time this portrait was painted.

(*Above*) Sir Philip Sidney, the Shepherd Knight, in 1577, by an unknown artist.

(*Left*) Francis Bacon in his glory, by an unknown artist. This portrait shows Bacon after Essex's death when, in the reign of James I, he rose, for a time, to the legal eminence his former patron had so unsuccessfully sought for him.

A view of Essex House from the Thames showing the watersteps by which Essex would take a boat when he wished to go upstream to Whitehall or Hampton Court, or across the river to the theatres.

Building up a Parliamentary Party. In this letter Essex asks Sir Edward Littleton to secure on his behalf the election of Sir Christopher Blount to the forthcoming Parliament of 1593 as one of the Staffordshire representatives. The body of the letter is written in the stylized hand of a secretary, but the complimentary close – 'your very assured frend' – and the signature are in Essex's own handwriting, as is the postscript:

'I psuade myself thatt my
creditt is so good with my contrymen
as the vsing of my name in so
small a matter will be enough to
effect yt. butt yete I pray yow vse me
so kindly in yt as I take no repulse.'

As well as being malproportioned, this view of Westminster–London begins
at Temple Bar (bottom right, letter S)– curiously omits any mention of
Essex House which lay, on this map, between Arundel House and Leicester
House near the spot described as Mylford Stairs. But the sprawling confusion
of the palace at Whitehall is obvious, as is the way in which the bishops' palaces
along the Strand were taken over by the nobility—with Burghley living in the

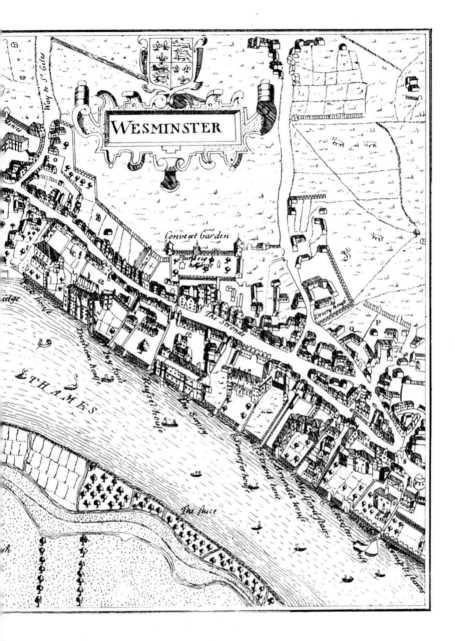

Convent Garden. Clearly shown are York House, where Essex was
imprisoned in 1599 and 1600 after his unauthorized return from Ireland, and
Drury House where the conspirators met to plan the rebellion of February
1601. A more happy stamping ground is marked by the letter N, the Tilt Yard,
where Essex displayed his jousting ability to such advantage.

William Cecil, 1st Lord Burghley, wearing his robes as a Knight of the Garter. This portrait is attributed to Gheeraerts.

Burghley's son, Robert Cecil, probably painted by de Critz just after the defeat of Essex.

Lord Admiral Charles Howard of Effingham, Earl of Nottingham, by Daniel Mytens. The battle behind him represents his triumph over the Armada.

Sir Walter Raleigh, painted in the year of the Armada by an unknown artist.

S. PAVLES CHVRCH

THAMESIS

The death warrant of Essex. The body of the document was, of course, written by a secretary, but Elizabeth's bold signature stands at the top, and in the bottom right corner the Lord Keeper, Thomas Egerton, has scribbled in Latin to certify that Essex was duly executed. The lengthy text, addressed to Egerton, states that Essex and Southampton have been charged with high treason, and sentenced to be hanged, drawn and quartered. The warrant spares Essex this sentence because he is a nobleman, stating instead that 'our pleasure is to have the head of the said Robert, Earl of Essex cut off at the Green within our Tower of London'.

(*Previous pages*) Visscher's Map of London – the western half of the city above, the eastern half below. This shows clearly all the main spots involved in the Essex Rebellion: south of the River Thames, the Globe Theatre where *Richard II* was performed: north of the river, Essex House, St Pauls, Leadenhall (the landmark nearest to the house in Fenchurch Street where Essex lunched), Queenhythe where the defeated rebels took to the water, and on the far right of the lower half, the Tower of London. At this end of London Bridge can be seen the impaled heads of execution victims: Essex, Blount, Danvers, Meyrick, Cuffe and Lee were all exhibited in this fashion.

and reprovision. And so isolated and unique were these oases of shelter that it was as the Islands that they were known. There was no need for a name so specific as the Azores. After all, what other islands were there between the New and Old Worlds?

The instructions given to the Earl of Essex on 15 June 1597 were quite specific. His expedition was to sail to the Islands, there to await and destroy the summer treasure fleet due from South America. But on the way towards this glorious and profitable objective they were to call at Ferrol, the naval port in the north-west corner of Spain just by Corunna and Cape Finisterre, where intelligence reports indicated that King Philip was assembling yet another Armada. If these reports proved true Essex was to destroy the ships being prepared, and also to land soldiers and engineers to wreak as much havoc on the port of Ferrol as possible. If the English fleet arrived so late that the Spaniards were already putting out towards their probable objective, Ireland, then the Islands sector of the voyage would have to be abandoned until this threat was dealt with. The Islands and the treasure fleet were the ultimate objects of the exercise, but not until all danger of reprisals against England or Ireland from the Spanish mainland had been firmly nipped in the bud. It could be fatal if Essex sailed casually past Spanish ports bustling with invasion preparations took his fleet – the flower and body of English maritime power – out into the Atlantic towards the Islands, and left the Spaniards free to attack the undefended British Isles at their leisure.

It could be fatal. Yet it was, in fact, precisely what Essex was to do. It was not entirely his fault. The individual profit motive which inspired the formation of this and every other English naval expedition meant that each captain would obviously be more intent on picking up easy booty in the Islands than on tackling Spanish warships nearer the mainland, but Essex's commission from the Queen was clear enough and he swore faithfully to carry it out: plunder, but only after the Spanish warfleet had been neutralized.

Things did not start well. Plymouth was the initial rendezvous, and Essex was to take the Queen's London and Chatham ships from the Straits of Dover down the English Channel, meeting up along the way with Sir Francis Vere and a thousand experienced soldiers in a squadron of ships from the Netherlands. After the success of Cadiz the Dutch were determined to seize this new opportunity for revenge and profit at the expense of their Spanish enemies.

The Dutch and English squadrons met up successfully, but then the wind blew steadily from the west and, unable to tack into it, the ships had to take refuge behind Dungeness. On 6 July 1597, after a fortnight at sea, Essex had still only covered a few score miles, and though a tempestuous storm then blew up which drove the ships dramatically into Plymouth, it was at the cost of severe strains to the vessels and tackle. Two weeks' stores had been consumed, and during the unexpected delay the troops waiting at the port had got out of hand. The soldiers were sick and restless. The captains had been up to their old tricks. A month's provisions had vanished.

Matters got worse when the whole fleet of some sixty ships bearing 6,000 fighting men finally put out to sea on 10 July 1597. The wind blew fiercer and fiercer, lashing rollers up out of the Bay of Biscay and scattering first the squadrons and then the individual ships all over the face of the waters. For four days the tempest whipped itself into a frenzy, so that each captain was driven willy nilly, he knew not where. It was a desperate affair of *sauve-qui-peut*. The men on Sir Walter Raleigh's ship fought hour after hour against the elements until they collapsed exhausted and commended their souls to God. Their bulkhead was ripped open and the bricks of their cooking galley ground each other to powder. When the gale finally blew itself out Raleigh found himself miraculously close to Plymouth, but Essex eventually had to limp into Falmouth, while other ships had been driven to Spain itself. The expedition was shattered.

John Donne signed up to sail with the Azores expedition. And his strange, modern, grating style of verse captured exactly the spirit of the tempest which wrecked Essex's real chances of success in the Islands and after which the Earl's fortunes were never again to thrive:

As sin-burdened souls from graves will creep
At the last day, some forth their cabins peep;
And trembling ask what news, and do hear so,
Like jealous husbands, what they would not know.
Some sitting on the hatches, would seem there
With hideous gazing to fear away fear.
Then note they the ship's sicknesses, the mast
Shaked with this ague, and the hold and waste
With a salt dropsy clogged, and all our tacklings
Snapping, like too high stretched treble strings;
And from our tattered sails, rags drop down so
As from one hanged in chains a year ago.[1]

Not until 20 July 1597 did the Earl of Essex crawl back to Plymouth with thirty other survivors that he had managed to round up, and after his previous buffeting in the Channel he seemed at the end of his tether. Even the usually hostile Raleigh felt impelled to write on Essex's behalf to Sir Robert Cecil: 'I beseech you to work from her Majesty some comfort to my Lord General, who, I know, is dismayed by these mischances even to death, although there could not more be done by any man upon earth, God having turned the heavens with fury against us, a matter beyond the power or valour or wit of man to resist.'[2]

It was a terrible catastrophe, but it was not Essex's fault. At the mercy of stormy weather, sixteenth-century mariners had infinitely less chance of controlling their craft or of escaping with their lives than the single-handed circumnavigators of the twentieth century. And the Queen was in a particularly forgiving mood, for in Essex's absence she had pulled off a most spectacular coup at Court, the triumph and memory of which was to keep her in good humour for weeks to come.

It had started out as a normal somewhat dreary episode of Court routine: the reception of an ambassador from Poland. Since he was apparently a handsome man, whose messages were expected to be well disposed towards England and her Queen, Elizabeth decided that the reception should be a public occasion in front of an audience of courtiers. Imagine her astonishment and annoyance when, having graciously kissed her hand, the ambassador stepped back ten paces and, drawing himself up to his full height, launched into a savage denunciation of the Queen of England and her ways. The fact that he spoke in Latin was no mitigation. His master, he said, was most bitterly incensed by the way in which Polish merchants were being mistreated by Englishmen and English ships. Poles trying peacefully to trade with Spain had been attacked, arrested and had their goods confiscated. The Queen of England had no right to claim this sort of privilege over other princes. Poland would trade with whom she liked.

The English Court listened horrified, not at the prospect of what retaliation a country as remote as Poland could carry out, but at the temerity of so obscure a man – of any man – daring to beard Elizabeth so openly in public on her home ground. Elizabeth too was horrified, first by the sacrilege committed, and then by the need to discover an appropriately crushing response. She found one: 'Expectavi legationem, mihi vero querelam adduxisti,'* she cried the moment the ambassador had finished speaking, and then in faultless Latin, without the slightest pause for preparation, she launched into a brilliantly eloquent and venomous speech, matching insult for insult and vindicating her policy with overwhelming arguments until the wretched Pole retreated in apologetic confusion. 'God's death, my lords,' she said with a twinkle and smile of triumphant contentment afterwards, 'I have been enforced this day to scour up my old Latin that hath lain long in rusting.'[3] She added that she wished Essex had been present to witness her victory, and Burghley took the hint to recount the whole episode in a long letter to the Earl down in Plymouth.

Other letters carried equally pleasant news: 'The Queen wishes you well, and has spared no expense in satisfying your demands. She will send you the *Lion*, and have three months' victuals more put into her, though she stuck at that at first.'[4] The ships driven down to Spain, indeed to Ferrol itself, returned before the end of July and started refitting for a mid-August departure.

But mid-August was two months after the original commission had been signed, and those two months had involved enormous

* I expected an embassy, but you have brought me a quarrel.

expenditure for which there was nothing to show, indeed a certain debit. Some of the valiant adventurers had been so discouraged by the buffeting they received in the storm that they had stolen quietly home. Others were really sick and – like Sir Ferdinando Gorges, the governor of Plymouth who was to have been the Sergeant Major of the expedition – they had to cry off. Gorges was one of the knights Essex had created at Rouen and he had been one of the commissioners appointed to oversee the division of spoils after Cadiz. He was to fight in the 1601 Revolt, but his participation then, as now in 1597, was curiously spineless.

The 6,000 soldiers, unused to the vicissitudes of a life at sea, were in a particularly poor state. Many were ill, and the morale of the others was at a low ebb. Essex, on his own authority, took the decision to discharge all of them except the 1,000 hard-core fighters from the Netherlands, a decision which, in the Queen's summery mood, aroused little comment at the time, but which ruled quite out of the question any serious attempt to incapacitate the Spanish ports. It was a decision Essex was later to rue, but, like the long-delayed departure, it was an understandable consequence of unavoidable misfortune. As Essex pointed out, as a result first of the adverse winds in the Straits of Dover and then of the storm in the southern part of the Channel he 'had been almost as long time at sea as I was first victualled for'.[5] With Raleigh he worked out an alternative plan for sabotaging the Spanish fleet by sending fireships into Ferrol harbour. The two men made a quick journey to London to urge the virtues of this scheme on the Privy Council and received a sympathetic but sceptical hearing. None of the Queen's own ships should be risked in such a hazardous enterprise, they were warned. The only vessels they could take chances with were the two Apostles, the Spanish galleons captured at Cadiz the previous year.

It was not until 17 August 1597 that the depleted and now virtually soldierless fleet finally got under weigh, dragged out to the open sea in search of a breeze by towboats. Under Essex the commanders of the expedition were Lord Thomas Howard, the brother of Charles Howard, the Lord Admiral; Thomas was now styled as Vice-Admiral; Sir Charles Blount of the golden chessman, who had recently on the death of his elder brother acquired the title of Lord Mountjoy, and who was appointed Lieutenant of the land forces; Sir Walter Raleigh whose title was Rear Admiral; Sir Francis Vere from the English forces in the Netherlands who was named Marshal and second-in-command to Mountjoy, a subordination to a younger, less-experienced but higher-ranking noble which infuriated Vere; and Sir Anthony Shirley, who took over as Sergeant Major from the sick Sir Ferdinando Gorges. These five men were appointed members of a Council of War on whose advice Essex was instructed to act. He should only follow his own opinion when his councillors were divided, and then only with the consent of the majority. This, Essex hoped, gave him in practice the unlimited powers he had wanted at Cadiz the previous year, for Councils of War were difficult things to arrange rapidly when the councillors were bobbing about in five different parts of a fleet several miles wide. Yet to guard against the Earl abusing his command, the royal commission laid down that all decisions of importance should be committed to writing, along with the names of those on whose advice the decision had been based. Elizabeth gave her Earl what he wanted, but could hardly have made clearer the suspicions she entertained.

The fleet that drifted finally and languidly down the Channel on 17 August 1597 consisted of the Queen's men-o'-war, including the two great Apostles, a score of transports and a Dutch squadron of twenty-two vessels. Overall it was a smaller force than had captured Cadiz the previous summer, but it contained more royal warships, seventeen as opposed to eleven, and was hopefully more efficient. Events were to prove otherwise. Seven days out of Plymouth another vile tempest blew up and split the fleet in two:

> Compared to these storms death is but a qualm,
> Hell somewhat lightsome and the Bermuda calme,

rhymed John Donne. Marvelling at the harsh succession of gales he wrote to a friend 'that even some of the mariners have been drawn to think it were not altogether amiss to pray, and myself heard one of them say, "God help us".'[6] This further storm was desperately cruel misfortune, and when the wind eventually subsided Essex discovered that Raleigh's ship and twenty others had vanished completely. Sir George Carew, the commander of one of the Apostles, the galleon *St Matthew*, had had to take his dismasted hulk home as best he could.

At half strength an attack on the Spanish fleet at Ferrol was out of the question, and Essex sailed straight south to the Rock of Gibraltar which had been fixed as an emergency rendezvous in the event of such a catastrophe. Small Spanish ships taken along the way gave reassuring but misleading reports that their war fleet was not due to sail until the following year, and fortified by this information Essex felt confident in sending Robert Knollys back to London with a message to the Queen.

'If her Majesty ask you why there was no attempt made upon the [Spanish] fleet at Ferrol,' Essex briefed him, 'you may say I neither had the *St Matthew*, which was the principal ship for that execution, nor the *St Andrew*, until my own ship was almost sunk, and I not able to make sail till Sir Walter Raleigh with his own ship, the *Dreadnought*, and very near twenty sails, were gone. We are now gone to lie for the Indian fleets, for, by Spaniards we have taken, we find the Adelantado is not put to sea this year.'[7] Adelantado was the Spanish title by which the Governor of Castille was known.

Elizabeth, still good-humoured, greeted Essex's news equably. But Burghley was not so pleased to learn that the main strategic purpose of the expedition had been so casually abandoned: 'I hope for nothing but the keeping up of the journey's reputation . . . but the fleet at Ferrol cannot be burnt.'[8] And his relative, Lady Russell, expressed the hopeful fears of those at Court for whom the prospect of glory that would boost Essex's ego still further was repugnant: 'I in no wise like of the enterprise toward. It may have good beginning, but I fear ill success in end.'

Raleigh was sufficiently of this faction for his sudden disappearance in the storm to be interpreted by the captains close to Essex as an act of deliberate sabotage. And the strange appearance at the beginning of September of a man-o'-war sent by Raleigh to

Essex seemed to confirm that the separation of the fleet into two was as much the result of conscious policy as of accidents of weather. For the messenger ship brought news that Raleigh had been pursuing activities on his own initiative and had discovered through scouts that the Spanish warfleet had left Ferrol and was bound for the Azores to protect the treasure convoys expected there. Without more ado Essex set sail with his ships for the Islands as well, sending back Raleigh's messenger with a sharp rebuke for what the Earl considered to be undisciplined and almost insubordinate behaviour. In fact, Essex's reading of Raleigh's motives was based on no more than suspicions fired and stoked by the military adventurers of the type whom the Earl loved to knight – to the Queen's understandable annoyance – and upon whose company and reassurance the Earl was coming more and more to rely. These swordsmen and captains were to make up a major proportion of his supporters in the rising of February 1601. In fact, Raleigh's disappearance was totally explicable in terms of the atrocious weather, and in reassembling such ships as he could discover and making independent enquiries about Spanish movements he was acting intelligently and responsibly. His fault was to discover and relay the wrong information.

For when Essex arrived at the Azores there was no trace of the treasure fleet, nor of the warships expected to protect it. Raleigh eventually arrived on 14 September 1597, and the two commanders greeted each other with every appearance of friendship. Inviting Sir Walter to dinner on his flagship, Essex spoke openly and apologetically of the suspicions he had entertained and how they were removed by this welcome, if overdue, reunion. Raleigh appeared to accept the apologies at face value, but the next week was to reveal how matters really stood between the two men.

At a council of war it was decided that while waiting for the arrival of the treasure fleet the English squadrons would land on the various islands, procure fresh provisions and pick up any easy plunder that could keep up the spirits of the expedition. After the long delays and damage caused by the succession of storms the private investors in the expedition were anxious to have some taste of the profits they could expect on their capital. It was agreed

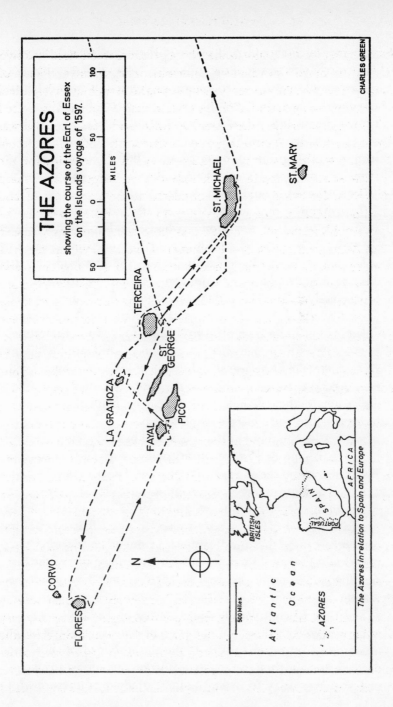

THE AZORES

showing the course of the Earl of Essex
on the Islands voyage of 1597.

MILES

0   50   100
50

CORVO

FLORES

LA GRATIOZA

TERCEIRA

FAYAL

PICO

ST.
GEORGE

ST. MICHAEL

ST. MARY

N

The Azores in relation to Spain and Europe

500 Miles

Atlantic

Ocean

AZORES

BRITISH
ISLES

S P A I N

PORTUGAL

A F R I C A

CHARLES GREEN

G*

that the Dutch should land on Pico, the largest island that was particularly rich in wine: the ordinary Dutch soldiers, preferring spirits, could, it was felt, cope more abstemiously with that particular type of booty than the sack- and sherry-loving English. Mountjoy and the other Blount, Sir Christopher, Essex's stepfather, should make for St Michael's, an island somewhat detached from the main group to the east. Lord Thomas Howard and Sir Francis Vere would tackle La Gratioza. And Essex, with Sir Walter Raleigh, would attack Fayal.

The starting point for all these sorties was Flores, the most westward island of the group, where the English fleet were sheltering. They had selected it as a rendezvous point because it was the least fortified and because it was the first land that the treasure fleet would sight. Commanders were left to work out for themselves the strategy they would adopt for landing on their respective islands, but Essex, in charge of the attack on Fayal, failed to explain his own plans to Raleigh fully. After the council of war Raleigh in the *Warspite* remained off Flores with the *Bonaventure*, the *Dreadnought* and the *Swiftsure*. Only just arrived, they needed a few days to refit. In the meantime Essex took to the high seas with the remainder of the squadron 'like a high constable to arrest all in the Queen's name that pass by in thirty leagues space.'[9] When he thought Raleigh would be ready, and when his high constabling had proved fruitless, Essex sent a ship back to Flores instructing the *Warspite, Bonaventure, Dreadnought, Swiftsure* and their accompanying vessels to make straight for their agreed object of attack, Fayal. But Essex himself did not make directly for Fayal. He decided to take a circular route that skirted the southerly course that the treasure fleet might be pursuing into the Islands. Hoping to win for himself alone the glory of the first sighting and capture, he kept Raleigh in the dark about his intentions.

So, when Raleigh with his ships arrived off Fayal after a rapid overnight voyage, there was not a sign of Essex and the rest of the squadron. Somewhat surprised, Raleigh dropped anchor and decided to wait, though the inhabitants of Fayal took advantage of his strange delay to make the most obvious preparations for defence and for the salvage of their valuables. Six groups of soldiers marched out of the little town and began digging trenches along the beach where, had he attacked immediately, Raleigh would have enjoyed an unopposed landing. And from the English ships could be seen little convoys of inhabitants taking mules laden with possessions out of the town and into the hills behind.

Raleigh's soldiers and sailors were at first astonished, then annoyed by their commander's failure to act. Having taken Fayal completely by surprise they had to ride at anchor in the sweltering sun watching their would-be victims grow stronger and less plunderable with every hour. Raleigh himself was infuriated, but Essex was his superior, and, after the misunderstanding caused by his previous independent initiatives, he decided that, for the time being, restraint was more advisable than honour or profit. He waited all day, all night, all of the next day, and still there was no sign of Essex. The temper of his men was changing from dissatisfaction to mutiny. A council of officers was called and their mutinous feelings were voiced loudly. Only one small faction led by Sir Anthony Shirley, Sir Christopher Blount and Sir Gelli Meyrick, Essex's steward, who had been left with Raleigh's ships, was in favour of waiting for the rest of the squadron. But Meyrick and his friends were the influential voices, for they were the very men whose gossiping had placed so uncharitable an interpretation upon Raleigh's earlier disappearance, and they could obviously do their disruptive work again. They insisted that Raleigh wait one more day for Essex to arrive.

Next morning there was still no sign or message from the rest of the squadron, and the wind shifted. Raleigh decided it was advisable to find an anchorage more to the north west of the island, but Blount, Shirley and Gelli Meyrick obstinately refused to budge. They remained off Fayal with five or six other ships while the rest of the group followed Raleigh to a point four miles further from the town. Their new anchorage was off a gentle beach behind which stretched prosperous and watered farming country. Raleigh decided to land a small party that could forage for provisions, but a group of Spanish soldiers suddenly appeared from the direction of the town. Raleigh ordered reinforcements for the foragers, and what had started as a reconnaissance patrol turned into a full-scale landing. The Spaniards were driven off, and once on dry land Raleigh decided to march on the town immediately. He was sick of waiting, and the opportunity was too good to miss.

There was no resistance as the English troops moved through the lush countryside until they came to a small fort defending the road into Fayal itself. Its cannon were efficient and from its walls musketeers sniped to deadly effect. The self-confident English advance was checked, until Raleigh himself dashed forward through the fire to emerge safely on the other side. The troops followed, and, the fort by-passed, they met no further opposition. Fayal itself, as they suspected, was empty, the inhabitants having taken good advantage of the three days' grace granted them to vanish with the most valuable of their possessions. The only defenders were barricaded firmly in the citadel above the town, and so Raleigh bivouacked in the deserted houses intending to launch a proper assault next morning.

And it was then that Essex sailed over the horizon tired and irritated after his fruitless combing of the high seas. He would have been annoyed enough to discover that Raleigh had stolen for himself the honour and glory of leading the invasion of enemy territory. But Shirley, Blount and Meyrick, still waiting at the original anchorage, recounted a tale of disobedience and insubordination that set Essex beside himself with fury. Raleigh's offence was deliberately insulting, they maintained, deserving immediate court martial – indeed summary execution.

Whipped into a passion by their allegations, Essex gave immediate orders for all the military captains and officers to be recalled from the town. As flyboats brought them through the morning back to Essex's flagship he upbraided all and cashiered some. He sent a summons for Raleigh to present himself on board the *Due Repulse* without delay, but Raleigh had no need of summonses. Unaware of the fate of his captains, he had gone back to the *Warspite* to prepare his report, and then set off for the flagship expecting the praise and thanks of Essex. He stepped on board the *Due Repulse* to be greeted with ominous silence, and did not discover what was wrong until he entered Essex's cabin.

There, flanked on either side by Meyrick, Blount and Shirley, Essex accused his second-in-command of a gross breach of orders and of flouting the articles of commission. To Raleigh's stuttered protest Essex read out the article of the royal commission ordering that none should land troops without the General's presence or express order.

For half an hour Raleigh defended himself, and his arguments were convincing. Essex had agreed they should land at Fayal. Raleigh had waited four days from receiving the order to make for Fayal, and had then assumed from Essex's continued delay that the General considered Raleigh's small party strong enough to land on its own – as, indeed, events proved it was. He had delayed landing for the day's further grace which Sir Gelli Meyrick had insisted upon, and the final landing grew out of a simple and necessary foraging raid. He did not mention the strongest defence of all for his initiative, that Essex's failure to inform his second-in-command of his whereabouts or intentions for four days was a blunder of the most basic kind.

The rest of the day passed with such bickerings, while the ships, sailors and soldiers waited for their leaders to agree on their future action. There was still the main fort to be captured. And the whole fleet was held up by the squabble, for upon reports that Spanish men-o'-war were in the neighbourhood, the plan to make individual landings had been abandoned and all the squadrons had made for Fayal. While Essex stormed up and down his cabin nothing happened, until, next morning, Sir Thomas Howard persuaded Raleigh to apologize to Essex; and, far harder, persuaded Essex grudgingly to accept the apology. Outward harmony was restored and it was decided to attack the fort immediately. A herald was despatched with a message demanding instant surrender – only to discover that the fort was empty. Unable to believe their eyes, the Spaniards had witnessed yet another inexplicable delay by the overwhelming English force threatening their little town, and had taken advantage of this one more night of grace to make good their escape. The quick-patched agreement between Raleigh and Essex was shattered once again. Why, asked Meyrick, Blount, Shirley and the others, had not Sir Walter taken the elementary precaution of setting a small guard on the garrison? Why, retorted Raleigh's partisans, was his lordship the General so sensitive of his honour? If he had not spent a day worrying over his reputation the ransoms of the fort's garrison would now be in English pockets. Why had he tried to court martial the only commander to achieve anything in the course of this long-drawn, profitless expedition? In disgust the empty town and fort were burned and the soldiers re-embarked. On 26 September 1597 the whole fleet sailed for La Gratiosa in hope of better pickings. But morale was low.

The worthies of the small community of La Gratioza came on board the English General's ship to plead for mercy, and Essex accepted their pleas in return for fresh supplies of wine, victuals and fruit. The island had little more to yield. Then on 27 September 1597 the Earl of Essex, commanding the naval might of his sovereign and mistress Queen Elizabeth, committed the supreme error in a chapter of errors and misfortunes. La Gratiosa was roughly in the centre of the eight Azores Islands. The Spanish treasure fleet was expected any moment to arrive from the west. Yet the Earl of Essex ordered his ships to move in precisely the opposite direction towards the comparatively remote island of St Michael, some twenty miles east of the first land which the Spanish galleons would sight. And his blunder was revealed almost as soon as the fleet arrived at St Michael on the dawn of 29 September, for just as the *Due Repulse* was dropping anchor, shots were heard from two ships that had been delayed off La Gratioza and had only now caught up with the body of the fleet. Their captains reported sighting the long-awaited Spanish treasure convoy arriving over the western horizon.

Amid frenzied preparations and over-optimistic anticipations of booty, the English fleet laboriously turned round and headed back the way it had come. But it was hopelessly, pathetically, late. Every inhabitant in the Azores knew that the English ships were waiting for the treasure convoy, and the moment the convoy had appeared off the western islands small boats had set out to warn its captains of the enemy presence. The galleons switched course rapidly and made straight for Terceira where a fortress guarded an inlet in which they could anchor and be unloaded.

Their course had been set for Terceira when the rump of the English force had sighted them, and the news of the sighting carried to Essex at St Michael was just speedy enough for the Earl to redeem his colossal error of sailing east. Had he made straight for Tercera he might have arrested some at least of the galleons before they put their cargoes ashore. But half way along the voyage back from St Michael to Terceira, the English fleet came upon three Spanish ships from Havana, cut off from the main body of the treasure convoy. Like a ratpack the whole English fleet set upon these three ships, which proved to be carrying quite sizeable cargoes of cochineal; these dried insect bodies, specially reared on Mexican and South American cactus plantations to form the basis for scarlet dyes and carmine, were valuable enough. But the hours consumed by capturing the three ships and arresting their crews put paid to what chance Essex had of preventing the main body of the treasure fleet landing their still more precious cargoes at Terceira.

When Essex and his ships finally reached Terceira the Spanish galleons were already anchored close under the guns of the fort there and had conveyed many of their valuables to the shore. Essex raged in fury at the prize that had been snatched so narrowly from him – but he had only himself to blame. A hastily summoned council of war flatly declined to attempt any seaborne assault against the galleons: they were too solidly protected by the batteries in the fort, and, in any case, they contained by now little booty of value.

And a landing by the troops seemed equally pointless. The Spaniards had made good use of the English delays to fortify themselves into virtual impregnability. The glittering prize that Essex and the other English captains had hoped and planned for through months of expense and adversity lay less than a mile away – and was completely untouchable.

It was a sour and bitter moment for the Earl of Essex. The adventure that was to have marked a brilliant step forward in a brilliant future had ended in tantalizing but total failure. In a hopeless attempt to salvage at least something from the ruins he gave orders for the fleet to return and sack St Michael's, the island on which they had scornfully turned their backs when news of greater profits from the treasure fleet had arrived. But by the time they had doubled back on their course yet again, the inhabitants had taken the same precautions that the inhabitants of Fayal had taken earlier while Raleigh had lain off that island awaiting orders from Essex. The garrison had put themselves in a state of readiness and most of the valuable goods and chattels had been moved out of the town. Though Essex did not know it, this was to be the last naval engagement of his career – and he mishandled it with the same energetic incompetence that had characterized his other military activities.

The landing had to be reconnoitred, and the honour of fulfilling this menial task provoked afresh the disputes between Essex and Raleigh. Sir Walter had already set out for the beach in a flyboat when the General called him loudly back. Essex then took Raleigh's place, and ignored all Sir Walter's shouts of advice to take his helmet and breastplate with him if he intended to go near the shore, where Spanish musketeers were waiting. Essex shouted back to the armoured Sir Walter that he would not dream of affording himself protection that the watermen who rowed him did not possess. All these altercations between the leaders took place in the full view and hearing of the rest of the fleet. Then Essex proceeded, quite unnecessarily, to risk his life among the breakers and musketfire of the beach, before returning to report that a landing was impossible against such well entrenched odds.

It was decided that the fleet should remain under the command of Raleigh off St Michael; and that that night Essex should take 2,000 soldiers round to the back of the island with flyboats and pinnaces and make a landing at Villa Franca, the other main community on the island. Then he would march to take St Michael from the rear, while Raleigh and the fleet kept up feints and diversions that would convince the garrison that a direct landing was about to be made.

The first part of the plan worked perfectly. Essex and his

troops landed and captured Villa Franca with ease, for it had been deserted. Raleigh kept up his programme of continuous alarm. But Essex did not then move on to St Michael. His troops were delighted to discover the deserted houses well stocked with food and drink. At a council of war the captains advised strongly against the hazards of a march and attack on St Michael, and Essex let himself be seduced by their arguments. It was a craven decision, revealing how easily swayed Essex was by those round about him. But he compounded his error by failing to inform Raleigh of his change of plan. He sat tight in Villa Franca while, for six whole days, the fleet on the other side of the island kept up the charade of shots and drums and trumpet calls. To the ever more mutinous irritation of his captains, Raleigh could only reply that after the misunderstanding and row off Fayal he simply dared not move without orders from Essex. And in fact, the fiasco off Fayal was being repeated again. Essex had changed his plans and had completely omitted to inform his second-in-command.

The criminal negligence and waste of the situation was underlined by the sudden appearance of a huge 1,800-ton Spanish galleon, a stray from the treasure fleet, which wandered by mistake into the middle of the English ships off St Michael. Different kingdoms, particularly the Spanish, bought armed assistance from all sorts of sources. So the cluster of vessels off St Michael looked to the Spanish captain like a collection of European merchantmen, which he assumed to be trading with or sailing on behalf of the King of Spain. Raleigh on sighting the galleon ordered his ships to assist the deception by not firing until the vessel was helplessly at their mercy. But a Dutch captain disobeyed him, weighed anchor, opened fire, and gave the Spanish commander just enough time to drive his vessel on to the beach and set fire to his cargo. By the time English flyboats could reach her the ship was a mass of flames too fierce to approach, and when she sank next day steam still rose from the sea as the molten spice and sugar in her hold continued to burn.

The Dutch captain's hastiness was foolish but understandable. The real crime in the eyes of the English fleet was the fact that no English soldiers were waiting on the beach when the galleon grounded, and the reason for that omission was the failure of the Earl of Essex to carry out his part of the assault plan. Their patience strained beyond endurance, a group of ships left the fleet to see what was happening on the other side of the island. There they discovered Essex and his troops living off the fat of the land. A message was sent for Raleigh and the rest of the ships to follow, and they weighed anchor and sailed off to the derisive hoots and catcalls of the garrison of St Michael.

Reunited in Villa Franca, both Essex and Raleigh warily avoided recriminations. With more and less justice each was itching to criticize and denounce the other but, aware that neither could completely exculpate himself of blame for the miserable series of fiascos of which this was but the last, they held their peace. Instead, while the fleet was watering and reprovisioning for the journey home, they drew up a report to the Privy Council in explanation and justification of their catalogue of failures, discreetly glossing over the various errors and incompetences of the commanders, and avoiding specific blame for the particular misunderstandings off Fayal and St Michael.

After a slight brush with a Spanish raiding party that allowed Essex to sprinkle a few more knighthoods among the gentlemen adventurers disappointed at the lack of action or profit that the expedition had afforded, the soldiers and sailors re-embarked, and on 9 October 1597 orders were given to sail for England. A brief storm gave the scattered ships an opportunity to lose contact with each other completely and sail for Plymouth at their own speeds without waiting for their general. Every adventurer reached home with a different story. But it was difficult, no matter what tale was told, to avoid the conclusion that the whole enterprise had frittered its time away with 'idle wanderings upon the sea'.

22

Lord Essex's Sickness

The Islands voyage had been a futile waste of time and money. It had failed in its real objective – to enrich its shareholders with Spanish plunder. And it had done worse than fail in the military objective which had been the government's main interest. The Spanish warfleet assembled around Ferrol, Finisterre and Corunna had not been destroyed. And the moment King Philip heard that Essex's vessels had left Spanish waters for the Azores he resolved to take advantage of the undefended English Channel and southern coast.

With rare speed and decisiveness he ordered that the preparations for a spring 1598 Armada be accelerated and that the invasion fleet sail immediately, while England's guard was down. It was the desperate gambler's fling of a man who, cheated all his life, and now close to death, had nothing to lose. He overrode fiercely the protests of the Adelantado who knew how ill prepared any warfleet would be that sailed next spring, let alone in this autumn's gales. The pious Philip threatened to 'hang his admiral at his wife's neck' if he did not put out to sea, and, despite the reports of imminent revolt among the inhabitants of Spain's Italian possessions, he added to the English expedition a squadron that was due to sail for Italy with three regiments of his finest troops. Spain's leading sea captains were summoned at breakneck speed to Ferrol, and in the harbour there assembled a warfleet that rivalled the great Armada of 1588: 136 vessels, sixty of them warships, bearing 9,000 experienced soldiers and 4,000 sailors. They were to be backed up from Seville by a further thirty ships carrying the troops originally intended for Italy, the finest infantry in Europe. Together the assembled fleets would sail to Blavet, a port in that part of northern France held by Spain, pick up more reinforcements in the shape of a squadron of galleys, and then capture the undefended English port of Falmouth. The troops would land, while the warships lay in wait for Essex's vessels and picked them off as they straggled home one by one.

Philip was correct in seeing that, provided his vast warfleet sailed rapidly and avoided storms, their lack of preparation would be more than compensated for by the total absence of defence along the English coast. So in the second week of October 1597 England lay totally undefended as two fleets converged simultaneously on her southern coasts. One was made up of the isolated, dispirited English vessels straggling back leaking and ill provisioned from the Azores. The other was the comparatively fresh and organized Spanish warfleet. It looked as though the consequences of the Earl of Essex's Islands expedition would be transformed from the futile to the catastrophic.

When Essex reached Plymouth on 26 October 1597 reports of the new Armada had already thrown the port into alarm and confusion. London had received the news three days earlier, and the capital was preparing to fight for its life. The militia all along the southern coast were mobilized and put on a twenty-four hour standby. Chains of beacons were prepared. Orders were sent to Picardy to recall immediately the English troops fighting there. Some £3,000 was despatched to the West Country, along with victuals and munitions to replenish Essex's battered ships.

Essex himself added to the general panic. 'The Spaniards are upon the coast,' he confidently informed the Privy Council, and he promised he would take his ships and soldiers to do immediate battle, 'though we eat ropes' ends and drink nothing but rain water.'[1] Then he passed on to London another rumour, that the Spaniards were making for Ireland. He would chase them at once, he proclaimed, either as commander, or under anyone else Elizabeth cared to place over him.

A weary note from Elizabeth took the hint and confirmed his continuing appointment as commander. But she did not refrain from pointing out that the whole crisis was Essex's own fault and that by his initial failure to attack Ferrol as he had been ordered, 'you have given the enemy leisure and courage to attempt us.'[2] He was not to go sailing off to Ireland on another wild goose chase 'whereby our own kingdom may lie open to serious dangers. . . .'

In the event, it was not Essex but the weather that came to England's rescue. The Spanish fleet reached its first French rendezvous at Blavet, then an enormous storm blew up that scattered it completely and forced its ships to run for home. They limped back to their Spanish harbours battered and leaking like the English vessels they had hoped to surprise. England, and Essex, had been saved by the tempest.

But Elizabeth, understandably, had little taste for such hair's-breadth and fortuitous salvations. And by the time the Earl of Essex reached Court, peevish and irritable after the long ride up from the West and the unexpected tensions of the last fortnight, she had listened to all that Raleigh's friends had to say about the Islands fiasco. She met her Robert with rebukes and criticism. Why had he failed to attack, let alone attempt to burn the Spanish warfleet at Ferrol? Why in the Azores had he let the laden and unsuspecting treasure fleet sail so close and still elude his clutches? Why had he acted towards Raleigh with such churlishness?

Essex bridled and responded with equal bitterness. He was infuriated that only a few days before his return to Court after long, expensive and dangerous labours on his sovereign's behalf, the Queen had decided to hand out rewards to those who had remained at home and criticized. Robert Cecil, who had been named Secretary on the last occasion that Essex was overseas, was now named Chancellor of the Duchy of Lancaster. It was a position that, in the sixteenth century, carried considerable power and patronage and could be of useful profit to its holder. Yet far worse than this reward to a political rival, an obvious snub to Essex, was the promotion, on 23 October 1597, of Lord Admiral Charles Howard of Effingham to the Earldom of Nottingham.

Elizabeth handed out few enough earldoms. There were more male peers alive in England on the day of her accession than on the day of her death.[3] So the conferring of Howard's new title was intended to take on special significance: and the wording of the patent that explained the reasons for the Queen's special favour underlined the maliciousness of her motives. Having set out, quite properly, the extent of Howard's services in dispersing the Armada of 1588 the patent also extolled his skill and bravery in the Cadiz expedition of 1596 as though Howard, not Essex, deserved principal credit for the success of the enterprise. To add insult to injury, the new Earl of Nottingham was to be Lord Steward of the Parliament due soon to meet, so that the Earl of Essex, who had previously walked in procession in front of Howard, would now have to fall in step behind. It was a trifle of precedence that threw Essex into a fury – and, to do him justice, was acknowledged by the whole Court as a deliberately calculated demotion. Processions like the one which opened Parliament were taken as profoundly symbolic of the whole English body politic, and the relative proximity of either Essex or Howard to the head was intentionally significant.

For a week Essex remained at Court brooding over the Queen's criticisms and insult. When they talked he met her rebukes with sharp retorts of his own and then he vanished. With mumbled excuses about illness and the need to get his own affairs in order after so prolonged an absence he disappeared to his house at Wanstead. Once there he shut himself in a room, refused to see visitors, and systematically developed debilitating melancholia. When his chaplain arrived to preach the Sunday sermon the Earl refused to go to chapel but remained ensconced in his chamber with his head muffled in cloaks and blankets like a ludicrous turban. It was an eccentric, ridiculous attempt to win Elizabeth's sympathy and, setting aside the waywardness of her own motives, it threw considerable doubt on Essex's mental stability.

The Earl's erratic handling of the Islands expedition – particularly his behaviour towards Raleigh – had been disturbing and was only partly explicable in terms of relative inexperience, lack of proper information on which to base a strategy, and the stresses and tensions of a war situation. He had revealed a definite and strange inability to co-ordinate for which no excuse could be made and which his sudden retreat to Wanstead seemed to confirm. And the remaining years of the Earl's life were to be marked by such an obvious, almost physical deterioration of judgement and faculties, that one is justified in searching for a psychological or physiological explanation of the change.

And there is one to hand. Contemporary gossip asserted that the Earl of Essex had syphilis.[4] This frightening new venereal disease was endemic in Renaissance courts, and it would be surprising if Essex had not caught it in the course of his *affaires*: foreign liaisons with battletrain prostitutes compounded the risk. Henry VIII probably died of syphilis caught in French brothels – and his daughter Elizabeth may well have suffered from an inherited strain of the disease. Whether Essex actually suffered from the disease can only be a matter for speculation, but the alleged source of the rumour is significant – Roderigo Lopez, the Physician to the Queen, ministered to the Earl before Essex started the witch hunt that ended in the doctor's execution in 1594. Lopez, it seems, did not keep his patient's secrets to himself and passed on stories to Don Antonio, the Pretender to the Portuguese throne, and Antonio Perez, the former secretary to Philip of Spain. Nor did these exiles treat the information in confidence, and Essex was apparently furious when the rumours got back to him having been passed round by the gossips of the Court. Lopez' betrayal of the syphilis could have provided one motive for the extreme vindictiveness with which the Earl hounded him to death over the alleged conspiracy to poison the Queen.

After initial and visible symptoms on the genitalia, syphilis goes into a latent period to re-emerge in a tertiary stage, one manifestation of which can be nervous disorder. The sufferer loses co-ordination, behaves erratically and eventually degenerates into total lunacy. Preceding that collapse are bouts of insanity

whose fury and unpredictability correspond closely to the fits
to which the Earl of Essex became increasingly prone after 1596.
Whatever their cause, they wrecked his hopes of becoming a
counsellor to whose advice Elizabeth listened attentively, they
were to mar his handling of the campaign in Ireland in 1599,
and they bedevilled the months in which his weird rebellion of
1601 took shape.

Worst of all, Elizabeth paid attention to them. She joined in
his game. Instead of ignoring the Earl's 'illness' in Wanstead as a
childish act of petulance, she worried, and let him know she
worried. Her comments were tart, but she made very sure they
were passed on, and she dropped hints to his friends. One decided,
on the strength of what she said, to write Essex an anonymous
letter:

> Hear me great lord, and with patience pardon me that am and ever
> will be ready pressed in all offices to thy service. Thou art full of wis-
> dom, bounty and valour, and dost perform all things with much
> honour: and yet methinks thou are least perfect in securely working
> thy own good, which in this age and time of uncertainty is most
> needful to be cared for. But by the way let me tell thee: thy own
> patience, I say, thy patience hath continually from the beginning given
> way to thy crosses.

The Earl was foolish to be provoked into leaving Court, said
the anonymous writer, it gave his enemies too much room to
manoeuvre. If he failed to attend Council meetings he could not
expect to influence the Queen's policy. And he should look to his
own friends more closely: 'take heed and remember that Christ
had but twelve [close friends] and one proved a devil.'[5]

The letter jolted Essex into returning to London, but he did
not grace the presence of the Queen or the Parliament then
meeting. He had some 30 MPs sitting in the Commons in his
interest – twelve of them were to take part in his rising – but he
made little use of their voices.[6] He stayed in Essex House, visiting
Court occasionally, but never the Council. He refused to tolerate Charles Howard, the new Earl of Nottingham, as his
superior. And he knew from tentative proposals through third

parties that Elizabeth was prepared to compromise to get him back – though he did not realize that it was not simply affection but the desire to present a common front to a recently arrived French diplomatic mission that made the Queen so anxious to have the Earl sitting again in her Council. Henri iv's embassies were adept at taking advantage of rifts in the courts they visited – and Essex was a known friend of France's.

Would Essex like to be considered for the Lord Admiralship? Would he like to become the Keeper of the Privy Seal? Essex was noncommittal. He wanted to know how definite the offers were.

Then in early December 1597 Elizabeth heard a new version of what had happened in the Azores. Sir Francis Vere had caught a chill when he returned from the Islands expedition, but once out of bed he made his way to Court and, having paid his respects to the Queen, proceeded loudly and forcefully to justify Essex's conduct. He posed questions which Raleigh and others listening in embarrassment were unable to answer. Elizabeth took him out of earshot to discuss the affair more closely and, according to Vere, dwelt fondly on the good Earl's virtues.

The next day Essex was summoned to Court, but declined the olive branch the Queen half offered. No, he would not attend Council meetings if the Queen were not present. No, he would not meet the French ambassador. No, he would not accept mediation from Raleigh. And he began to utter grave threats of disorder if he and Nottingham were required to appear publicly together. He demanded combat with Nottingham or with one of his sons or relatives. He demanded that the terms of the patent extolling Nottingham's conduct of the Cadiz expedition be changed. And on 21 December he stumped off again to Essex House in a huff. Fortunately for him, Nottingham himself had indulged in a similar fit of sulks several days earlier and had vanished to Chelsea pleading sickness.

The Queen relented. She would bestow on Essex the title Earl Marshal of England. Nottingham's title and the published reasons for it would remain unaltered – but Essex's new title would give him precedence over Nottingham on public occasions. Cecil would work out a suitably laudatory patent in time for Christmas.

Essex did not like the patent, of course. 'The conclusion also is merely impertinent and may, I think, be well left out,'[7] he told the Secretary and insisted that it be changed. On 28 December 1597 the revised version was read out for all to hear in the Presence Chamber. Essex had won through.

The new Earl Marshal was jubilant. He saw his fresh title as a clear victory. He had defied the Queen and made his defiance public. She had submitted and made her submission public. But it was a victory only in Essex's own childish terms. He took no account of the fact that his defiance had not been a face-to-face confrontation but a tiresome moodiness that did no credit to his own reputation or reliability. And that Elizabeth's so-called submission had consisted solely in granting a dignity that cost her nothing. The Earl Marshal was as much a servant of the Queen as the Earl of Essex had ever been: and Elizabeth was likely to allow him less not more power in his new position. He might possibly have gained a restatement of Elizabeth's affections – but it had been at the expense of his credit as a stable counsellor whose advice could be relied upon. Indeed the episode might well have caused Elizabeth to ponder on what had happened to the attractive young man who had won her affections half a dozen years previously.

His company was no longer worth paying for. Indeed he was a definite liability. His youthful pride had degenerated into grasping vanity; his ambition to serve the Queen had become a crude lust for power; his military ambitions had become an uncritical thirst for war for war's sake – or rather for the sake of the authority he was only granted in warfare; he had not outgrown his military companions, indeed he seemed to take refuge in their tavern swaggerings, for he found the coarseness of their oaths and their facile code of values more comforting than articulate discussions or actions that led to confrontations with real-life situations; and under their influence he was paying more attention to his popularity with the common people than with the Queen – though through no real love or understanding of them. They were just cheers and shouts he found it easier to respond to than the real individuals he needed to come to terms with to construct real power.

The French ambassador who met Elizabeth's Council after its differences had been settled, found the Earl of Essex agreeable company but suffering from delusions of grandeur: 'he is a man who in nowise contents himself with a petty fortune and aspires to greatness.'[8] It was an ominous note on which to start 1598.

23

Felix and Bolingbroke

Absence from the Court was dangerous. It was while Robert Devereux had been abroad fighting for his country that his rival Robert Cecil had taken his great steps forward. In 1596, while Lord Essex was away at Cadiz, old Burghley had won for his son the secretaryship. And in 1597, as the Earl was sailing fruitlessly round the Azores, the little hunchback had secured himself the most remunerative Chancellorship of the Duchy of Lancaster. He had used it to build himself a strong following in the 1597 Parliament and was forming a network of clients to rival the alliances which Gelli Meyrick was constructing for Essex in Wales. The Earl's military ambitions were all very well. Some were hailing him as the successor to Drake. But his sorties abroad had definitely lost him ground at Court, and it was there that ultimate power and profit resided.

So the opportunity that presented itself at the beginning of 1598 was a precious one. Robert Cecil was to travel to France to continue with the wily Henri IV the negotiations begun with the French ambassador in London. He would be gone several months. His old father Burghley was failing. Robert Devereux could take advantage of Cecil's absence to regain some of the influence he had lost with Elizabeth.

Unfortunately, Essex was not completely alive to the chance before him – and Cecil was. The Secretary spent the weeks before his departure assiduously wooing the Earl. With Raleigh he had before the Islands voyage gone to great pains to wine and dine the Earl in his own home. Now he did the same and, furthermore, spent long hours arguing on Essex's behalf with the Queen. He persuaded her to offer the Earl all the cochineal and indigo captured in the Azores at a knockdown price of £50,000 (18s per pound compared to the market price of 30s per pound); and to stop the bottom falling out of the market all further importation and sale of cochineal was forbidden for two years. A few days later he induced Elizabeth to grant Essex a further free gift of £7,000 from the proceeds, the only unconditional cash grant she is recorded ever to have made. Her gifts usually took the form of rights to patronage or economic monopolies – like the Farm of Sweet Wines.

What bait Cecil dangled before the Queen to coax her to such generosity is unknown. But the Secretary made no attempt to hide his motives from Essex. In friendly, cunningly honest conversations with the Earl he extracted the promise that Essex would do nothing to seek office or favour that might be detrimental to Cecil's own interest while Cecil was in France.

For all his ambition and paranoia Robert Devereux was a simple man. He agreed to Cecil's request, and having agreed, he felt honour bound to stand by his word – as his rival knew he would. Like Elizabeth, the little Secretary could sniff out the Earl's predictability.

Cecil left Court for France on 11 February 1598, and in his absence Essex became Secretary. Going beyond his promise to Cecil, he squandered the influence this temporary position gave him on personal matters, and made no effort to prove that he possessed the qualities that the secretaryship required. He renewed an *affaire* with Mistress Bridges, one of the Queen's ladies in waiting, and he connived at his friend Southampton's secret liaison with Mistress Elizabeth Vernon, another of the Queen's maids of honour, whose lovers could expect to incur her Majesty's most extreme displeasure. Southampton was, furthermore, in disgrace for getting involved in a gambling brawl.

Then the insatiable Lettice, now married to Sir Christopher

Blount, pestered Essex to use his temporary eminence on her behalf to contrive for her to be received at Court. So, like a good son, Robert in turn spent long weeks pestering the Queen to receive Lettice and to heal up the bitterness that went back to the Earl of Leicester's days.

Elizabeth prevaricated. The former Lady Leicester visited Court and waited in the Privy Gallery for Elizabeth to walk past, but the Queen decided not to come and sent an excuse for her absence. After several more abortive attempts to contrive a meeting the Queen was invited to dinner and Lettice stood ready with a jewel worth £300. But again Elizabeth sent excuses, and she would not agree to a later, more public encounter. The Earl of Essex's mother had to be content with a brief formal reconciliation, and her son gained nothing from his efforts but intense royal irritation.

Then by the end of April 1598 Robert Cecil was back, and Essex could salvage nothing from his short period of authority except the consolation that Cecil's mission to France had been as fruitless as his own efforts as temporary Secretary. Cecil and his fellow ambassadors had travelled some 300 miles seeking the deliberately elusive Henri IV, only to discover that he had been negotiating secretly with Spain and was intending to make a separate peace, leaving England to fight on alone. The news brought into the open the debate that had been simmering for many months at the English Court. How long could the Spanish War go on? Essex, predictably, argued strongly in favour of battle to the bitter end. He argued that when Burghley and Cecil talked of peace they were forgetting with whom they were proposing to negotiate – Popish Spain, whose word could not be trusted and whose priests would not rest until Protestantism was destroyed. Passions grew heated at the succession of Council meetings that debated the problem, Burghley maintaining that it was less Spain than Essex who breathed forth war, slaughter and blood. He took out the prayer book he carried everywhere and pointed accusingly at Psalm 55, verse 23: 'Bloodthirsty and deceitful men shall not live out half their days.' England no longer had her back to the wall fighting for survival, and she simply could not afford the expense of war for its own sake.

Outside the Council Chamber the debate widened to question the motives behind Essex's desire for war. One bright young satirist compared the Earl to the Roman, Sulla, and discovering that Sulla's agnomen 'Felix' rhymed well with Essex, pilloried not only his warmongering but his thirst for popular acclaim. For as the Earl found his arguments in the Council ignored he was turning for support to the public.

> This vizard-fac'd pole-head dissimulation,
> This paraqueet, this guide to reprobation,
> This squint-ey'd slave, which looks two ways at once,
> This fork'd Dilemma, oil of passions,
> Hath so betray'd the world with his foul mire
> That naked Truth may be suspect a liar,
> For when great FELIX passing through the street,
> Vaileth his cap to each one he doth meet,
> And when no broom-man that will pray for him,
> Shall have less truage than his bonnet's brim,
> Who would not think him perfect courtesy?
> Or the honeysuckle of humility?
> The devil he is as soon: he is the devil,
> Brightly accoustred to be-mist his evil:
> Like a swartrutter's hose his puff thoughts swell,
> With yeasty ambition: *Signor Machiavel*
> Taught him this mumming trick, with courtesy
> To entrench himself with popularity,
> And for a writhen face and body's move,
> Be barracadoed in the people's love.[1]

Less apparently vicious but far more dangerous was Shakespeare's description of Bolingbroke in *The Tragedy of Richard II*. The obvious similarity of Bolingbroke's behaviour, and attributed motives, to Essex's was underlined by the fact that the scene in which Bolingbroke deposes his monarch was omitted from the version of the play published in 1597. And Essex himself was known to enjoy the play, going several times and applauding enthusiastically.

Ourself and Bushy, Bagot here and Green
Observ'd his courtship to the common people,
How did he seem to dive into their hearts
With humble and familiar courtesy,
What reverence he did throw away on slaves,
Wooing poor craftsmen with the craft of smiles
And patient underbearing of his fortune,
As 'twere to banish their affects with him.
Off goes his bonnet to an oyster-wench;
A brace of draymen bid God speed him well,
And had the tribute of his supple knee,
With 'Thanks, my countrymen, my loving friends';
As were our England in reversion his,
And he our subjects' next degree in hope.

To deny such insinuations was to countenance them, but they were dangerous. In a world ordered from above, those who sought for power from below were traitors to the established order. Essex decided to make a bid for respectability by setting out the guiding lines of his policy in the war debate. He carefully devised a letter to Anthony Bacon that expounded his views on the wisdom of making peace with Spain, and then had copies made for Bacon to circulate.

The letter became known as Essex's *Apology* and infuriated the Cecils. Essex's bland denials of all complicity in the circulation of the document infuriated them still more. For the Earl published the same rhetorical argument he had used in Council meetings. Having set out how desirable peace was, he came to the reluctant conclusion that Catholic Spain could not be trusted. The Spaniard was simply looking for a breathing space. It was a theme that played on the most nagging suspicions of the beleaguered Protestant island. And the Earl took advantage of his audience's chauvinism to play up the virtues of his military record and to cast aspersions on the motives of those who had not tasted battlefield action. He personally had gained nothing from warfare, he complained,

in which I have impaired my state, lost my dear and only brother, the half arch of my house, buried many of my nearest and dearest friends, and subjected myself to the rage of seas, violence, general plagues, famine and all kind of wants, discontentment of undisciplined and unruly multitudes, and acceptation of all events, in which I did not only leave my known enemies elbow room to see their own and their friends' advancement, but was fain sometimes upon trust in their protestations, after new reconcilements, to make them the receivers, censurers and answerers of all my despatches.

The imputation was aimed obviously at the Cecils – but when they protested Essex himself protested disingenuously. A corrupt servant, he said, must have copied some loose sheets he left under his bed's head.

The Earl was sailing very close to the wind – and the storm came on 1 July 1598. The Council were discussing the appointment of an English governor for Ireland. Rebels there led by Hugh O'Neill, Earl of Tyrone, spurred on by their Catholic priests and with the promise of Spanish help, had made a nonsense of English claims to own the country. English settlers and soldiers scarcely dared show their faces a score of miles from Dublin, the sole English garrison of significance.

Successive English governors had come to the same sad end as Essex's father, Walter the first Earl, and though Lord Burgh, the Lord Deputy sent over in April 1597, was more honest and industrious than most, he had died in that same winter, poisoned, some said, by corrupt officials in rebel pay.

The need for a new Lord Deputy was urgent, but no one was anxious to take on the burdens that had laid low so many good soldiers and administrators. When the matter came up for discussion on 1 July 1598 the Earl of Essex proposed Sir George Carew for the hotseat, and launched into a most flattering catalogue of Carew's good qualities. Yet his eloquence did not impress, for Carew, a friend of Cecil's, was known to be an enemy of Essex's, and that, indeed, was the reason for the Earl's nomination. He wanted to see one of his opponents out of the way, preferably in a situation where he might come to harm.

Such malice against Carew and the Cecil faction was cunning too transparent to be worthy of the name, and Elizabeth laughingly dismissed the Earl's arguments. But he had not the wit to realize that his crude strategem had been seen through, and he returned to the fray arguing still more passionately. Impatient, Elizabeth grew heated too and matched his vehemence, pouring scorn on his suggestions. Essex lost his temper, jutted his bearded jaw fiercely at the Queen, and then turned his back on her contemptuously. Furious, Elizabeth stood up, reached out and caught Essex a fierce box on the ear. He could go and be hanged for his insolence, she screamed.

Essex whirled, his hand on his sword. Nottingham stepped between the two combatants. Essex was beside himself shouting that he would never and could never endure such an insult from any man, and especially not from any woman: he would not have accepted it from her father King Henry VIII's hands and he would not accept it from hers. He strode out of the chamber seething as Elizabeth, whitefaced and quivering, silently watched him go.

Which of her councillors had Elizabeth ever previously struck as if they were silly maids-in-waiting? The Court found it hard to remember. Which courtier or subject had ever made to draw his sword on his sovereign? The Court was certain no one had ever been guilty of such treasonable impertinence. Such physical violence on the Queen's part and such assumption on Essex's argued a private relationship very different from the theoretical remoteness of monarch from subject.

And the sequel to the sword hilt incident showed that Elizabeth and Essex were locked together in a way that had nothing to do with the Irish problem that had been the ostensible cause of the row. For Essex was not banished from Court or sent to the Tower for his threat to assault the Queen. He protested his indignation as he had after the Islands voyage and retired to the country in an exactly similar fashion. There he sulked awaiting the Queen's messengers. And it was indeed the Queen who made the first move. She sent one of her gentleman attendants, Mr Killigrew, to visit the Earl as if on his own initiative.

Sir William Knollys wrote to his nephew to urge him to accept such oblique olive branches: 'if in substance you may have a good peace, I beseech your lordship not to stand upon the form of treaty.'² But Essex was holding out for more. He had got what he wanted by sulking the previous winter after the Islands voyage. He would maintain his right to a similar victory now.

Lord Keeper Egerton wrote to warn the Earl that fits of pique were not devices that could be used indefinitely – and that there were real dangers to such self-imposed exile. It might work with Elizabeth for the time being, but it gave his enemies at Court dangerous freedom of action. Was the Earl sure he had worked out his policy from every angle, or was he surrendering to self indulgence? 'The difficulty, my good lord,' he wrote in a most perceptive sentence, 'is to conquer yourself.'³

Essex was stung into a reply that was later to be held against him. To Egerton's solid warnings against the foolishness of allowing such freedom to those who wished him ill he could retort with only rhetorical devices. And then he launched into an imprecation that in the speech of a Member of Parliament would have been punished as treason direct: he questioned the divine authority of the monarch: 'What, cannot Princes err? Cannot subjects receive wrong? Is an earthly power or authority infinite? Pardon me, pardon me, my good lord, I can never subscribe to these principles.'

It was heresy. To question the power of the sovereign, God's Vicegerent on Earth, was to question God Himself. Even when Parliament mobilized troops at the beginning of the Civil War they maintained that they levied for the 'protection' of the sovereign as his servants, not in any way as rivals to his authority. But Essex could not lay claim to any bold democratic advance in political theory. His outburst lacked the sustained conviction of a Wentworth or a Cromwell or the intellectual consistency of a Pym. When his Elizabeth was on his side then the Queen could do no wrong, and anyone who dared so much as criticize was guilty of *lèse-majesté*. Committing such treasonable speculation to paper was simply an unpremeditated outburst of frustration on his part.

And he was scarcely more restrained when writing to Elizabeth herself:

When I remember that your Majesty hath, by the intolerable wrong you have done both me and yourself, not only broken all laws of affection, but done against the honour of your sex, I think all places better than that where I am, and all dangers well undertaken, so I might retire myself from the memory of my false, inconstant and beguiling pleasures. I am sorry to write this much, for I cannot think your mind so dishonourable but that you punish yourself for it, how little soever you care for me. But I desire whatsoever falls out, that your Majesty should be without excuse, you knowing yourself to be the cause and all the world wondering at the effect.[4]

The Earl was pushing his fortune to the very limit, and all over a comparatively trivial matter of pride. He heard that Lord Grey was being most kindly received by the Queen in the favourite's absence. So he lay in wait for Grey near the royal apartments, accosted him roughly and warned him to watch his step. Was Grey becoming a friend of the Cecils? If so he should declare himself, for there could be no neutrality between the friends of the Cecils and of Essex. The fact that Essex had knighted Grey on a military expedition abroad made his conduct more unpardonable in the Earl's eyes.

Himself a proud and irascible man, Grey answered back with equal violence. No, he would not alter his friendships to please Essex's prejudices. Yes, he had tasted the good favours of Robert Cecil, and he saw no reason to act ungratefully for them. In that case, cried the Earl, Grey should look to that direction for all his rewards, for from Essex he could henceforth expect none.

Like his written outburst against royal power the Earl's all-or-nothing dismissal of Grey marked a dangerous step of no return. He might accuse his enemies of conspiring against him, but such ruptures as occurred were of his own creating. He was the one demanding unconditional allegiance or hostility from those on the fringe of the competition. He was the one who talked like a general gathering his troops into the laager. He was the one who plotted and threatened and suspected the worst of those who did not accede to his every wish. And he was actively stirring up aggravation and hostile passions at a most inopportune moment, for old Lord Burghley lay dying. His death would leave a power vacuum into which Essex could not hope to be drawn so long as he stayed out of contact with Elizabeth and persisted in antagonizing everyone at Court or on the Council who did not hang on his every boast or fury with slavish devotion.

On 25 July 1598, the old statesman who had served Elizabeth for forty years was too weak even to sit up in bed. On the evening of 4 August he summoned his children round about him, blessed them, prayed for the Queen and handed his steward his will. At eight o'clock next morning he died peacefully – and when Elizabeth heard the news she retired to her private chambers to weep alone.

Sir William Knollys wrote Essex the obvious letter: 'Your lordship's being from Court at this time is, in my opinion, very unreasonable both for the common good (many weighty causes now depending) and your Lordship's own private; wishing, that there be no disposing of office or place without your lordship's allowance.' Word of Essex's 'cannot Princes err?' outburst must have reached Knollys for he concluded: 'Remember, I beseech you, that there is no contesting between sovereignty and obedience; and I fear the longer your Lordship doth persist in this careless humour of her Majesty, the more her heart will be hardened; and I pray God your contending with her in this manner do not breed such a hatred in her as will never be reclaimed.'5

The Earl ignored the hint. He attended a Council meeting, but refused to say a word until the Queen agreed to listen to him first. And this being refused he stumped off angrily. He was in danger of losing such offices as he possessed, for his refusal to carry out his duties as Master of the Ordnance was proving a grave embarrassment to plans to reinforce the English troops in Ireland. He had little chance of securing the Lord Treasurership or mastership of the Court of Wards which Burghley's death had left vacant.

Then events moved to a sudden crisis. On 14 August 1598, Sir Henry Bagenal, Marshal of the English Army in Ireland, gathered all his troops together and staked everything on one dramatic gesture. With 3,500 infantry and 500 cavalry he marched out of

Armagh to relieve the small English garrison holding the fort at the Blackwater against Tyrone and the Irish rebels. But before Bagenal could reach the Blackwater, the rebels had outflanked him and were lying in wait around the Yellow Ford over the Callan River which the English force had to cross to reach their objective. The slaughter was terrible, and at the end of the day some 2,000 English soldiers lay dead, together with Bagenal himself and thirty of his best officers.

The massacre of the Yellow Ford provided the spark needed to fire the entire Irish powder keg. As the news spread, Ulster was overrun by the rebels. Every local chieftain gave his allegiance to Tyrone. Connaught burst into flames. And in Leinster rebel bands marched into the English Pale, pillaging, burning and killing up to the walls of Dublin itself. Edmund Spenser, the author of *The Faerie Queene*, was just one of the hundreds of English colonists who woke one night to discover his house in flames, and destitute he had to fly with such members of his family as survived to take refuge in one of the few English strongpoints. Tyrone was King of Ireland in all but name. Except for a handful of beleaguered English garrisons he controlled the entire country. All that was needed to end completely English claims of occupation was for Spanish troops to land with the artillery Tyrone lacked.

The terrible news reached Elizabeth as Essex was falling into a real and not a diplomatic sickness. Their quarrel had lasted two months. She sent her own physician to attend him and instructed Killigrew, Fulke Greville and Lord Henry Howard to carry her good wishes to his bedside. When the Earl recovered sufficiently from his fever to come to Court on 10 September 1598 she welcomed him warmly and the breach seemed healed.

It was not, of course, and Essex was wrong to interpret the reconciliation as in any way a victory. In the face of the Irish crisis Elizabeth realized the futility of her favourite's caprices and decided to end them rapidly. She ignored his attempts to secure Burghley's former offices of Lord Treasurer and Master of Wards. And when he criticized her and the Council's prescriptions for Ireland she took him at his word. If Essex knew what was best for Ireland then Essex should go to Ireland. If he criticized all the names the Council put forward as Lord Deputy, then he should have the post himself.

By the end of November 1598 it was decided that Essex was next year to lead a spring and summer expedition to bring Tyrone to his knees. Orders were sent out to muster masters in all the shires to prepare the largest English army ever assembled for the Irish Wars. Captains unemployed since the return of the Islands expedition in 1597 hustled round to offer their services. Through January and February 1599 Essex became once more the centre of English affairs as he made his preparations. And in March his commission and instructions were signed by Elizabeth.

But he had taken on a dangerous task. Planning and organizing the expedition meant that he had little time to see Elizabeth – and once he set off he would be out of touch with events as he had been at Cadiz and in the Azores. He set out the hazards before him in an unusually perceptive letter:

Into Ireland I go. The Queen hath irrevocably decreed it. The Council do passionately urge it. And I am tied in my own reputation. . . . I am not ignorant what are the disadvantages of absence; the opportunities of practising enemies when they are neither encountered nor overlooked. . . . The Court is the centre, but methinks it is the fairer choice to command armies than humours. In the meantime enemies may be advanced. . . . These are my private problems and nightly disputations.[6]

They were not the only difficulties Essex could not sleep for worrying over. Elizabeth had been badgering him for weeks over the vast sums of money he owed her. She discharged him of £10,000 worth of debts to help him meet the costs of outfitting his expedition, but made it clear she expected repayment of the rest, as she had expected it of his father. The Devereux must meet their obligations one day. She indignantly refused to approve the appointment of the Earl of Southampton as his Master of Horse in Ireland because Southampton had made pregnant her lady-in-waiting Elizabeth Vernon and had added insult to injury by marrying the girl. She refused to appoint Sir Christopher Blount, Essex's stepfather, to the Council for Ireland. External events made matters worse. One Doctor John Hayward had published a book about Henry IV that opened with a dedication that revived the comparison between Essex and Bolingbroke. It ripped open a painful wound, and it was only after bitter arguments that Elizabeth agreed to sign a licence that would allow Essex to return from his command to England whenever he judged the Irish situation permitted. Did she fear perhaps that he would use his Irish army against her?

At two o'clock on the afternoon of 27 March 1599 the Earl of Essex rode down the Strand in the direction of Chester, the first mustering point of the troops sailing to Ireland. Crowds followed and cheered his retinue for four miles crying 'God save your lordship' and 'God preserve your honour'. The weather seemed set fair for the journey when suddenly, at Islington, the sky darkened and a downpour of rain and hail drenched the cavalcade. Contemporary chroniclers who described the triumphal send-off took the storm as an omen of evil.

24

The Irish Enterprise

'A Prayer for the good success of her Majesty's forces in Ireland.'

Almighty God and most merciful Father, which by thine holy Word declarest . . . how much thou hatest all resistance and rebellion against thy divine ordinance: vouchsafe (we humbly beseech thee) to strengthen and protect the Forces of thine anointed our Queen and sovereign, sent out to suppress these wicked and unnatural Rebels. Be thou to our armies a Captain, Leader, and Defender. Let thine holy Angels pitch their tents round about to guard them, and give them victory against all such as rise up to withstand them. Let not our sins, O Lord, be an hindrance to thine accustomed mercies towards us, neither punish our misdeeds by strengthening the hands of such as despise thy Truth, and have wickedly cast off the rightful yoke of their due allegiance. . . .

> *Imprinted at London by the Deputies*
> *of Christopher Barker, Printer to*
> *the Queen's most excellent Majesty.*
> *Anno 1599*

When the Earl of Essex landed in Ireland in April 1599 he needed all the prayers he could get, for the challenge before him demanded leadership organized at a level he had not previously attained. The sea expeditions had been tough obstacles and he had not cleared them altogether cleanly. Ireland was finally and catastrophically to lay him low, as it had his father before him.

The terrain confronting him was a trial in itself: 'uneven, mountainous, soft, watery, woody and open to winds and floods of rain, and so fenny as it hath bogs upon the very tops of mountains, not bearing man or beast but dangerous to pass: and such bogs are frequent all over Ireland.'[1] Essex hoped for an Arcadia of meadows and babbling brooks through which he could lead his tangerine soldiers, but his hopes were rapidly deceived. Over the course of the century's campaigns, Irish dysentery and marsh fever had claimed more English victims than the darts and swords of its native inhabitants,[2] and his army was to be destroyed in the same way.

The Earl had a small base to fight from. England claimed to rule the whole of Ireland, but Essex's father Walter was but one of a succession of English governors who discovered what a fiction that claim was:

An old distinction there is of Ireland into Irish and English Pales; for, when the Irish had raised continual tumults against the English planted here with the [Norman] Conquest, at last they coursed them into a narrow circuit of certain shires in Leinster which the English did choose as the fattest soil, most defensible, their proper right and most open to receive help from England. Hereupon it was termed their Pale, as whereout they durst not peep.[3]

This Pale which constituted the only significant English settlement enclosed less than a twentieth of Ireland's population and land area. In times of peace the English authorities could hope for the support of well-disposed Celtic chieftains living outside, and count on the reasonably enthusiastic loyalty of the Anglo-Norman gentlemen within the Pale counties of Dublin, Meath, Westmeath, Kildare and Louth – provided they were not expected to display that loyalty outside those counties. But the Government's only paid agents beyond the Pale were the isolated mayors of corporate towns, and sheriffs whose best hopes of survival in times of disorder lay in quiet compromise with the local insurgents or flight to Dublin. And Dublin itself was but a frontier city which the wild O'Byrnes from the Wicklow glens could reach between sunset and dawn.

It was a precarious perch for a Viceroy, and lent little substance to the viceregal powers that Elizabeth bestowed on Essex as her plenipotentiary. He could award knighthoods, proclaim traitors, issue pardons by letters patent under the Great Seal, levy forces, in fact fulfil all the royal prerogatives except that of coining money. On paper at least it was the most powerful office Elizabeth had in her gift and an office she could only afford to give to a man worthy of complete trust. Essex would have to rule through a Council, a judicious blend mixed by the Queen to include able English administrators and loyal Irish lords like Ormonde and Kildare, but his powers were those of a king in theory; and in practice those of an expeditionary general: the better he fought, the more he ruled.

But how was he best to fight? Advice was not lacking. 'The only way to regain and recover the entire dominion of this cursed land,' explained one anonymous minute-writer in 1599, 'is by edifying strong castles and forts upon the heaviest retreats and fastnesses of the rebels, thereby to curb and check their vagrant incursions and depredations . . . for we see by manifold experience what madness it is for a Deputy or General to lead royal forces against naked rogues in woods and bogs, whom hounds can scarce follow and much less men.' He derided the armed progresses of pacification that successive English governors had led across the countryside.

They have produced no other effect than a ship doth in a wide sea, who leaves no longer print or impression in the water than for the very instant, the waves immediately filling the way she makes, so as the same cannot be found. Wheresoever forces are conducted against these rebels they forthwith retire and hold themselves close in bushes and bogs without engaging any fight but upon advantages: and no sooner shall our camp remove or dislodge but they forthwith possess and overspread the ground we held. It is strange that Deputies are not restrained from running still this wild goose-chase.[4]

Not quite so strange considering the expense of the only real alternative that the writer could suggest. Lacking money and time to erect 'strong castles and forts', the Earl of Essex was committed in advance to the wild goose-chase, though that did not excuse the aimlessness of his chasing. His successor as commander of the English army in Ireland, Lord Mountjoy, proved that the wild goose could be caught. And Essex had been given good warning. Hearing of his appointment, a captain with experience of Irish campaigns had written to tell the new commander what rebel tactics he should expect: 'skirmishes in passes, bogs, woods, fords and in all places of advantage. And they hold it no dishonour to run away: for the best sconce and castle for their security is their feet.'[5] The anonymous minute-writer belaboured the point: 'their ordinary food is a kind of grass. Neither clothes nor houses generally do they care for. With this their savage life they are able to wear out any army that seeketh to conquer them. It is no more possible to defeat them at once than to destroy so many wolves and foxes: the which may be effected by tract of time and means convenient, but not to be attempted by plain force in the open field.'

For Essex was confronted with a land as easy to overrun as it was difficult to hold: a land of mountains and few roads, where three felled trees could block a company's march through a wood, or two holes in a ford leave a regiment floundering. 'The passages are every way dangerous,' wrote Gainsford who marched with Essex into Ulster, 'both for unfirmness of ground and the lurking rebel, who will plash down whole trees over the passes and so intricately wind them or lay them that they shall be a strong barricade, and then lurk in ambush amongst the standing wood.'[6] There was no specific resistance centre whose capture could produce a collapse, and any attempts at blanket reprisals and devastation simply fortified the hatred of the population as a whole. An Englishman might sneer in 1599 that the rebels' manoeuvres more resembled 'a morris dance by their tripping after their bagpipes than any soldier-like exercise',[7] but the dance they led Essex was not to be sneered at. 'On the bog they likewise presume with naked celerity to come as near our foot and horse as is possible and then fly off again knowing we cannot or indeed dare not follow them,' wrote Gainsford. 'And thus they serve us in the narrow entrances into their glens and stony paths, or if you will, dangerous quagmires of their mountains where 100 shot shall rebate the hasty approach of 500: and a few muskets (if they durst carry any) well placed will stagger a pretty army.'[8] As John Harington sourly remarked, the rebels stirred from the woods no 'further than an old hunted hare doth from the covert for relief'.[9]

Not that the Irish army was small, ill-equipped or incompetent. Soon after Essex arrived the reports of local English agents were collated in an attempt to estimate the enemy's armed strength and the curiously precise figure of 17,997 was arrived at. Further analysis of the reports allocated exactly 8,922 of those men to the northern heartland of Ulster, and they were for the most part good warriors. In 1596 Sir Henry Wallop, the Treasurer at Wars, had written to tell Cecil that for the first time in Elizabeth's reign the Irish could field an army experienced and disciplined enough to meet the English in formal confrontation. And the Massacre of the Yellow Ford in 1598 confirmed Wallop's opinion. By the end of the century the Irish had over fifty years constant guerrilla experience. Their generals had seen the English or Spanish armies from the inside, and Tyrone, during a period of allegiance to Elizabeth, had been able to train a substantial cadre of troops with English subsidies. Keeping their numbers constant but turning them over rapidly he had trained musketeers who could fire more accurately than the Englishmen alongside whom they were hopefully intended to fight.

He was a cunning man, was Hugh O'Neill, Earl of Tyrone, overlord of Ulster, the undisputed paramount of Northern Ireland. And in a century of raging Irish conflagrations he inspired a fire that outburnt all others. As a young man he had spent six years in England living the life of a young nobleman attached to the household of Leicester. He returned to Ireland when he was twenty-eight, leaving behind him the memory of a 'high dissembling, subtle and profound wit'. Though the chronicler Camden deplored Tyrone's later rebellions he was forced to admit that the young earl's 'understanding was very great, his soul large and fit for the weightiest business. He had much knowledge in military affairs, and a proud dissembling heart.'

'Dissembling' was the most frequent charge brought against this lively little Irishman by Englishmen who, captivated by his charm on first meeting, were later betrayed by his primary loyalty to his native country. Essex, never a sound assessor of character, took a decision even rasher than usual when he chose to stake his career upon half an hour's conversation with this least assessable of men. For Tyrone's rise had been unpredictable. In the twenty years after his return from England in 1574 he was subsidized as an Irish chieftain controlling most of what is now Armagh, and in acknowledgement of his loyalty Elizabeth confirmed his Earldom of Tyrone by letters patent in 1587. But in 1593 he was tempted by a title greater than any the Queen of England could bestow. His ailing cousin Tyrlong, the head of the O'Neill clan, withdrew from his chieftainship of Ulster and Hugh was elected to succeed him. As he sat in the old stone throne in the open field of Tullaghogue where generations of Ulster chieftains had been crowned before him, the Earl of Tyrone was in a unique position that might have marked a new era in Anglo-Irish relations. This client of the English Queen had been chosen to embody and champion the national aspirations of his people. He was respected by both natives and invaders as no other was before – or since.

But his daughter was married to his most powerful neighbour, Hugh Roe O'Donnell, the fighting Prince of Donegal, whom the English had imprisoned by specious trickery in 1587. And escaping from his captors on Christmas night, 1591, Tyrone's twenty-one-year-old son-in-law had called upon his people for revenge. They rose in bloody revolt and at once the two faces of Tyrone's dual chieftainship became irreconcilable contradictions. He was compelled to choose between the Queen in London and his son-in-law at home, and his people left him little time for decision. In 1594 he joined forces with young O'Donnell and on 28 June 1595 Elizabeth issued a proclamation declaring that the fighting prince, Tyrone and all their followers were proscribed as traitors.

It was these 'traitors' which Robert Devereux was in April 1599 sent to bring to justice. He could not complain at the strength or condition of the troops given him for the task. They numbered some 16,000 foot and 1,300 horse. He could employ five or six thousand of them for mobile campaigns, leaving 5,000 in defence of the Pale, garrison 3,000 in Connaught and station as many in the South. Some of them were Anglo-Irish or Irish with a record of conspicuous loyalty to the Crown, but the bulk were English levies, for in 1596 the Privy Council had decided against the wisdom of recruiting native troops in large numbers. They might be cheaper and more accustomed to local conditions, but their persistent desertions simply weakened the English forces while swelling the number of trained and armed warriors in the rebel ranks.

And leading the cream of the English shires were the officers who followed Essex and who, for once, were curiously appropriate to the chosen field of warfare. Impetuous young bloods might cause more confusion than their valour could counterbalance in the Low Countries, France or the Azores, but in Ireland the rule book of war no longer applied and a hot-headed rush might accomplish more than a well-polished formation. Old soldiers were 'vexed to see so many raw youths press for the greatest charges',[10] but the old soldiers had few achievements to boast of in Ireland. It was young captains like John Harington, Josias Bodley and Gervase Markham who gained such glory as there was to be salvaged from Essex's Irish expedition. And all three of these gentlemen were fired by their campaigning to write descriptions of their experiences, Markham later pursuing his literary career so far as to write the first handbook 'for the destruction of Moales or Moles, which dig and root up the earth': 'if you take green leeks, garlic or onions and, chopping them grossly, thrust it into the holes, the very fume or savour thereof will so astonish and amaze the moles that they will presently forsake the earth and falling into a trance you may take them up with your hands.'

But it was to take more than chopped garlic to winkle the Irish from their holes, and impressive though its strength appeared on paper, there were serious deficiencies in Essex's army. It was the old trouble of establishing a national army on a private enterprise basis.

Many of the soldiers had sold their equipment before even they sailed to Ireland, and the Privy Council decided too late to stop that abuse by sending the coats and weapons that Essex's levies would need in special ships.[11] But at the root of the trouble were the officials. Special 'Commissaries of Victuals' appointed by the Privy Council with extensive powers to speed up the distribution of foodstuffs proved no better than the contractors they were meant to oversee. Whole cartloads of oatmeal were left in the Dublin castle cellars to be 'utterly spoiled' by the rising tide.[12] And the soldiers were charged so much for their food, clothing and gunpowder that it took them eighty days to fight out of their debts.

Their officers were more prosperous – and some had laid the foundations of their prosperity before even they reached Ireland. In Chester a 'robbers' cave' had sprung up since the intensification of the Irish wars, to which 'cave' officers would take lists of the troops, weapons, and even horses that they were required to parade before embarkation. On parade day a near-identical company to the one described in the officer's muster book was provided for the inspection of the muster master. His roll signed and certified, the captain could pay off the stand-ins and the agents who made a good living from arranging such performances, and then proceed to Ireland where he could file a claim for the travelling expenses of ferrying one hundred men across the Irish Channel. Once in Dublin it was only too easy to discover natives with authentic English equipment or to hire men from other companies who would enable the charade to be played out almost indefinitely. One critic thought Elizabeth would have had a good bargain if she paid such rogues a thousand pounds to stay out of her army.[13] And soldiers who tried to expose their captain risked being hanged as mutineers once the muster master's back was turned.[14]

Essex's Irish campaign was to divide itself into three parts, though he can receive no credit for planning such convenient divisions. The first was a long march south from Dublin through the province of Leinster into Munster and back again. The second was a short march due west from Dublin towards Athlone and back again. The third was a hesitant advance towards Ulster and the northern rebel heartland which, after parleys with Tyrone

The Expedition of the Earl of Essex in Ireland in 1599

N

Lough Foyle

ULSTER

Louth
Bellaclynth
Ardee
Navan

Dublin

Maryborough

Athy

Wicklow

LEINSTER

Arklow

Limerick

Kilkenny

Askeaton

MUNSTER

Cahir
Clonmel
Waterford

Conna

Dungarvan

Southern Expedition: May 9 – July 2 .... — — —
Western Expedition: mid-July ....—·—·—
Northern Expedition: Aug. 28 — Sept. 9 ..- - - - - -

10 0   20   40   60

MILES

CHARLES GREEN.

near Dundalk, also ended back in Dublin. It was the third sortie that both Elizabeth and Essex had expected would be the English army's first and last, for from London nothing seemed simpler than an immediate march north from Dublin into Tyrone's own country, a direct confrontation with the main body of the rebel force, and then a pacificatory tour of Ireland mopping up isolated pockets of rebel resistance. It was so obvious that Tyrone had foreseen it long before Essex sailed into Dublin harbour and had made preparations accordingly.

When the Council of Ireland met their new Lord Deputy for the first time on 15 April 1599, they had to inform him that rebel forces in Leinster, Munster and the south were being strengthened by detachments sent from Tyrone, and that until those forces were dealt with no expedition to Ulster and the north could hope to succeed. Nor was there sufficient transport available efficiently to supply any army campaigning north of Dublin. Tyrone would have to be left undisturbed in Ulster until high summer when there would be more pasture available and when the rivers, still rising in the April rain, had become more manageable.

Essex let the Council vote down his plans to cut at the root of rebel strength in the north and was probably relieved by their insistence that he 'shake and sway the branches'[15] of resistance else-where first. He was more concerned with personal matters: he made a great show of appointing the Earl of Southampton to be his Master of Horse, in deliberate defiance of the Queen's pro-hibition. Yet he did make sure that Elizabeth should be fully aware that the reasons for delay were none of his own making in a letter dated 28 April 1599, and signed by the whole Council. London accepted the reason for the delay, though not Southampton's appointment, and in a letter to the English ambassador in Paris Cecil marvelled how Essex had 'wrought miracles to have settled and distributed an army of 16,000 foot and 1,300 horse and to have accommodated them with all necessaries in a country full of misery and disorder. For the time of year not serving to pass into Ulster to break the head of the rebellion till the month of June, within twenty days his lordship began a journey into Leinster and from there intends to pass into Munster with a purpose to secure these provinces, that thereby the main action of Ulster may be proceeded with less distraction.'

Either Cecil's admiration of the Lord Lieutenant in Ireland was fabricated for the benefit of the dubious French Court, or his memory was conveniently short, for he later spared Essex's initial dilatoriness no criticism. Nor was the Lord Deputy's own memory or honesty above reproach, for when the recriminations started later he tried to shuffle off responsibility for the southern expedition on to the Earl of Ormonde and got Elizabeth to rebuke that commander accordingly.[16] The seventy-year-old Irishman, long inured to the caprices of successive English governors, easily proved that he had been nowhere near Dublin when the decision to march south was taken; but it would have helped Essex to have the benefit of his advice. For his Council was without its experienced treasurer, Sir Henry Wallop, who died in agony on the evening of the new Lord Deputy's entry to Dublin – and also the Earl of Kildare, drowned a few days later in an Irish Channel storm. On 9 May 1599 Robert Devereux marched out on the first stage of the campaign that could have proved the pinnacle to his career, but in fact began its débâcle. His expeditionary army, some 3,000 foot and 300 horse who had left Dublin a few days earlier, was waiting for him near Kilcullen in County Kildare. A strong force, especially the cavalry who were to make themselves feared throughout the countryside in which they marched. 'Amongst the heathen there is no such wicked soldiers,' complained Bishop William Lyon of Ross in Carbey, speaking particularly of the Irish horseboys that the English cavalrymen employed to forage for them. They 'fetch in horse-loads of corn of the poor people day by day, they [the Irish poor] having no other sustenance to relieve them and their families than a little cow about which they have taken great pains and travail, and if they come to rescue it from the horseboys they fall upon them and beat them and cut them in the heads most lamentable to see.'

The campaign began well. On 11 May the castle of Athy surrendered with little attempt at resistance, and the old Earl of Ormonde arrived with 700 foot, 200 Irish cavalry and two kinsmen, Lords Cahir and Mountgarret, who had both dabbled with rebel activities and who now fell on their knees begging forgiveness for their infidelity. They were small fish, but Essex made the most of his pious rebukes and gracious indulgence. He marched on to revictual the fort at Maryborough.

In a defile at Blackford, near Stradbaly, his scouts caught sight of an enemy force shadowing their advance, and, somewhat surprisingly, the rebel commander MacRory O'Moore sent heralds to the English headquarters. He challenged fifty Englishmen to a sword and buckler tournament with fifty of his own picked champions, a challenge which Essex jumped at. But it proved the first of the many non-encounters that were to drag through the summer of 1599, for the Irish failed to feature at the rendezvous.

Annoyed, Essex tried deliberate provocation, and headed his army at the pass of Cashel. It was terrain ready made for an ambush, rough, boggy and wooded, and there was little hope of confrontation with the enemy on the more open detour that his captains must originally have suggested. The confrontation nearly came at a trench around which the rebels had 'plashed trees' to form a woven barrier of branches. Essex sent ahead a special 'suicide squad' of forty shot and twenty swordsmen to draw the rebel fire but this party attacked with such success that the vanguard were able to push straight through on to the plain beyond. Had they been less forceful the Irish might have moved in closer, but overwhelmed by the speed of the English breakthrough the snipers fell back. Essex's young gentlemen captains attempted to pursue them, but only lost their hats in the process, earning the skirmish the title of 'the Pass of Plumes'.

On 18 May 1599 the English again attempted to force confrontation in the pass that led them to the castle of the recently contrite Mountgarret at Ballyragget, but again resistance melted. Essex left one hundred men to garrison the fortress then moved on to the rush-strewn reception that Ormonde's retainers had laid on for him in the town of Kilkenny. On 22 May the town of Clonmel puffed up a similarly fulsome and meaningless display of loyalty, and riding among the cheers and smiles and garlands the new Lord Lieutenant decided he had pacified the province of Leinster. With the enemy before him, behind him, he knew not where, he decided to push on towards Munster.

He was told that some of the rebels were ensconced in Cahir Castle led by the younger brother of the Lord Cahir who had knelt before him at Maryborough. He had supplies sent up from Waterford and then marched the ten miles from Clonmel to the island on which the castle stood in the River Suir. Under covering fire an advance party occupied an orchard near the walls, and when the garrison fled managed to cut down a good number in the darkness. It was a small triumph but it proved to be the only conclusive action in Essex's entire Irish campaign, and his last success in battle or anything else. Leaving his sick in Clonmel the Lord Lieutenant marched onwards through worsening weather – to hear news of the disaster that had overtaken Sir Henry Harrington in Wicklow.

Left with less than seven companies of inexperienced troops to contain the fierce O'Byrnes of Wicklow, Sir Henry had camped in the valley of the Avonmore on the night of 28 May 1599. Withdrawing hastily when morning revealed the O'Byrnes gathered in force he left troops to cover his retreat who had but recently deserted from the rebel ranks, and who, not surprisingly, showed little stomach for a fierce rearguard action. They broke, and their panic spread to the main body of English troops who turned tail and ran as well, not halting until they reached the walls of Wicklow.

Tidings of the disaster lent a derisive note to the huzzas with which Limerick greeted Queen Elizabeth's representatives on 4 June 1599. And after a month of fruitless marching through drizzle and mud the morale of the English troops was sagging. Essex felt compelled to reproach them for their lack of enthusiasm when on 8 June they shilly-shallied through an ambush laid on their march to Askeaton Castle. There was no point in going further west, for the rebels were too clever to let Essex sandwich them between his army and the sea, and they had slipped round to his rear. The English had no choice but to retrace their steps, heading for the fortress of James FitzThomas at Conna near

Lismore in the hope of 'giving the rebel an inexcusable provocation'. A slim hope, for FitzThomas had burnt down his walls and fled by the time the English troops got to Conna on 17 June. Nothing – not even a castle – would induce the Irish to stand up and fight.

Essex marched to Waterford for the solace of speeches, feasts and sycophants. Orators extolled the valour of the Lord Lieutenant who rode so proudly through their streets on 21 June, but his troops' one concern was to drown their sorrows in 'the best *aquae vitae* in Ireland' for which Waterford was renowned. Many were sick with marsh fever or dysentery, and those who were still fit were thoroughly demoralized by their fruitless ramblings through mists and drizzles and bogs. Essex ferried them across the Barrow River into Wexford, but viewing their condition and remembering the fate of Sir Henry Harrington, he decided he could not risk a direct march to Dublin through the Wicklow hills. Fighting off a rebel detachment at Arklow he moved back up the coast to the capital and was sleeping again in Dublin Castle at the beginning of July 1599.

His two months of wandering through the hills of southern Ireland had been little short of catastrophic. His 16,000 foot with 1,300 horse had been cut down to 11,250 and 925. The men were tired, sick and resentful. No rebel force of consequence had been destroyed. No rebel leader of consequence had submitted. 'The Gaels of Ireland were wont to say that it would have been better for him that he had not gone on this expedition to Hy Connell Caura,' commented the Annals of the Four Masters, 'for he returned back without having received submission or respect . . . and without having achieved any exploit worth boasting about, save only the taking of Cathair Duine lasgaigh.'[17]

And Elizabeth rightly dismissed the capture of Cahir as no more than taking 'an Irish hold from a rabble of rogues'. The important task was taking an axe to Tyrone, 'that tree which hath been the treasonable stock from which so many poisoned plants and grafts have been derived.'[18] Why had the Earl entrusted the cavalry in deliberate defiance of her orders to the profligate Earl of Southampton? The letters from the Queen that Essex found waiting for him in Dublin were fierce and caustic and Elizabeth did not confine her displeasure to despatches. She made sure all London knew how much she disdained the Earl's efforts.

Hearing of the royal disapproval from the epistles which their friends at Court wrote, Essex's young followers clustered closer about their leader. They resented criticism from courtiers who would not risk their own life and health in a country whose mysterious hazards could only be understood by those who had known them personally. And drinking morosely together in the Dublin hostelries they struck up those conversations of resentment that the next eighteen months were to elaborate and intensify to a point where restraint was impossible: they were misunderstood, and misunderstood by men of ill-will, malignant influences which conspired against them and which they could only combat by hatching conspiracies of their own.

Essex lashed out fiercely at the men involved in the Wicklow débâcle. Sir Henry Harrington was confined at the Queen's pleasure – for as a Privy Councillor he could not be tried. Piers Walshe, an Irish lieutenant who had wrapped himself in the colours and fled, was executed. The other officers of the foot were cashiered. And all the surviving soldiers were condemned to death, the sentence being carried out on one in ten of them.

After that vigorous and bloody blame-shuffling the Lord Lieutenant set out on 25 July on a short expedition due west into the King's and Queen's Counties. Maryborough was revictualled once again; a rebel force under the Anglo-Irish mercenary Richard Tyrrell was beaten off; the O'Connors' corn was burnt 'so that all the country was on fire at once' and some cows were captured. But news from the north west of Ireland soon after Essex returned to Dublin put his raid into its proper perspective. Sir Conyers Clifford had been defeated in the Curlew Mountains as he marched to relieve the besieged castle of Sir Donogh O'Connor, one of the loyalist adherents to the English crown among the Irish chieftains.

Entering the Curlew Hills on 5 August the English force of 1,496 foot and 205 horse were set upon by a detachment from the army besieging O'Connor in his Collooney castle. Making full use of barricades, bogs and woods the rebels broke up the English vanguard, who wheeled and panicked the troops behind them. Sir Conyers Clifford fell fighting valiantly, but few imitated his courage. His body was left to have its head hacked off as a present to the fighting Prince of Donegal, who secured at the same time the surrender of Sir Donogh O'Connor. It was a catastrophe almost as crippling as the ambush that had destroyed Sir Henry Bagenal's army at the Yellow Ford a year earlier.

Essex summoned a Council of War on 21 August 1599. Before him was Elizabeth's latest letter ordering him to advance into Ulster and withdrawing her permission for him to return to England until such time as 'the northern action be tried'. There was a note of hysteria to her rebukes, for intelligence of a threatened Spanish invasion of England had prompted mobilization under Nottingham, Mountjoy, Thomas Howard and Raleigh. The chronicler Camden later alleged that this levy was a defence against the possibility of Essex returning violently from Ireland, and some evidence is lent to his charge by the fact that he was in Cecil's confidence and that there is a note in Cecil's handwriting on the copy of the letter ordering the Lord Lieutenant to march into Ulster – 'to command him not to come over'. Whitehall speculation found it easy to represent Essex's perambulations around Ireland as a means of gathering together disaffected swordsmen willing to follow their master to London in the redress of his alleged injustices.

Elizabeth's original intention had been for Essex to march right through Ulster to the northern coast and establish a garrison on Loch Foyle. But by late August 1599 Essex scarcely had enough men to fight his way through to Loch Foyle, let alone leave a garrison there. 'Every town and place of garrison is an hospital,' he wrote to the Privy Council, 'where our degenerate country-men are glad to entertain sickness as supersedas for their going to the field . . . and we can never make account what numbers we have of them.'[19] In fact his useful force of 'strong and service-able troops' now totalled little more than 3,500 foot and 300 horse with the expectation of 2,000 reinforcements reluctantly granted by Elizabeth.[20]

The Loch Foyle dash was clearly out of the question, and Essex's

Council were opposed to expeditions north of any sort. But the Queen's Lord Lieutenant now had little choice. On 27 August 1599 he sent Henry Cuffe back to England with news of the Council's opposition but of his determination to confront Tyrone, come what might. And the next day he wrote again. 'I am even now putting my foot into the stirrup to go to the rendezvous at Navan; and do as much as duty will warrant me and God enable me.'[21]

God and duty kept him going for just ten days, and by the sixth day the hopelessness of his task had become apparent. As the English army reached Ardee in Louth, on 3 September, Tyrone paraded his troops for the Lord Lieutenant's inspection out of musket and assault range. They outnumbered Essex's force by at least two to one. An envoy was sent to demand the release of an English officer held by the Irish, and replying, Tyrone said he would be glad to make submission. Would Essex speak to his constable, Henry O'Hagan?

O'Hagan reached the English headquarters on 5 September and requested a parley. Essex cried he could only parley with swords. 'If thy master have any confidence either in the justness of his cause or in the goodness and number of his men, or in his own virtue, of all which he vainly glorieth, he will meet me in the field so far advanced beyond the head of his kerne as myself shall be separated from the front of my troops, where he will parley in the fashion that best becometh soldiers.'

A gallant challenge, except that Essex was thirty-two and Tyrone was fifty-four. Next day Essex paraded his troops in an outspread St Andrew's cross, his horse set well on the flanks and rear of the open ground. But Tyrone knew better than to be tempted by the Lord Lieutenant's empty heroics. The rebels' overwhelming strength put any English advance out of the question, and that was all Tyrone needed to achieve. No odds would tempt him to direct confrontation.

He sent back O'Hagan on 7 September to request another parley. By this time Essex was withdrawing to Kells, and to his right lay the valley of the River Lagan. O'Hagan suggested that the two leaders meet there by the ford of Bellaclynth, and when

Essex appeared with his cavalry on the southern hill a rebel detachment was waiting on the gentle slope opposite. Between them flowed the Lagan and there, with the water lapping at his horse's belly, waited the solitary figure of Tyrone, his head humbly bowed in submission. Essex rode down alone to the water's edge.

It should have been a great moment, the moment Elizabeth had spent so much money and effort and men to make possible, the moment Essex had staked all on achieving, the moment that would finally redeem his reputation and by that redemption reunite mistress and favourite. The Lord Lieutenant sat proud on the river bank while the rebel shifted and finicked his horse to stay steady in the stream below. The commander who had led the cream of his Queen's armies to the Netherlands, France, Spain and the Azores looked down on the Irish chieftain whose pelt-clad men had never strayed beyond their native hills and marshes. The glory of it appeared to vindicate all Essex's hopes. He had proved, as he had always believed, that he was the master of all situations. And Tyrone's grovelling humility proved, as Essex had always believed, that no problem could not be resolved by the personal charm and influence of Robert Devereux.

The rebel was so contrite and, with it all, so civilized and reasonable. Not at all the uncouth savage Essex had expected. He had come alone, as he had promised, with but a token bodyguard on the northern hill.

But behind that hill was the entire Irish army, and behind the southern hill the English force, no more than half the size, tired, diseased and demoralized. That was the reality of the situation, the reality Essex allowed himself to forget as the simple chivalry of the confrontation, the gentle lilt of Tyrone's voice and the moderate logic of the Irish terms seduced his judgement. He was not a conquering hero graciously conceding to the pleas of a vanquished foe. He was the leader of a beleaguered and disintegrating force whose every concession was an admission of defeat so total that hopeless defiance or suicidal attack might have seemed more honourable. And he forgot what political implications his conference might have back at the English Court. He was not a sovereign negotiating privately with a fellow monarch.

His unwitnessed conversation was treasonable by definition in sixteenth-century terms. Essex was the leader of a Court faction whose reliability was uncertain and whose loyalty was doubted, talking privately with a rebel. His behaviour was open to the most uncharitable constructions. He was at worst a traitor, at best a fool.

For nearly an hour the two men talked, then returned to their comrades with promises of peace. They rode back down to the ford, each with his own entourage, and there appointed commissioners to conclude the truce next day. That done, Essex dispersed his army and retired to Drogheda, feeling sick.

And sick he must well have felt when he contemplated the truce at greater leisure and had time to imagine Elizabeth's reaction to it, for only form threw a thin disguise over naked surrender. While Tyrone swore an oath to the terms, Essex simply gave a written assurance, a distinction that can have afforded but scant balm to the Lord Lieutenant's wounded dignity. The Irish rebels were to remain in possession of everything they held on the date of agreement, 8 September 1599, and the English had to agree not to establish any new garrisons or forts. The truce would last six weeks in the first instance, then again six weeks if both sides agreed, and so on at six weekly intervals until May 1600. Within those six weekly periods either side could open hostilities at fourteen days' notice – which suited Tyrone ideally. He was expecting an expeditionary force from Spain before winter's end.

But Essex, of course, was not concerned in the last resort with what happened to Ireland that far ahead, for he had accepted the lord lieutenancy primarily as a means of re-establishing himself in Elizabeth's confidence. Tyrone, the rebels, the settlers, the Pale were no more than pawns in a chess game and they were not his real concern. It would have helped his overall strategy to win them, but he had not. And indeed, military failure apart, his absence from Court had been disastrous. In May Robert Cecil had been appointed to the mastership of the Court of Wards, the profitable office that had so greatly augmented old Burghley's fortunes and with which Essex had hoped to strengthen his. And, when a letter from Elizabeth arrived refusing to accept the terms Essex had agreed with Tyrone, it confirmed to the Earl what he had long suspected: that his Elizabeth was surrounded and seduced by men of evil and corruption. He must return to her side. There seemed nothing left for it but to make a direct appeal to the Queen.

With Southampton and Blount the Earl conferred in Dublin Castle. Southampton and Essex were for picking a thousand or so men and marching on London, said Blount later, giving himself the credit for scotching the scheme. A more likely deterrent was the condition of the troops and Essex's own panic. He had simply lost his nerve. Ceaseless attacks of dysentery had undermined his morale; scarce-veiled criticism from the Privy Council and the Irish Council had sapped his will. The parchment tantrums and sarcasm which each post brought from Elizabeth demoralized him still further. She could hardly suspect his loyalty, she wrote, since she had entrusted him with the care of an entire kingdom, but why had Essex not told her the exact terms of his secret conversation with Tyrone, the great Irish traitor? She feared his handling of her troops had proved not only dishonourable and wasteful but 'perilous and contemptible'. Unless Essex had forced the rebels to allow the stationing of English garrisons throughout Ireland he had pieced up but a 'hollow peace'. The invective rolled on remorselessly. And Elizabeth did not know yet that the Earl had taken it upon himself to dub over eighty knights in the last few weeks, bringing the number of titles awarded by Essex in the course of his scarcely illustrious campaigns to 170, over a quarter of the total in the whole of England. When the Queen found out, her rage would know no bounds. Essex could stand it no longer. This land of mist and bogs had ruined his father, and now it had ruined him.

He called a meeting of the Irish Council on 24 September 1599 and handed the sword of state to Archbishop Loftus and Sir George Carew. One hour later he was aboard ship for England taking with him the Earl of Southampton, Sir Henry Danvers and a small group of assorted young knights, captains and gallants. They made up a band more noteworthy for their swordplay than for their wisdom, and Ireland had given scope for neither. They looked for better sport ahead.

25

'A hatred in her as will never be reclaimed'

Landed in England, the Earl of Essex rode hell for leather towards London. With his band of swordsmen he galloped through the North Wales valleys, not pausing as the route passed near Chartley and his estates. Surprise was all. His truce with Tyrone had been fault enough. To desert his command at an hour's notice without even warning the Queen and Council was tantamount to treason. He was staking all on a personal confrontation with Elizabeth – and for her to catch wind of his coming would be fatal.

So Essex, Southampton and their companions kept their spurs in their horses' flanks. And as they rode across the Vale of Evesham, through the northern Cotswolds and down into the Vale of the White Horse they anticipated gleefully the consternation their arrival would cause. How the hunchback Cecil would be discomfitted! No longer would the Queen be defenceless against his sly whisperings. Essex could represent events in Ireland as they had truly happened; the jibes of the Howards and Raleigh would be answered.

And yet the galloping band must have been uneasy. They needed the reassurance such anticipation could give, for they were out on a limb. If their coup did not work the cost of failure would be high. Jingling bridles and thundering hooves and oaths laughed into the wind might keep up their spirits on the journey. But when they reached Court the galloping would have to stop. Would surprise be enough? Could the Earl of Essex sustain the momentum of this mindless, headlong dash when the Queen and Council had overcome their astonishment and started to question more coolly the reasons for the unsanctioned truce and the spur-of-the-moment departure?

The speed of the journey spared such worries. Up over the Chilterns they galloped and then down along the final stretch towards London. In the early hours of Friday, 28 September 1599 Essex and his followers clattered over the cobbles of Westminster down to the Lambeth ferry. They had heard the Court was at the palace of Nonsuch, ten miles south of London. They left their horses on the north bank of the river to be brought over in a second convoy, but as their ferryman shipped his oars near the steps of Lambeth Palace they saw another group of horses tethered under the trees. They were waiting for riders who had gone into town – so Essex commandeered them for the final stage of the adventure, leaving Sir Thomas Gerard to bring their own horses on when the next ferry tied up. There was no time to lose. It seemed Lord Grey had already heard news of their arrival and was riding ahead of them to warn Cecil.

Down south towards Nonsuch the sweaty group galloped. It was a wet autumn and damp leaves from the trees that shaded the road caught in their hair. Mud from the horses' hooves splattered up in their faces, matting their beards and caking the lace on their soiled torn garments. Morasses in the unmade road slowed their progress and Sir Thomas Gerard caught up, bringing the now spare horses. Waiting at the ferry he had heard definitely that Lord Grey was in front of them, and having told the news to Essex he rode out furiously ahead.

He caught up with Grey and asked him whether he wouldn't rein in and talk with Essex who was just down the road. But Grey dug his spurs in his horse and rode ahead still harder. He had business at Court, he explained. At least 'let my Lord of Essex ride before, that he may bring the first news of his return himself,' begged Gerard. Should he take that as a personal request from the Earl himself? asked Grey superciliously, galloping ahead as ever.

'No,' cried Gerard in a sudden fit of temper. Nor would his master ask for any favours from the hands of Grey. He pulled up to wait for his companions.

When Sir Christopher St Lawrence, one of the more blood-thirsty of the Irish adventurers, heard Gerard's story he was even more incensed than Essex. He would ride ahead, slay Grey, reach the Court and murder Cecil too, he bellowed. The emotions of the group were reaching fever pitch – but Essex still retained some grip on reality. It was the sort of threat that had maintained their morale through four days and nights of hard lonely riding. But he knew it would defeat what small chance of success their desperate enterprise still had. He told St Lawrence to bide his time. They rode on.

Grey reached the palace of Nonsuch ten minutes before his pursuers. When they thundered into the courtyard and leapt from their horses there was no sign of him. Yet the guards to the royal apartments seemed completely astonished by the sudden apparition of Essex. Grey must have taken his news elsewhere, presumably to the apartments of the little Secretary. Essex still held the initiative. Pushing the pikemen and chamber attendants aside he strode towards the royal apartments – flushed, sweating, splattered with mud from head to toe, his spurs jingling, his sword banging on his thigh in his haste.

He brushed through the Presence Chamber to the Privy Chamber and right on through that, without knocking, into the royal bedroom. The Queen had no idea, as she turned at the sound of scuffles and commotion, that the Earl of Essex was in England, let alone in her palace, let alone in her own private bedchamber to which no male subject had ever been invited. And as the Earl of Essex advanced – damp, dirty and breathing heavily – she had no idea whether he had come from Ireland alone or did not perhaps have the whole English army at his back. Perhaps even now Nonsuch was surrounded by armed guards in the Earl of Essex's pay. Certainly he had broken somehow through all the security arrangements that were supposed to protect her.

She was only just up – grey, wrinkled, her wig off, her hair straggling down over her unmade-up face. She had not finished dressing properly. She was alone and defenceless, deprived of the physical artifices that turned a wizened old woman into a robed, crowned, painted Queen. Essex had stripped away the façade that was Gloriana and had dared to thrust himself unprepared and uninvited upon the vulnerable, decaying woman that wore the mask.

He knelt before her and kissed her hands. She was chilled by the damp and cold of his riding clothes. What did he want? She played for time. She greeted him gently, smiled kindly at his incoherent speech of explanation and complaint, patted him softly on the head, and suggested he revisit her when both had had time to prepare themselves more fully for a meeting. To her suggestion he agreed and shambled off, telling the crowd of courtiers who had gathered in awe outside the royal apartments that 'though he had suffered much trouble and storms abroad he found a sweet calm at home'.

An hour later, at eleven, he returned, clean, spruced up and with more of a grip on himself. The Queen too was more in command of the situation – but still did not know exactly the circumstances of his return. They spoke together in private for an hour and a half, he pouring out his heart, his worries, his fears: she leading him on, discovering exactly why he had left Ireland, whom he had brought with him, what he expected to achieve.

Outside the royal apartments his travelling companions waited anxiously, and as the minutes passed their hopes grew. Their patron had secured the long, private audience he had always maintained would clear up the problems between himself and the Queen. Elizabeth was listening to him, obviously talking warmly with him. She must be glad to see her favourite back and to hear from his own lips the full account of his actions. Cecil, Raleigh, Grey and the Howards stayed discreetly hidden. When Essex emerged smiling to eat with Rutland, Rich, Mountjoy, and his other friends it seemed that the coup really had come off. Courtiers and ladies flocked round the returned hero to hear tales of battle, the Irish and the truce concluded with Tyrone. The Secretary ate quietly and apart with Raleigh, Grey, Cobham, the Howards and Shrewsbury. Their cold silence was ominous, but hardly threatening. At moments of crisis like this, when all hung on the knife-edge, it was the Queen alone who decided. Cecil might have laid his plans thoroughly and be prepared for the worst eventuality, yet what mattered were the workings of Elizabeth's mind.

As usual they were convoluted, and far more complex than Essex at least could guess. Elizabeth had greeted him. She had smiled on him and granted him a long and sympathetic audience. Yet she was thinking hard and fast. Until she knew exactly what Essex's motives were she had had to fear the worst and presume he really had returned from Ireland with force enough to impose his will upon her. When it became clear that he had no such intention, that his hope was to win her over with sweet talk, that his weapons were arguments, not swords, then she knew she was safe. Far from Elizabeth being at Essex's mercy, he was now at hers. And once she discovered that, she was implacable.

Essex was summoned for a third audience that afternoon, and Elizabeth showed what she really thought of his capricious, self-indulgent impulse. That morning it had been Essex who had done the talking. Now the boot was on the other foot, and while Rutland, Mountjoy, Rich and the knights confidently waited for the news that their patron had been handing out more advice to the Queen, Elizabeth was in fact cross-examining Essex icily. His jaunty answers became less confident. He began stuttering. He contradicted himself. He could not explain his bungling in Ireland. He could not justify his sudden departure from Dublin. There was no excuse for the rudeness of his arrival that morning. To the Queen's questions he could only mumble answers or flare resentfully with complaints against Cecil. Elizabeth was remorseless. And the more she pressed, the more unconvincing Essex became. Confused by the sudden, and to him inexplicable, transformation in her behaviour he tried to argue back, until with scorn she dismissed him from her presence. She had no further wish to see him, and although even in the intensity of her cold fury she could not have intended it, this was a final dismissal. Elizabeth was never to see her Robert again.

The Earl was sent to be examined by the four councillors that could be found at Nonsuch, while messengers rode post haste to bring others to the palace next day. For an hour Essex talked with Cecil, Hunsdon, North and Knollys, trying to convince them with the same arguments that had worn so thin with Elizabeth. They were unimpressed, and repeating his rehearsed speeches yet again, even Essex must have realized the hollowness of his justifications. When he pressed them for reassurance they were evasive, refusing to commit themselves. But late that evening, when Elizabeth had had a chance to read the report the councillors had drawn up after their meeting with Essex, word came from the Queen that the Earl was to keep to his chamber. Nor was he to leave the confinement without express royal permission.

The Essex party that had swollen in the few confused hours of that day since Essex's arrival suddenly collapsed. And one of the few visitors that the lonely Earl received in this unexpected imprisonment was Francis Bacon. Yet the visit was not a friendly one. Although Essex did not realize it, this too was a meeting as decisive as his own final interview with the Queen. Bacon did not waste time pointing out the many ways in which Essex had ignored his advice, nor that if anything could have prevented this tragic débâcle it was the politic course of action towards the Queen that Bacon had urged consistently on his patron. He contented himself with repeating gently the tenor of his previous advice – and begged Essex to drop the pretence that the botched-up truce with Tyrone was in any way a brilliant or glorious accomplishment. Essex listened in silence, then shook his head. It was the last time he was to talk to Francis Bacon as a friend or ally. Crippled Anthony remained true to the bitter end, but Francis was not a pilot to stay on board with a captain who ignored his directions. He was already seeking a new helm to guide when the Council met next day.

The councillors had ridden to Nonsuch with the dawn, and all morning they deliberated until, after lunch, Essex was summoned from his quarters. When he entered the Council Chamber his former colleagues rose to greet him: but when they sat down he was told to remain standing bareheaded at the end of the table, and the clerks were sent out of the room to ensure that, if a great man were to be humbled, it would at least be among his peers. Cecil read out a list of charges drawn up as principal offences by Essex against his Queen. There were six:

that Essex had been contemptuously disobedient to Her Majesty's instructions in returning to England.

that many of his letters from Ireland had been presumptuous.

that he had departed in Ireland from the instructions given to him before he left England.

that his flight from Ireland had been rash and irresponsible in view of the situation there.

that he had been overbold in breaking into Her Majesty's bedchamber.

and that he had created an inordinate and unjustified number of idle knights while he had been in Ireland.

For five hours the Privy Councillors cross-examined Essex on these six points. And when he had left them it took but fifteen minutes to reach a decision. Even his kinsman Knollys could not defend the Earl's indiscretions. They carried their verdict to the Queen and she pondered it alone.

The next day was Sunday, and while Essex prayed privately, the Queen pursued her devotions in public. It was on Monday, 1 October 1599 that Elizabeth made her pleasure known. Egerton, the Lord Keeper, along with the Lord Treasurer, the Lord Admiral and the Secretary were instructed by Elizabeth to inform the Earl of Essex that he must leave Court and be committed into the custody of the Lord Keeper at York House – the mansion off the Strand where Francis Bacon had been born when his father, Sir Nicholas, had been Lord Keeper. The captive earl could take two servants with him but would be confined to the house, was denied permission even to walk in the walled garden, and could receive no visitors, not even relatives or his wife. No reason was given for the sentence. The Queen's reasons would be made public later. Essex would have to wait in solitary confinement for his case to be considered further.

That afternoon the Earl of Worcester's coach carried the Earl of Essex with his new jailer, Lord Keeper Egerton, back along the road to London down which the party of travel-stained horsemen had galloped with such high hopes only three days previously. Their gamble had failed – and now their leader was paying the stakes.

Essex was suddenly alone, and locked up within York House beside the River Thames so near and yet so far from both the palace at Whitehall and his own Essex House, he suddenly fell prey to one of the black attacks of religious melancholia which, together with short bursts of tragically erratic activity, were to characterize the last sixteen months of his life. He had never been a consistent or predictable man. His character was one of extremes. After the frenetic excitement of his Dublin to London dash, his days and nights in the saddle and his plottings and boastings with his friends, something snapped, and he sank into blank, despairing self pity. Egerton, the Lord Keeper who was his unwilling jailer, was not an unpleasant man. Indeed, he had proved, and was now again to prove himself, a firm friend to Essex within the limits of his loyalty to the Queen. He did all he could to lighten the load of the Earl's sudden confinement. Yet in the long weeks of waiting for the Queen's final decision Robert Devereux, in perverse defiance of any kindness offered, grew sicker and sicker.

He absolutely refused to be consoled. When a packet of letters delivered after his departure from Dublin finally reached him at York House he sent them away unopened. When, through the good offices of Egerton, friends got permission to visit him, he refused to see them unless the Queen herself expressly ordered them to attend him. He spent long hours on his knees reading the Bible. He wrote to Southampton, but his letter was not a personal or friendly document: it was little more than a sermon. With the blithe inconsistency that was becoming more and more his hallmark he warned the young Earl that if he persisted in pursuing worldly delights he would be guilty of perfidious treachery to God. 'It was just with God to afflict me in this world,' he concluded sententiously, 'that he might give me joy in another.'

With Essex's approval, almost in expectation of the demise his letter anticipated, Southampton and his wife took up residence in Essex House. But the stream of visitors calling to express sympathy with the imprisoned Earl soon drove Lady Southampton off to the country, accompanied by Essex's sister, Penelope Lady Rich, Mountjoy's mistress. Southampton evidently set little store by his friend's warning against worldly delights, for one newsletter writer reported that Southampton and Rutland 'pass away the tyme in London merely in going to plaies every day.' Though their theatre-going might not have been entirely frivolous: 1599 was the year of *Julius Caesar*, and Shakespeare, Southampton's friend, was working out the moody soliloquies of *Hamlet*. While Essex moped in York House his wife, Frances, gave birth to the daughter conceived before Robert left for Ireland; and at the christening its godparents were Southampton and the Countesses of Rutland and Cumberland.

Essex took positive pleasure in being cut off from these various social developments. He revelled in his solitary devotions, and also in the bodily torments caused by dysentery caught from an infection in Dublin – 'the Irish flux'. He was eating and sleeping less. Extracting a strange delight from his misfortunes, he was doubtless pleased to hear that the behaviour of his followers had made it likely that the Queen, whenever she pronounced further on the Essex affair, would take an even sterner view of his misdemeanours than she originally intended. The succession of visitors expressing their condolences at Essex House was not well thought of. Reports of bawdy tavern songs and slogans scrawled on walls in support of Essex and deriding Cecil increased the royal ire. Carousing men would break into cheers when they passed York House. London was suddenly flooded with swordsmen and captains tired of Irish service. They brawled in taverns and duelled in the streets. They proclaimed their allegiance to their ill used General to the world and drank boisterously to his health and to the confusion of his enemies. Elizabeth summoned the chief among them to Court and, having thanked them graciously for coming to visit her, had them ordered sharply back to their regiments. Yet she could not deal so easily with the ordinary people of London who were demanding a reason for the disfavour that their great hero was being subjected to and was so painfully suffering. When it was heard that Lady Essex, scarce risen from childbed and dressed in widow's weeds, had tried to visit the Queen only to be turned away and told to visit Court no longer, sympathy for the fallen Earl grew dangerously. Public reasons for Essex's strange punishment became vital.

And so, on 29 November 1599, two months after the sentence pronounced privately at Nonsuch, a public pronouncement was made by the Privy Council meeting in Star Chamber. As well as the majority of the councillors, most of the nation's judges were in attendance. Lord Keeper Egerton rose to protest against the rising flood of rumour and slander that was threatening good order in the kingdom. Men who were no better than traitors were distributing vile libels in Court, city and country. He mentioned no names, but his subject was obvious – the prisoner in his own house, the Earl of Essex. Becoming more specific, he presented his audience with a description of how seriously the government viewed the Irish situation and how disappointed they were that having supplied the army there with all it required, the commander had returned home so suddenly and contrary to royal command.

Lord Treasurer Buckhurst took up the tale. He listed the huge expenses that the Irish expedition had run up and how there had been so little obvious result to show for it all. He could have gone through all Spain with such a lavishly equipped and sizeable fighting force, he maintained. And he went on to present a list of demands allegedly made by Tyrone – and allegedly agreed to by Essex – that made a mockery of the whole enterprise.

The further censures of other councillors added to the weight of government condemnation. There were no explicit accusations of guilt and no formal sentence pronounced. There was no reference to the Queen having passed any judgement on the Earl or having come to an ultimate decision about his fate. Everyone present knew he was a prisoner in York House: and everyone had heard the persistent rumours that he would be committed to the Tower. The long series of government denunciations had been by way of a public relations exercise, not an opening statement of prosecution.

But there was no doubt at all that a mighty man had fallen, and fallen from a height he could never hope to regain when, four days later, orders were given for Essex's household to be dispersed. One hundred and sixty servants were turned away from Essex House to find jobs elsewhere. Their master had no use for them in a solitary confinement whose outcome was still uncertain. And whenever it ended he would no longer possess the means or motive for living in his former state.

At the end of 1599 the Earl of Essex was very definitely down. But a small group of men were determined that, hard though his battering had been, he was very far from out.

26

Confinement

Francis Bacon had deserted the Essex cause; and in York House the Earl himself seemed reconciled to relinquishing his former ambitions. A week after his retirement there he had announced his intention of leading a private life in the country if the Queen ever saw fit to release him from custody. And through the months that followed, a combination of piety and diarrhoea sapped still further any desire he might have had to fight back from the humiliation that his return from Ireland had brought down upon him. The Star Chamber denunciations had been arranged to calm the passions of the public, not those of Essex. In the first week of December 1599 he seemed at death's door and took communion in preparation for an imminent meeting with his Maker.

But men who had nailed their own colours to the Essex mast did not intend to give up the fight so easily. Chief among them were the Earl of Southampton and Lord Mountjoy. Weeks before the Star Chamber denunciations they had met together to plot out the various courses open to them. Mountjoy had taken over a secret correspondence Essex had opened with James, King of Scotland. He reaffirmed to James that Essex and his friends supported James' claim to the throne on Elizabeth's death and denied strongly allegations made by enemies that Essex had ambitions to the Crown of his own. With Southampton he discussed whether the best course was to arrange an escape to France, where Essex would certainly be sheltered if not welcomed by Henri IV; to raise a rebellion among the many who were true to the Devereux name in Wales; or whether the most effective expedient would be to organize a proper coup at Court. Had the Earl brought more men with him from Ireland and organized his surprise arrival aggressively, it would be Cecil, Raleigh and the others that would now be lying in custody. Mountjoy and Southampton brought one of the murderous Danvers brothers into the discussion, and he agreed to help in any plan to spring the Earl from captivity.

But for two reasons all these plottings came to nothing. The greatest obstacle was Essex who, when he was told of the escape plan, said firmly 'he would rather run any danger than lead the life of a fugitive.' And the other obstacle was Mountjoy himself, for the Queen was about to name him to take command of the Irish army that Essex had deserted. While in London his talk remained bold enough, and he went so far as to promise Southampton four or five thousand men from his Irish command in the event of a Scottish force coming south to rescue the Earl; but once he got to Dublin his commitment became vaguer. He became engrossed in the real problems and challenges that Ireland set him – and which he, to his credit, overcame: and away from the heady whisperings and plottings of the Essex circle he began to see his former friends in true perspective. Their cause was not only risky, it was catastrophically unrealistic. Their only hope of success was the chance that his own Irish army might join in any uprising – and no reward Southampton could offer could compensate for the massive risks which that involved. Moreover, the strange disintegration of Essex's own personality ever since the Nonsuch débâcle threw further major doubts on the reliability of the enterprise's centre and corner stone.

As 1599 drew to a close the captive Earl seemed more determined than ever to quit the land of the living. On 10 December reports were circulated of his death, and funeral bells sounded through London – to the intense annoyance of the Queen. When the Earl's bed was made he was so weak he had to be lifted out in the sheets. His only pleasure seemed to be the chastisement of abstruse theological discussion. When his old tutor from Cambridge, Doctor John Overall, visited him the Earl started bemoaning the sins and lewdnesses of his short past life. Nothing, he felt, had offended God so much as his failure properly to observe the Sabbath. Might a man make lawful recreation on the Sabbath after evening prayer? he earnestly asked his clerical visitor. Doctor Overall, with the worldliness of all good Cambridge divines, quoted instances which showed that certain innocent diversions would not be accounted mortal sins. 'Well,' sighed Essex piously, 'if it may be so, yet it is safer to forbear; and hereafter I will forbear.' He continued his attempts to persuade Southampton to repent of his former errors, writing 'you must say with me, "There is no peace to the wicked and ungodly; I will make a covenant with my soul".'

Elizabeth showed sympathy when faithful reports brought news of Essex's pious and apparently unswerving change of heart. When bulletins from his sickbed grew graver she ordered eight of her most experienced physicians to minister to him – and their pessimistic diagnosis brought tears to her eyes: 'they found his liver stopped and perished . . . his Intrailes and Guttes were exulcerated.' She sent her own doctor to the sick Earl with a special broth and a message that she would visit him herself if such a condescension would not be regarded as a blot on her honour. She did not add that Cecil and other Privy Councillors had almost certainly caught wind of the plottings among the Earl's companions and had passed them on to her – nor that a full indictment based on the Star Chamber denunciation was being prepared for Essex to answer personally and in public.

A preliminary date for the hearing was set for 7 February 1600. After Christmas 1599 and through the early weeks of 1600 the Earl seemed to make a positive recovery and on 6 February the Star Chamber was prepared for a proper trial. The ushers had to put up a special barrier to keep back the crowds that started collecting – until at nine o'clock in the evening an unexpected proclamation announced that the trial had been postponed. Cecil, it was given out, was the man responsible for this. He had visited the Earl of Essex and persuaded him to send a letter of humble submission to the Queen, who had promptly cancelled the entire proceedings.

It was a strange little manoeuvre – though the reasons for it were obvious. Although the government had reason enough to regard Essex with disfavour, they could not have hoped to sustain specific charges of a more serious nature. Cecil gained a certain public credit by intervening on Essex's behalf, and the Queen was at that very moment entertaining an important embassy from the Protestant Netherlands. It would not have helped the negotiations to haul up one of the Protestant cause's most renowned champions in public court. The Earl of Essex's conduct and the government's disapproval of it certainly warranted fuller treatment than had been granted until then – but a full-scale Star Chamber arraignment was not the way.

One man *not* relieved by the last-minute postponement was Lord Keeper Egerton. He did not enjoy his jailer's job, and Essex was a far from easy prisoner. When the Earl's illness had grown really severe he had been moved into Egerton's own chamber, and then on 21 January 1600 Lady Egerton died. It was too much for the Lord Keeper. Almost in imitation of Essex he became a recluse and did not reappear in public until the Queen sent a sharp message to remind him of his official duties. Not until late March did relief come, when all the Essex womenfolk were ordered to leave Essex House and Essex was moved back into his own home under the charge of Sir Richard Berkeley. Egerton was finally relieved of his uninvited guest.

Yet for Essex little had changed but his surroundings. His wife was allowed occasionally to visit him by day, and he could write letters. But Sir Richard Berkeley had all the keys of the house and only a skeleton staff of servants were retained. For ten more long weeks the solitary confinement continued, and not until 5 June 1600, eight months after Essex was first committed to custody, was the full hearing and inquiry into the Earl's misdemeanours held.

It took the form of a special commission held in the seclusion of York House under the chairmanship of Egerton, the Lord

Keeper. Business started early. By eight in the morning the eighteen members of the Commission, most of them either councillors or judges, were seated around one long table. Brought before them Essex fell on his knees, but not one of his former colleagues gave the slightest sign of acknowledgement. Only Whitgift, the Archbishop of Canterbury, whispered that the Earl might have a cushion to soften the harshness of the floor.

There was no definite precedent or legal form for the proceedings, for its main purpose was publicity, and to that end had been gathered together an audience of some 200 spectators of eminence and substance. It was not a proper trial, but neither was it a simple commission of enquiry, for there were no witnesses, and the bulk of evidence came from four lawyers briefed with the government's case. The first to speak was the Queen's Sergeant at Law. He presented Elizabeth's own feeling about the case: how she had discharged Essex of £10,000 worth of debt before he went to Ireland, had given him as much again to help with his personal expenses of outfitting, yet was unwilling for the man who had so ungraciously repaid these kindnesses to be proceeded against in an ordinary Court of Justice. As if to emphasize the royal graciousness Essex was invited to rise from his knees and then to sit on a stool at the conclusion of this speech.

The next lawyer was Coke, the Attorney General, and his comments dug deeper. Having set out the enormous powers which the Queen's commission had granted Essex in Ireland – he had even been given authority to pardon treason against the Queen's own person – he set out the five specific crimes with which the Earl was charged. It was not the same list that had justified Essex's imprisonment back at Nonsuch the previous October. References to 'presumptuous letters' and the over-bold intrusion into Her Majesty's bedchamber were not mentioned. And Essex's Irish misconduct was detailed more closely: he had appointed the Earl of Southampton General of Horse in defiance of deliberate instructions: he had marched south into Leinster and Munster when his orders were to march north into Ulster; he had knighted an indiscriminate and unworthy number of warriors: he had held a conference with Tyrone – though the exact nature of the conference was carefully skirted: and he had returned from Dublin without royal permission. When Coke had finished scathingly elaborating these points there was little the third lawyer, the Solicitor General, needed to add. And the content of the fourth lawyer's speech was equally superfluous. Yet strangely his was the most significant voice of all, not for what he said or how he said it – but for who he was. The Crown's fourth speaker in the presentation of its case against Essex was none other than the accused's own *éminence grise* and former comrade, Francis Bacon.

The fiercest devotion to truth and justice could not condone Bacon's presence among his former patron's chief accusers, and the vicious irrelevance of his speech to the specially Irish charges laid against Essex emphasized how personal his motives were. He brought up that two-year-old letter of the Earl's in which had occurred the outburst 'Cannot Princes err? Cannot subjects suffer wrong?' And alleging that Essex had made efforts to get Hayward's *History of Henry the Fourth* suppressed before he left for Ireland, Bacon suggested this was because 'forbidden things are most sought after'.

They were far-fetched charges and only contributed towards a feeling of sympathy for Essex that was strengthened as the Earl began to speak on his own behalf. Humbly he thanked the Queen for sparing him public trial; he recounted the spiritual remorse that had afflicted him during his long eight months of imprisonment, and professed a loyalty to his sovereign that he held dearer to him than anything else. He would tear his heart from his body with his bare hands rather than betray the trust of Her Majesty, he protested.

So far, so good. But warming to the sound of his own voice deployed once again in public and to the sight of the obvious effect he was having, the Earl of Essex went on to answer, point by point, the various charges laid by his accusers. This was not at all what the special Commission had been called for, and the Lord Keeper hastened to interrupt him. None of the lawyers, he pointed out, had charged the Earl with disloyalty, but with contempt and disobedience. So Essex was wasting the Commission's time in trying to establish a loyalty that had never formally been called in question. Essex fell silent, duly reproved.

Then it was time for the eighteen Commissioners to pronounce their verdict – and they did so, one by one. The performance dragged on through the afternoon and late into the evening, and as the endless speeches droned through the soft midsummer twilight it became obvious that the point of the Commission had been simply to re-express the Queen's displeasure – not to reach any definite conclusion. One after the other they rose, discoursed long and loud on the Earl's shortcomings and the Queen's generosity and clemency, and agreed that Essex should remain a prisoner until Her Majesty saw fit to release him. It was nearly nine o'clock before the Earl got back to his apartments worn and weak, his plight no nearer resolution than it had been that morning. For two more long weary summer months he would have to endure the frustration of confinement within his own home, until on 26 August 1600, almost a year since he had departed so precipitately from Ireland, he was summoned once again to York House and there told by the Lord Keeper, the Lord Treasurer and Mr Secretary Cecil that it was the Queen's good pleasure finally to set him at liberty. But the release was far from unconditional. The Earl of Essex should hope no more to come to Court. Liberty for him was a retired life in the country. His days of greatness were over.

27

'The licence of sweet wines lies at anchor aloof'

The Earl of Essex's trouble was that he simply could not afford to retire. The Queen might refuse to see him again. Her councillors might ban him from Court. He might express the wish to retreat to the depths of the countryside, to Chartley, to Lamphy or to the Oxfordshire estates of his uncle, Sir William Knollys. But he just did not possess the means to leave public life; his inheritance and his past career had run up such colossal debts that the only way to keep creditors off his back was to show signs of seeking the income to repay them. If he left Court he would have to leave the principal source of his revenues behind him, and while rural retreat might cost him little it would cost his creditors a lot. He had jumped on the roundabout of Court favour and spun it so fast that he risked destruction if he tried now to jump off. He had

> Stepp'd in so far, that should I wade no more,
> Returning were as tedious to go o'er.[1]

His exploitation of his Queen had rebounded in his face. His father had left him more dependent than most Elizabethan noblemen on a Court-centred existence. He had increased that dependence, gaining more and more credit on the strength of his skill at balancing on the tightrope that led to Elizabeth's favour. Indeed his talent for that particularly hazardous form of acrobatics was virtually his only asset, and he had no other resources, no lands or ships, that might act as a harness or safety net if his sense of balance deserted him. Well, now it had deserted him and he was falling hopelessly, with no prospect of a hand-hold he could snatch at to prevent his descent.

His income was made up from a variety of sources granted him by the Queen over the last dozen years of favour: he was a Privy Councillor, Master of the Ordnance, Master of the Queen's Horse, Earl Marshal of England and had had a number of military commands. But chief of all his revenues was the income he derived from holding the right to levy customs charges on the import of sweet wines from the Mediterranean and Levant, and it was on the security of the generous duties this patent brought in that the Earl had been borrowing heavily in recent years. Elizabeth had granted Essex the Farm of Sweet Wines on Michaelmas Day, 1590, and granted it for a term of ten years. Now at the end of August 1600, the lease was due for renewal in a few weeks' times, and unless renewal was secured the Earl faced certain bankruptcy. Apart from loss of the sweet wines' considerable revenues, he would have to meet the demands of creditors no longer content to wait for good times projected into an increasingly unlikely future.

It was a desperate dilemma. The religious melancholia of the Earl's confinement in York House must have been in part a defence mechanism against the worries that the threat of bank-ruptcy raised. He was almost better off imprisoned and protected against the need to cope with the complex hopelessness of the situation. But now he was thrown into a world that his captivity had made him less suited than ever to deal with. And, to add to the cruel problems of adjustment that all released prisoners face, he had an impossible time limit. A few weeks in which to win back not only the favour of the Queen, but to win from her one of the richest gifts in her possession. Denied the personal access on which his fortune had been over the years built up, he had to destroy a solid mistrust on Elizabeth's part that had withstood nine months of the most abject and crawling remorse from Essex. The task was hopeless.

Yet like Prometheus, he had no choice but to attempt it. He made a token withdrawal to the country and began petitioning the Queen. He had written to her from captivity in York House and Essex House, but now his letters took on a new urgency: 'Haste paper to that unhappy presence, whence only unhappy I am banished. Kiss that fair correcting hand which lays new plasters to my lighter hurts, but to my greatest wound applieth nothing. Say thou comest from shaming, languishing, despairing, SX.'

He got friends to pass the note to the Queen by way of Lady Scrope, who remarked to Elizabeth that Essex's punishment had now lasted almost a year: Lady Scrope ventured to express the hope that Her Majesty would rebestow her favour on a humble subject who sought forgiveness with such true remorse. But Elizabeth made no answer, sighed and withdrew to her private apartments.

Faintly encouraged Essex tried again and more directly:

This day se'night, the lease which I hold by your Majesty's beneficence expireth, and that farm [of sweet wines] is both my chiefest maintenance and mine only means of compounding with the merchants to whom I am indebted. . . . If my creditors will take for payment as many ounces of my blood, or the taking away of this farm would only for want finish me of this body, your Majesty should never hear of this suit. For in myself I can find no boldness to importune, and from myself I can draw no argument to solicit.[2]

Essex affected nonchalance towards his financial difficulties, but with £5,000 of his debts due for immediate repayment, his lack of concern hardly rang true.

His next attempt betrayed his growing panic more honestly: 'my soul cried out unto your Majesty for grace, for access and for an end to this exile . . . for till I may appear in your gracious presence and kiss your Majesty's fair correcting hand, time itself is a perpetual night, and the whole world but a sepulchre unto your Majesty's humblest vassal.' He would have to get still humbler.

In desperation he resorted to the most far-fetched measures.

Francis Bacon had approached him shortly after the long York House hearing and, more to hedge his bets than to make amends for his treachery on that occasion, suggested that he concoct a series of letters that would purport to have passed between his brother Anthony and Essex. The gist of Anthony's remarks would be that the Queen had no intention of destroying Essex entirely or of withholding from him all hope of office and profit. To this Essex would reply that he was most eager to make up for the errors of his past ways, but that he could not possibly convince the Queen of this while enemies denied him access to her. Francis would then make sure that this correspondence fell into Elizabeth's hands.

It was a transparent device – rendered the more implausible by paragraphs that Francis inserted into each letter in lavish praise of his own abilities and honesty. Elizabeth certainly saw right through it, for she called Bacon to her one day and remarked how moved she had been by the dutiful writings of the Earl of Essex. Francis smiled quietly to himself. But then Elizabeth went on to remark that all the Earl's letters seemed simply devices to ensure that his patent to tax the sweet wines was renewed. It was Elizabeth's turn to smile, for she had nothing to lose from a waiting game. 'The licence of sweet wines,' wrote one observer of the London scene, 'lies at anchor aloof and will not come in.' A few days earlier the same writer had heard rumours that the Queen was repenting of her anger with Essex and that he would soon be back in favour. 'You may believe as much of that as you list,' he commented tartly, 'but I ne'er a whit: for till I see his [Essex's] licence for sweet wines renewed ... or some other substantial favour answerable to it, I shall esteem words but as wind and holy water of court.'³

In the last set of correspondence between Bacon and Essex there had occurred a most significant phrase which gathered into one mythical comparison the exact nature of the Earl's career to that point, and foretold with cruel precision the tragedy of his final months; for by September 1600 the Earl of Essex had less than half a year to live. 'I was ever sorry,' wrote Bacon, 'that your lordship should fly with waxen wings, doubting Icarus' fortune.' In his reply Essex affected not to understand the analogy, being 'a stranger to all poetical conceits'. But it must have struck him to the heart, for like Icarus he had indeed ventured to achieve the impossible and, intoxicated by initial success, he was now flying too close to the sun. At the end of October 1600 Elizabeth made known her final decision about the Farm of Sweet Wines: the grant to Essex would not be renewed, and she would keep the revenues for her own purposes.

The catastrophe had occurred. Debts which Essex had carried cheerfully, and had been allowed to carry while hope of future reward glowed brightly, suddenly became millstones threatening his destruction. He was no longer the Queen's prime favourite but just another courtier, indeed he was poorer than any other courtier, for he was denied access to the royal presence and had made himself the declared enemy of the very men of influence who could now gain him that access. His only immediate friends were people who had relied on him, not powers in their own right. And after a year out of office it was no longer possible plausibly to claim that Essex was the hero on whom the government's salvation depended. Mountjoy was making a success of the Irish campaign. In the Netherlands English troops had won a brave victory at Nieuport. Secret negotiations with both the French and Spanish seemed to be bringing closer the peace that it was Cecil's great ambition to achieve. What rôle was there for Essex in this new scheme of things? the doubters asked. And Essex, asking the same question himself, was equally taxed to discover an answer.

He had come to the end of the road. All paths before him were blocked. The Queen's displeasure seemed absolute, and Essex panicked. Royal favour, the lodestar by which he had guided his career ever since he came to Court, was no longer true to him, and without it Essex's course went haywire. His behaviour had been growing more and more erratic in the course of the last years, and tertiary syphilis seems a plausible clinical explanation for this; with the ending of his lease on the patent of sweet wines, something crucial snapped. The final three months of Essex's life were a confused jumble of fears, rages, sly plottings and crude irrational outbursts of emotion, culminating in the tragic and dismal fiasco of the 8 February rebellion. Never a man to react calmly to adversity, Essex went into a flat spin, striking out wildly in all directions and disciplining his actions only within the limits of an hysterical persecution complex. Unwilling to adjust to the enduring fact of the Queen's displeasure, and incapable of recognizing in his own personality the defects that were the reasons for her distrust, Essex resorted to a crude mechanistic explanation of his misfortunes. His enemies were to blame for his failures. They had poisoned his Elizabeth's mind against him and had conspired to prevent the personal confrontation that would set all wrongs to rights. He failed to realize that this false rationale was the very same simplistic interpretation of events that had brought him back from Ireland – and had been proved then to be so disastrously wrong.

And his friends, for reasons either sinister or stupid, fell happily into the same delusion. Their leader was out of favour because Cecil, Raleigh, Cobham, the Howards, Grey and their ilk were all men of evil intent who had combined to destroy Essex. The corollary of this 'heroes and villains' thesis was obvious. Cecil, Raleigh, Cobham, the Howards, Grey and their ilk must be destroyed before their canker spread; and when the evil they represented was purged, then true virtue could flourish once more. Given their premises their logic was irresistible – and their ensuing violence totally justified.

Yet in cold point of fact their premises were totally false. Essex's record both as a man of state and a commander on the battlefield was unimpressive. Elizabeth, nasty, vicious and selfish as she might be, was not at fault in punishing him so severely in 1600, but in allowing him such authority before then for such fickle insubstantial reasons. The dramatic shift in the balance of Court power in Cecil's favour after Essex's return from Ireland was long overdue and was of Essex's making, not Cecil's. Someone had to fill the power vacuum left by Essex's own shirking of his responsibilities, and Elizabeth rightly and reluctantly allowed more power to her little hunchbacked secretary. There was no substantial evidence of any stronger conspiracy against the Essex faction than was natural when men feel themselves threatened and group together in defence of their personal interests. Essex was the man who plotted. And of all the courtiers whom Essex and his cronies suspected of 'unbalancing' the Queen's mind, only Cecil possessed the record of balanced advice that would incline Elizabeth to pay the slightest heed to his opinions. The others were insubstantial figures, and Elizabeth would only be moved by Cecil after lengthy thought – and then usually for different motives of her own.

Grey, Cobham and Raleigh might be vicious enemies of Essex and Southampton, but one of Essex's followers had, after all, made as if to kill Grey during that autumn dash to Nonsuch. Raleigh, it is true, had once written to Cecil urging the elimination of Essex, but he had been politely ignored. And Cecil, allegedly the spider at the centre of the whole malicious web, was not a man to tie himself to allies every bit as fractious and volatile as his rivals. He appreciated the support against Essex of men like Raleigh, Grey, Cobham and the Howards, but he was, perhaps, unique in realizing that power in the Elizabethan Court came from Elizabeth alone and that any attempt to replace that source of power with a group or faction, no matter how strong, was doomed by definition to failure. He was quite content for Essex to be Elizabeth's undisputed fancy man, for it did not threaten his work and was manifestly what the Queen wanted. It was only when the Earl had aspired to responsibilities for which he was obviously unsuited that Cecil had worked against him. And even then his work was not especially malicious, but consisted simply of labouring for Elizabeth in a fashion that made him indispensable and showed up Essex's failings.

When Essex and his comrades, faced with the absolute but hardly unpredictable refusal by the Queen to renew the patent of sweet wines, complained to each other that they were victims of a conspiracy, then they were, in fact, the victims of their own delusions. And, had they been more intelligent, one could also accuse them of conscious hypocrisy. For such plotting as had been going on until that point in time had been carried out by members of their own party.

Sir Charles Danvers and the Earl of Southampton had been trying to reimplicate Mountjoy in the plans they had laid before he went to Ireland. It was suggested that Mountjoy should write an open letter to Essex complaining at the way in which certain factions at Court had gained control of the government and that he should call on the Earl to make a stand for justice. When Essex made his stand Mountjoy would then weigh in with the Irish forces his earlier promise had committed him to supplying.

But the new Commander in Ireland showed himself understandably unenthusiastic towards such a project. So Danvers and Southampton turned to the consideration of other expedients, forcing an entry at Court, or else manipulating the Parliament that was expected shortly to be called.

More feelers were sent towards Scotland. It was suggested to King James that Robert Cecil was negotiating secretly with Spain so that the English throne would pass on Elizabeth's death to the Infanta, the King of Spain's daughter. The Spanish royal family was, after all, connected to the Tudors by a blood relationship going back to John of Gaunt. And in the early years of her reign, Elizabeth had been prepared to exploit the possibility of marriage to her dead sister Mary's husband, Philip of Spain. It was not inconceivable, suggested Essex's messengers to King James, that James' own claim to the throne might be set aside to suit the purposes of an agreement with Spain. And in that case, since any such agreement would be the work of Cecil and the peace party, then James' surest ally must be the Earl of Essex. So scared was James by the suggestion, that he agreed to send south a special embassy whose official purpose would be to ask Elizabeth to name her successor – and whose private object would be to negotiate with Essex about the best means to achieve their mutual ambitions. The King of Scotland committed himself further to the Earl in a short note on parchment, seven lines long, that Essex put in a little black bag and wore mysteriously round his neck.

It was all sinister stuff, and it more than justified the suspicion with which Elizabeth viewed Essex. The Earl himself felt guilty about the entire proceedings and carried out most of his plottings through Southampton, Danvers, Gelli Meyrick, or Henry Cuffe. The crippled Anthony Bacon was still living in Essex House, but partly through fear of betrayal to his brother Francis, and mainly no doubt because Anthony was, for all his spy rings and agents, a basically straightforward Englishman who was loyal to the Queen, Essex did not implicate him in his rebellious plottings.

There was, as yet, no definite conspiracy to revolt – indeed the great weakness of the rising of February 1601 was precisely the fact that it was not properly planned but just 'happened' haphazardly – but the passions stirring in Essex House were becoming more and more rebellious. And chief among the stirrers of these passions was Essex's professor of Greek-turned-secretary, Henry Cuffe. When in August 1600 Essex had proclaimed his intention of retiring to a life of rural solitude Cuffe had criticized his master's pusillanimity with such bitter scorn that Essex had ordered Gelli Meyrick to turn Cuffe out of his household. And it was only because the fiery Meyrick was of the same opinion as Cuffe that the former don was still in Essex's service when the Queen refused to renew the patent of sweet wines, and fighting men came into their own again among the Earl's followers. Now, as Christmas 1600 approached, Cuffe became some sort of Iago, organizing the secret discussions and formulating the plans that were to come to such ill-starred fruition on 8 February 1601.

Swept along by a tide of feverish resentment that each whispered cabal quickened and aggravated, Essex and his friends were reaching a point of no return. They were becoming the helpless victims of suspicions of their own devising. Cecil certainly possessed an extensive network of agents and correspondents, but no evidence uncovered at the time or since then suggests that he was using it against Essex with any real viciousness. But Essex had passed the point where he could rationally assess either his own actions or those of others, and as the cold winter evenings drew darker round Essex House, grimly cut off from the social flutterings and gaiety that characterized the Court's preparations for Christmas, he began to attribute to his rivals the most malevolent intentions and intrigues. His suggestion to James of Scotland that Cecil was plotting to give the English throne to Spain was more than just a ploy to win Scottish support for his own plans. He began seriously to believe it and to snatch from the air vague improbable strands of evidence to lend substance to his fantasies.

Cut off from the political realities of life at Court, Essex pieced together the weird fabric of a conspiracy aimed not simply against himself or James but against the Queen, the Council and the Parliament, Church and people of England as a whole. Cecil, he decided, was negotiating secretly with the Spaniards. It was the one charge proved solid by later events, yet on Essex's part it was sheer conjecture, and the true reasons for the negotiations borne out by the subsequent peace treaty of 1604 were very far from the sinister motives that he attributed to the little Secretary. Cecil, Essex was convinced, was plotting to replace Elizabeth with the Infanta of Spain, and to back up this conviction he had the evidence of a snatch of conversation between the Secretary and another councillor. Cecil was reported to have said that he could prove the Infanta's claim to be stronger than that of any other competitor for the throne. In fact, as the councillor in question made clear at Essex's trial, the remark had been taken disastrously out of context, and the one piece of evidence on which Essex had so confidently based his entire conspiracy theory was turned against him. For Cecil had actually been discussing means of counterbalancing such Spanish claims.

Yet to this fatally false inference Essex added others. The leniency which Elizabeth had recently asked local authorities to show towards Jesuits and other Roman Catholics was taken not as an expression of her abiding aversion to religious persecution, but as another sign that Cecil had poisoned her mind. The appointment of Raleigh to be Governor of Jersey was not seen as an attempt to rid the Court of a hothead whose passions could explode as dangerously as Essex's, but as a means of guaranteeing that the western defences were in the hands of the pro-Spanish faction. Cobham's appointment to be Lord Warden of the Cinque Ports was now explained in a similarly sinister fashion. Who controlled the Treasury and Navy? Why, Buckhurst and

Lord Admiral Nottingham, both friends of Robert Cecil. The Lord President of the North was Thomas, Robert Cecil's elder brother and inheritor of the Burghley title. The man most likely to succeed Mountjoy as Lord Lieutenant of Ireland was Sir George Carew, another creature of Cecil's.

These soundly based and plausible facts, and the most baseless and implausible inferences Essex drew from them, were woven together into the tissue of threatening conspiracy. To question why Essex did not use such influence as he still possessed to present his suspicions immediately to the Queen is as pointless as wondering how on earth he could convince himself and his followers that such a rickety mishmash of farfetched imaginings was reality – and not the tragic product of a deluded mind.

Such doubts as any of them may have entertained were dismissed when, on 9 January 1601, the Earl of Southampton encountered Lord Grey riding near Raleigh's residence in London. Grey and Southampton were sworn personal enemies and had occupied the Privy Council's energies for the last year in attempts to prevent them duelling together. Now, on this chilly January morning, Lord Grey set firmly about Southampton with his sword, and in the ensuing scuffle between the rival retainers, Southampton's page had his hand lopped off before help could arrive. Grey was a choleric, unpleasant man as mistrusted by his so-called friends as by his many enemies, and Elizabeth had him promptly clapped in prison for his vicious and unprovoked attack. Yet Southampton, Essex and their friends refused to take the incident at its childish face value. Grey was a supporter of Cecil, and if his sympathies seemed scarcely reciprocated by the Secretary then there were Machiavellian explanations for that. The murderous attack not only confirmed their conspiracy theory, but gave the plot a further twist. Their enemies were now planning violence against them. Essex must strike first before it was too late. Attack was the surest form of defence. From 9 January 1601 the Earl of Essex's intentions became actively aggressive and unashamedly violent.

28

The Rebels

Armed and open rebellion it was to be. But who were the men that so readily resolved to unsheath their swords and risk their lives in the cause of an unbalanced young aristocrat? Were their motives as widely political as the consequences that their action threatened? And how could they not only share but conspire to make still wilder the delusions from which the Earl of Essex was suffering?

Without false sympathy, one can describe all of them as victims of a system. Like Essex, their most immediate conscious impulse was economic. Though owning exploitable property, most had chosen, for the social attractions and the economic rewards that the Elizabethan Court system offered, to pursue the royal presence. They had at different stages attached themselves to Essex's rising star and had developed the tastes and liabilities that went with such meteoric political progress. Now apparently deprived of all hope of royal favour and future profit they had little to lose from a desperate fling. The rewards at stake seemed to them to be well worth the risks: but whereas assessment of the profits their coup might bring was an economic operation, or to be more precise a matter of pure greed, assessment of the risks involved demanded personal calculations too subtle for most of the conspirators. Indeed, it was precisely because Essex and his followers had consistently shown themselves incapable of gauging the complexities of the Queen's mind and the qualities necessary to win its confidence that they now found themselves excluded from favour.

Yet one cannot satisfactorily explain a rebellion in terms of the erratic motives of men whose motives and actions have consistently shown that they are erratic, for that begs the question of how those men first gained both the aspirations and the power which erratic incompetence denies itself in normal circumstances. The real explanation lies in the social and political structure that Essex and his followers were seeking not to destroy but to gain control of, and since that social and political structure was one of personal, semi-absolute monarchy, the answer must be sought in Elizabeth's own handling of the situation. If the drama of Essex and his Elizabeth turned out to be a tragedy then the blame for that was primarily Elizabeth's, for she had made it possible to stage the drama in the first place. She had simply miscalculated. Setting too much store by Essex's financial dependence on her good favour, she had encouraged the Earl and his friends to aspire to rôles to which they were manifestly unsuited – for her own personal motives that could not even plead the excuse of genuine emotion. Elizabeth was playing games when she spoke of love to Essex: when she grew agitated over her favourite's failings it was her hurt pride and vanity, not real feeling, that caused her distress. Essex was the victim of the ageing Elizabeth's refusal to acknowledge her age, and his fellow rebels were victims of the whole Elizabethan Court system which promoted men to power from a limited hereditary caste and then judged their fitness for political and military responsibility by standards of Court behaviour totally irrelevant to the real qualities their power demanded. Most of her life Elizabeth proved herself capable of seeing Court politics for the charade it was, and only surrendered real responsibility into the hands of men of competence like Burghley. But in old age she was herself deceived by the pretence she had exploited so long, allowed Essex and courtiers like him a taste of real power, and then snatched it back too violently when she realized her mistake. She proved herself incapable of managing the demotion her own self-indulgence had made necessary. Essex was at fault for setting his ambitions too high and for pursuing them so remorselessly, but Elizabeth was even more to blame for not seeing more searchingly into her favourite's nature. The Essex rebellion was the revolt of hope denied, and for both encouraging and frustrating that hope so ineptly, Elizabeth was herself to blame.

The men who conspired with Essex in January 1601 were, with the odd exception of Machiavels like Cuffe, simple men with expectations beyond anything their abilities or records could justify. Their simplicity was proved by the very crudeness and incompetence of their rebellion; and their elevated expectations by the extreme lengths to which they showed themselves prepared to go. Their individual circumstances were various but followed a depressingly common pattern of financial desperation. They had invested heavily in the rat race for Court favour, and had received insufficient return on their money.

Eight of them, with Essex, were aristocrats: the Earls of Southampton, Rutland, Sussex and Bedford, and Lords Mounteagle, Cromwell and Sandys. Southampton, Rutland, Sussex, Bedford and Mounteagle were all young men – and Rutland, Southampton and Bedford had, with Essex, all been wards of old Lord Burghley. In 1601 all were chronically short of money, either because their inheritance had been slender or because they had spent recklessly since inheriting. Rutland was particularly extravagant, having in the years 1597 to 1601 alone wasted at least £12,400 of his fortune on his personal pleasures. Though one of the richest young noblemen in England his debts at the beginning of 1601 totalled nearly £5,000. And he had to pay over a quarter of his annual £3,000 income in annuities to two unmarried sisters. He had been raising ready cash by mortgaging the rents due from his estates, and having spent the money received in this way now had little prospect of squeezing further extra revenues from his own lands. Married to Frances Sidney, Lady Essex's daughter by her first marriage to Sir Philip Sidney, he could hope for little income from his wife's family – and so he looked for profit from his stepfather-in-law's dangerous enterprise.[1]

Southampton rivalled Rutland's extravagance. With a similar annual income from his lands, some £3,000, he was, in 1601, in debt to the tune of £8,000 – a third of a million pounds in modern values. To raise money he had in the last four years been not mortgaging but actually selling his estates, and for £20,000 had disposed of a third of his inheritance. An inveterate gambler he was proud once to have staked, and lost, 3,000 crowns at one throw.[2]

Bedford was another member of the big-spending set that envious courtiers classed as 'fantastycalls' – but he had had the misfortune to reveal his extravagant nature before he had inherited full control of his wealth. So his relatives had secured bonds that prevented him selling off the family estates, and he was driven to employ Rutland's device of mortgaging future rents for the sake of ready cash. By 1601 the short-term nature of the expedient was painfully obvious to him and he was deep in debt with no prospect of lawful salvation.[3]

Cromwell, a distant noble relative of the young Oliver who had been born two years earlier in Huntingdon, was no better off. A man with military pretensions, he had sued long, expensively and unsuccessfully for the governorship of Brill, one of the towns England held in the Netherlands, and had been compelled to sell land worth £10,000 to finance that suit and his participation in Essex's various military adventures abroad. His trip to Ireland in 1599 had nearly ruined him, and wielding a sword in rebellion was fighting out of his troubles in the only way he knew how.[4]

Lord Mounteagle, whose craven performance in the Essex rebellion was rivalled only by the cowardice with which he betrayed the Gunpowder Plotters four years later, hardly had the stomach to squander money with the heartiness of his comrades. But his immediate ancestors had given him no chance. His maternal grandfather had dissipated the vast bulk of lands that Mounteagle should have inherited in Lancashire, Yorkshire and Lincolnshire through his mother. And his father sold or tied up the other side of the family inheritance with mortgages and bonds that left Mounteagle practically penniless and propertyless.[5]

Like Mounteagle, the Earl of Sussex was involved in the

preparations that led up to the rebellion, but then vanished discreetly from the scene of the disturbance. And his withdrawal must have been through cowardice, for he certainly had little to lose. Having inherited debts totalling £12,000 to the Crown alone he wasted some £20,000 raised from land sales, and still owed Elizabeth £5,000 on the day of the revolt, plus an unknown and probably larger sum to private creditors.[6]

Lord Sandys was similarly poverty-stricken. An embittered, middle-aged man, he had wasted a lifetime hanging round the Court in hope of preferment that never came, and had gone to Ireland in the futile expectation of winning the fortune he needed to pay off debts that totalled £3,100 in 1598. His income at that time was less than £800 a year – and he had been compelled to sell off the bulk of his family's property in Northamptonshire, Berkshire and Gloucestershire. Saddled with large annuities he was bound to pay to the spinster and widowed ladies of his family he was in 1601 in a hopeless financial plight.

Sandys' onerous obligations to his female relatives were common to all the plotters except Cromwell. Essex had the expensive tastes of his mother Lettice to finance. Southampton also paid a large annuity to his mother. Mounteagle had a step-grandmother and Rutland a stepgrandmother and aunt, to all of whom were due, by law, at least a third of the estates left by their deceased husbands. If the ringleaders of the Essex revolt were bankrupts it was not entirely the fault of their own extravagance.

Their followers were no better off. 'Seize the Queen and be our own Carvers!' was one of the battlecries of the swordsmen who followed Essex on that fatal February morning, and a rough look at their finances shows how much in need they were of a good joint to carve. Sir William Constable was heavily in debt and in real danger of arrest by his creditors. Sir Edward Littleton was in fact arrested for that very reason as he swaggered through the streets in the rebellious cavalcade. Sir George Devereux, idle, garrulous and senile, sponged off his nephew Earl Robert as he had sponged off his brother Walter before him. Sir Ferdinando Gorges, the Governor of Plymouth who had tried so un-successfully to keep track of the Cadiz plunder in 1596, was so poor that when imprisoned after the rebellion he could not afford the supplementary charges levied for the additional comforts normally provided for gentlemen behind bars. Richard Chomley even advanced as an excuse for his participation in the rising that thanks to his father's handling of his estate he 'doth owe more than he can pay'. His father had actually taken him away from Cambridge in order to marry him off to a wealthy heiress. Sir John Heydon was 'as poor as ever Irus was'. Thomas West was cursed with 'a very broken estate'. Sir Robert Cross was an unsuccessful pirate. George Brooke and Sir Griffin Markham were both suitors who had spent heavily to gain offices that were eventually denied them.

The rebellion was in many ways an outburst of financial desperation by men who had gambled and lost in the lottery for Court favour and profit – the patronage backlash. But there were other conspirators whose motives were more religious than economic. Robert Catesby and Francis Tresham fought for Essex in February 1601, and four years later they became the leading spirits in the Popish Gunpowder Plot which was to stow Guido Fawkes under the Houses of Parliament on 5 November 1605. Catesby was the inheritor of lands in Northamptonshire, Oxfordshire and Warwickshire worth some £3,000 a year but 'was very wild; and as he kept company with the best noblemen in the land, so he spent much above his rate, and so wasted a good part of his living.'[7] Tresham, his cousin, was an extravagant young man who was also mistrusted as 'unstayed and wild' – and both were committed Roman Catholics. Both, too, were good friends of the treacherous Mounteagle – and of John Wright, Christopher Wright, John Grant, Robert Winter, Thomas Winter and Sir Edward Beynham, all of whom played conspicuous parts in both the Essex and the Gunpowder conspiracies. That these nine men were all closely involved in two plots less than five years apart is remarkable, but not especially significant so far as the Essex rebellion was concerned. All were militant and discontented Catholics dedicated to changing the status quo and willing to exploit any means to achieve their ends.

After the rising the government were to make much of the

Popish connections of some of the rebels. Sir Christopher Blount, Essex's stepfather, and Sir Charles Danvers, both Catholics, were cross-questioned particularly closely to discover what promises to Papists the Earl had made; and Blount's 'confession', which the Privy Council made public, seemed to suggest that Essex was a Roman Catholic sympathizer: he had promised 'toleration' of religion, said Blount. In fact Blount made clear in a passage that was not made public that the Earl 'was wont to say that he did not like any man be troubled for his religion.'[8] Essex was a pious Christian, but like Queen Elizabeth he could not share the sixteenth century's passion for 'making windows into men's souls'. Blount, Danvers and Catholics like those who were later to plot with Guy Fawkes, took the Earl's expressed toleration to mean that the Roman religion could be practised more freely and openly in England if the rising succeeded. But though they were probably right to assume that, their hopes were not exclusive. Puritans too could expect from the Earl more freedom for their Low Church practices, and, indeed, it was towards the re-reformed doctrines that Essex himself tended. He opened the courtyard of Essex House to preachers excluded from their own churches because of their Puritan beliefs and he was, not without reason, regarded all over the Continent as the fiercest and most militant defender of the Reformation in England. He had at Court indulged in spasmodic but spectacular displays of Protestant piety, adopting, for example, after the Cadiz expedition, a daily timetable most liberally sprinkled with sessions on his knees in the chapel. But the truth of the Earl's religion was that he was less a partisan than a man anxious, even desperate, for support, and quite prepared to count a Catholic sword as useful as a Protestant one.

For despite his occasional fierce bouts of piety the Earl of Essex definitely thought in terms of swords, and was counting heavily on his campfire comrades, those soldiers of fortune who could not settle to the routine of peacetime activity and whose concepts of honour set no duty higher than battle in defence of their patron, Essex; particularly as his foe was the unmilitary little Secretary, widely and rightly suspected of working towards a peace that would end the long-drawn-out war with Spain. Captain Thomas Lee had been one of the party who rode back so rapidly and secretly from Ireland in 1599. William Green was a discharged captain who had convictions as a cutpurse, picklock and thief. Owen and John Salusbury were young Welsh squires who had served with Essex on both his Irish and his maritime expeditions. John Selby was a discharged captain, and Piers Edmonds was another veteran of the Essex campaigns, a Corporal General who, it was alleged, had been a bed-companion of Southampton's. As unemployed soldiers none of their motives for following the leaders who had taken them into previous encounters can have been very complex:

> All the unsettled humours of the land,
> Rash, inconsiderate, fiery voluntaries,
> With ladies' faces and fierce dragons' spleens,
> Bearing their birthrights proudly on their backs.[9]

The economic and religious grievances of the men who plotted rebellion with Essex make up a fair picture of discontent at the turn of the sixteenth century: a vague, fractious, scarce-licked malaise to which subsequent constitutional conflicts were to lend more form. But Essex in his anger was as much a throwback to the feudal barons of past centuries as a herald of the more ideological disputes that were to come. And his following reflected the feudal nature of his power. The Devereux came from the Welsh borders – and Essex's chief steward, Sir Gelli Meyrick, was a fiery Celt who knew personally the various tenants of his master's Welsh lands. While Essex, Southampton, Rutland and the other courtiers in the conspiracy plotted the best strategy to pursue in London, Sir Gelli was out riding from farm to farm on the Essex estates whipping up grass-roots support. His efforts were aided by the illness and death on 19 January 1601 of the Earl of Pembroke, President of the Council of Wales, who was the absentee Constable of Bristol and Brecknock, Steward of Brecon and Dinas, Porter of Brecon, Steward of Monmouthshire's Trilateral Castles, Custos Rotulorum of Monmouth and Glamorgan, and Vice Admiral of South Wales.[10] Nominees carried out the administrative duties that went with those titles, but the long illness and final death of so eminent a government representative left a vacuum in which Meyrick could work more easily. His whipping up of Celtic discontent on Essex's behalf made an obvious parallel with the way in which Bolingbroke had allied with Glendower's fiery Welsh forces to depose Richard II – and the analogy was certainly noticed by spectators of Shakespeare's play. Since the death of Roger Williams, Meyrick's rough cattle-raiding mentality had provoked the ridicule of Essex's more sophisticated courtier colleagues, but when the sudden decision was made early in January 1601 to turn discontent into active rebellion then Meyrick's allies from the Celtic fringe were welcomed as useful reinforcements. They were particularly useful for being prepared. Meyrick had been hoping and planning for an armed confrontation since Essex's confinement, and as well as sparing Cuffe from the consequences of their master's pious moods had spent the summer of 1600 preparing the valleys for battle. 'The summer is half over, time is precious. Let us not lose the start we have gotten,' he had written to Sir Henry Bromley at Holt Castle on 29 July 1600.[11] Richard Broughton, Essex's old tutor, came up to London at Christmas to help co-ordinate the activities of Essex House and the Essex estates.

Most notable among the Welsh supporters of the Essex cause were John and Owen Salusbury who had been to Cadiz, the Islands and Ireland with the Earl – and who showed themselves ready to fight for him to the death when the rebellion came. With them to London they took in January 1601 Sir John Lloyd, one of the knights Essex had created in Ireland, and Peter Wynn from the Wrexham area. Meyrick billeted them in lodgings 'on the back side of St Clements'. Another Welsh swordsman was Ellis Jones who had fought behind Essex's colours under Meyrick's command in the Low Countries, Cadiz and Ireland. Had the outbreak of the rising not been precipitated by the alarmed Privy Council then the Welsh contingent would have been even larger. The great Roger Vaughan of Radnor whipped together a party of local squires who armed themselves and began riding on

London at the beginning of February, only to hear at Colebroke that the rising had already broken out and had been suppressed.

Such were the several elements that made up the Essex revolt: bankrupt nobles, failed courtiers, persecuted Catholics, unemployed soldiers, and Welsh retainers. After the rising's collapse the Privy Council listed in all eighty-five prisoners, of which more than a third – thirty-two – were rapidly discharged without bonds, without indictment, arraignment or fine. Only six men were executed, hardly a fearsome number of hardcore rebels – which only revealed yet again the uncanny knack that Essex and his friends possessed for miscalculating the response to their cause. But there was a strange plausibility to their coup. For small though the body of men that they mustered at the beginning of February 1601 turned out to be, and wild though their plottings were, they did come closer to success than modern assumptions about an Elizabethan monolith of government conventionally allow. Had they put to better use that last month of scheming between 9 January, when Grey assaulted Southampton, and 8 February, when the rising occurred, then they might well have toppled Cecil, executed their enemies, got control of Elizabeth and even made Essex king – as some of them, though not Essex, certainly wished to do in their more hopeful moments. Puritan ministers allowed to preach in the courtyard of Essex House were applauded when they voiced the extreme Calvinist doctrine that men of authority and responsibility were entitled, in certain circumstances, to restrain, correct and, if necessary, depose sovereigns who failed in their duty towards God and their subjects.

Essex House, with its agents and messengers coming and going, had for a long time represented an independent power in London. In January of 1601 it came to be an open and unashamed anti-Court, as riders galloped in from Wales, Ireland and Scotland and as nobles like Southampton and Rutland passed and repassed in urgent huddles. Unemployed captains from the Irish and Dutch Wars drank, caroused or slept in the courtyard. Known Catholics and Puritans showed their faces outside the gates with impunity. The tone of the sermons preached to the growing mass of humanity who congregated around and within its walls became ever more inflammatory. Essex himself set the tone of the increasing recklessness, flourishing a hollow imitation of the boisterousness that characterized his days of favour and uttering ever more insolent statements about Cecil, Raleigh, Grey, Cobham – and the Queen herself. Elizabeth, he said, with a viciousness that was to be amply repaid, had a mind as crooked as her body. It was a two-pronged barb, for whatever might be said about the workings of her mind, it was sacrilege enough to imply that her physical beauty no longer measured up to that of a young Virgin Queen.

In sharp contradiction to all Essex's complaints about unjust persecution, Lord Treasurer Buckhurst sent a friendly note to warn the Earl against the dangers that his behaviour could lead him to. Buckhurst was an elderly man who had never been a particular friend of Essex's, but neither had he been a particular opponent. And it was certainly not in his interests to see Secretary Cecil fill the power vacuum that Essex's absence from Court had caused. So he sent his son to the Earl to explain how he and friends were working for Essex's restoration to favour – but were finding their difficult task made still more difficult by the strange goings-on at Essex House. The Queen, he explained, was especially alarmed by three things: the swaggering swordsmen whose rakehell reputations boded ill: the lavish entertainment offered to nobles and others as if Essex was courting popularity – a cardinal Elizabethan sin for all but the Queen: and the increasing numbers and outspokenness of the Puritan preachers whose courtyard sermons were attracting vast and unruly crowds.

It was a sensible, courteous and friendly word of warning. But Essex was so far committed to violence that he could only treat it as a shot across the bows, and he responded accordingly, with a sharp note that made no allowance for Buckhurst's good intentions. His plottings had long since ceased to discuss ends but were concerned solely with means. He had appointed a special committee to plan out a strategy of rebellion, and early in February 1601 two long conferences were held in Drury House,

Southampton's residence occupied by Sir Charles Danvers in Drury Lane across the Strand, to discuss the best means of deploying the arms and forces at the rebels' disposal.

To avoid attracting suspicion, Essex himself was not present at the discussions, but he appointed as a co-ordinating chairman the Earl of Southampton. The committee members were Sir Charles Danvers, Sir Ferdinando Gorges who had been summoned from Plymouth, and two of the Devereux' Welsh following, John Lyttleton and Sir John Davies. Davies, who was to be sentenced to death for his rôle in the rising, was a man like Gelli Meyrick who owed all he had to the Earl of Essex. He was a soldier of fortune who had fought in the Netherlands with Roger Williams and had met the young Earl either there or on the 1589 raid on Portugal. Like so many of the captains prepared to swagger through the streets and shout Essex's name he had been on the expeditions to Cadiz and the Islands; he depended on the military livelihood which Essex's anti-Spanish belligerence made possible, and which Cecil threatened to cut off. But Davies was more than a simple man of arms. On becoming Master of the Ordnance in 1595 Essex gave Davies the title of Surveyor, effectively to carry out the Master's functions and to act as the Earl's representative. Unfortunately Davies appears to have taken the actual administration of the royal munitions as lightly as his patron, concentrating his energies on ousting officials thought to be favourable to Cecil and replacing them with cronies of Essex. So through 1600 the Ordnance Office in the Tower was less consumed with the problems of supplying the Queen's forces with powder and shot than with the feuds between the representatives of the factions contesting power at Court. But Davies proved a tough and wily fighter both in the Ordnance department, and in the conspiratorial conferences at Drury House, the first of which was held on 2 February 1601. On the same day the Queen issued an order releasing Lord Grey from the Fleet prison where he had been confined for less than a month after his assault on Southampton. It only seemed to prove that Essex and his friends could no longer count on the protection of the law against their enemies, and even fresher urgency was lent to their discussions.

Sir John Davies produced for consideration two long documents in Essex's own handwriting. The first was a list of some 120 noblemen, knights and gentlemen whom the Earl believed he could count upon in the action that lay ahead. The committee members took their absent leader's word for the strength of the loyalties he could call on. Then Davies invited discussion on the second item, a list of specific points on which Essex desired the committee's advice, and this was crucial to the success or failure of the whole enterprise. Sir Gelli Meyrick, Essex himself and the other noble leaders of the action could, with their stewards, be guaranteed to assemble on any given date in the near future a reasonably large body of armed and mounted men in the courtyard of Essex House. The question was where best to direct that force. There seemed three major possible destinations: the Court, which was the ultimate aim of the whole enterprise; the City, where Essex had always in the past raised substantial bodies of men and where he had reason to believe that one Sheriff Smyth was already working on his behalf: and the Tower of London, the capture of whose fortifications and armaments would add immeasurably to the military strength of the enterprise. The Court lay west of Essex House, less than a mile down the Strand. The City lay east of Essex House, also a mile along the Strand but in the opposite direction. And the Tower lay even further east, beyond St Paul's Cathedral, the City and London Bridge.

Capturing the Tower meant gaining effective control of the City, so the real point at issue was whether to try to attack both Court and Tower of London simultaneously, or to concentrate on a single objective in the hope that control over one would lead to the surrender of the other.

The majority of the committee favoured a two-pronged attack, but Sir Ferdinando Gorges opposed it, maintaining that they simply did not have sufficient forces at their disposal for such an ambitious and complicated assault. He moved them on to discussion of the other points Essex had asked them to examine – more detailed consideration of the way in which the Court itself could be captured. What were its key strategic points? Who best could capture them and how many men would they need? Where could Essex himself assemble with his bodyguard near the Court so as to cause least suspicion? Who were the enemies at Court who should first be taken into custody? Debate battered fiercely and vaguely round these points. Southampton did not possess the experience or the personal presence to draw definite conclusions from the arguments that chased each other round the room; for while few of the committee members seemed reluctant to issue prescriptions, there was a strange reluctance when it came to assigning specific rôles or responsibilities in this the active and most crucial part of the whole rebellion. The meeting broke up disputatious and undecided.

Next morning they reassembled, and overnight Sir John Davies had had the wit to work out a definite plan to seize the Court. He put this forward as a concrete basis of discussion. A number of the less-suspected and frowned-on conspirators, with their followers, should enter Whitehall Palace at discreet and irregular intervals as though they were carrying out their normal attendance at Court. Once safely inside the Palace they should each move to a key point – Davies to the Hall, Danvers to the Presence Chamber, Sir Christopher Blount to the gates and Gorges to the gate at the preaching place. At a given signal all were to act simultaneously. Danvers and his followers, with the help of Davies, were to seize the halberds of the royal guards – which they often left lying un-attended outside the Presence Chamber – and to capture, too, the guard chamber. Many of the guards were, in any case, former servants of Essex's. Blount was to gain control of the Great Court Gate and make sure no government reinforcements got in – or warnings got out. Then Essex and his noble colleagues would enter the palace in freedom and dignity and make their way to the royal presence. Raleigh, the Captain of the Guard, would be arrested along with whatever councillors the Earl decided to punish. Special heralds would proclaim the news of the coup to the people and particularly to the City. And then a Parliament would be summoned at which all who had been hostile to the Essex cause would be tried and would receive their just deserts.

Given the decision for a coup, Davies' was a thoughtful and

quite feasible plan. But it provoked a most feverish outburst of opposition from Sir Ferdinando Gorges; and when actually confronted with the personal participation their project involved, the other councillors were curiously lukewarm in support of Davies' suggestions. Quite willing to plot and boast they were suddenly cowed by their realization of the mess their blusterings had landed them in. Gorges was a half-hearted revolutionary, as they all were, but at least he had the honesty to express his fears in violent and disruptive criticism: 'I utterly disliked that course, as besides the horror I felt at it, I saw it was impossible to be accomplished.'

Southampton could sense the general cravenness but could not put his finger on it, losing his temper and turning savagely on Gorges for frustrating the one seriously considered course of action proposed to them: 'we shall resolve upon nothing, and it is now three months or more since we first undertook this.'[12]

Gorges, just up from the West Country, retorted that he knew nothing of their past preparations and that the Earl of Essex's best course was to talk to his friends in the City, like Sheriff Smyth, who had made such fair promises of support. The meeting dissolved in confusion: 'we broke up resolved upon nothing, and referred all to the Earl of Essex himself.' The one attempt at conscious organization had failed, and now events were to move too quickly for Essex, or any special committee, to gain control of them.

It was Tuesday evening. On the following Friday Lord Mounteagle, Sir Charles Percy, Sir Jocelyn Percy and others of Essex's friends dined well and went over the river to the Globe Playhouse where the Lord Chamberlain's company performed. The revellers asked the company if they would stage a special performance of Shakespeare's play about the deposition of *Richard II* for their pleasure and, they were sure, for the pleasure of the populace as a whole. They offered to supplement the takings of the door by 40s.

The actors were reluctant. *Richard II*, they said, was one of the oldest productions in their repertory. They'd forgotten the lines and doubted whether a revival would attract much interest.

Shakespeare himself may well have been reluctant to have one of his early historical panoramas wheeled out at a time when he was working on plays like *Troilus and Cressida*. But 40s was a substantial guarantee, and the gentlemen had interested friends. So next day, on the afternoon of Saturday, 7 February 1601, a special performance of *Richard II* was presented to an enthusiastic audience of Essex's followers, notable among them being Lord Mounteagle, Sir Gelli Meyrick and Sir Christopher Blount.

It was crude and open provocation for a carousing company of swordsmen so deliberately to arrange and applaud the production of a play that was not only controversial for depicting the deposition of a reigning sovereign – drama still retained the ritualistic aura of magical representation that lingered from pagan mimings and the Mystery plays – but which had also been linked so inescapably to the Earl of Essex himself. The Privy Council had only a few weeks previously examined yet again Doctor John Hayward who had actually been imprisoned in the Tower for the dedication to his *History of Henry IV* that alluded too obviously to the similarity between Essex and Bolingbroke. Added to the obvious warlike preparations at Essex House, the inference of this special performance was clear, and the Privy Council justifiably took alarm. The Court was virtually unprotected.

An emergency Council meeting was held at the home of Buckhurst, the Lord Treasurer, who had tried to warn Essex a few weeks earlier of the suspicions his activities were causing, and who was now confined to his house with a late winter chill. It was a damp February evening, dark already, and councillors who rode past Essex House had seen flickering lights and heard the hubbub of a large unruly assembly. There were reports of strange horses being stabled in hostelries and small wild Welshmen sleeping in the straw of cellars and attics because normal accommodation was suddenly overflowing. Trouble was brewing, and tomorrow was a Sunday when the city apprentices and workmen would be away from work and ready to join in any disturbances. The last time the Council had been faced with a crisis like this, some thirty years previously when they suspected that the Catholic Earls of the North were up to no good but had no firm evidence to go on, they had brought matters to a head by summoning the conspiring lords to the royal presence: the summons had faced the plotters with the alternatives of submitting, or declaring their rebellion before their plans had properly matured. Now on that anxious evening on 7 February 1601 the Privy Council decided on a similar course. A messenger was sent requesting Essex to present himself before them.

The returned playgoers were now back at Essex House and half way through supper. The Council's messenger was turned away with an excuse. He arrived back at the Lord Treasurer's house to tell the waiting councillors what he had seen. Essex's offhand dismissal sounded ominous. A stronger deputation would obviously have to be despatched to show the Earl the authorities meant business; and so out into the night went Secretary Herbert.

He knocked at the gate of Essex House and was admitted to the Earl's presence. He repeated the request that Essex should present himself at once before the Privy Council. Essex blustered, protesting ill health and repeating his old complaints about persecution by his enemies. He feared for his safety and his life if he ventured beyond the walls of his home, he said. Mr Secretary Herbert had to return to the Council alone and since it was, by then, getting on for midnight the councillors decided to adjourn and meet again early next morning.

Meanwhile, back at Essex House, fast talking was going on. The government obviously had wind of the conspirators' plans. If they delayed too long the whole enterprise would be nipped in the bud. Sir Charles Danvers was for escaping while the going was good. Essex should 'fly with some hundred gentlemen to the sea side, or into Wales, where he might command some ports.'[13] Yet it seemed a poor conclusion to the weeks of preparation. Could not Essex attack the Court by night? He had 300 men ready armed and waiting for his summons. But that would secure only the Queen. Cecil, Cobham, the Howards, Raleigh and Grey might be sleeping anywhere. No plan could succeed unless they were captured. Temple, one of the Earl's secretaries, was sent to the City to find out how matters stood there, and he was back in next to no time reporting that Sheriff Smyth could raise a thousand London militia to fight for the cause next morning. That was the answer – a night of preparations, then an early morning march up the Strand to the City; juncture with Sheriff Smyth's thousand men and any of the populace that cared to tag along, then a triumphant march back down the Strand, past Essex House to the Palace of Whitehall and seizure of the Court. The small royal bodyguard would be helpless against the vast, armed and resolute army of Essex's supporters – and there would be no time for the Privy Council to organize resistance.

Nobody thought to ask exactly who this Sheriff Smyth was, where he proposed to raise a thousand men from, and what faith could be placed in his word – or in the word of the secretary who had been Essex's intermediary. The time for rational discussion was long past.

Tomorrow they would venture.

29

The Rebellion

Before dawn on 8 February 1601 messengers were hurrying through the streets of London to summon Essex's supporters to his banner. Old Lord Sandys was roused at six. And at about the same time young Rutland left home to join Southampton at his lodgings.

The rebellion was to be a rush job. There was still no news of the embassy James had promised to send from Scotland. Welsh supporters were still on the road. Rutland had not received a boatload of arms he had ordered from the Continent. But the Council's alarm left the conspirators no choice but to act immediately. And as they hurried through the grey, deserted, dawn streets, most of the rebels had high hopes of success. Only Sir Ferdinando Gorges displayed the half-heartedness that had characterized his participation from the start. In the dim first light he had received a message from his West Country kinsman, Sir Walter Raleigh, inviting him to a meeting. Essex suspected Gorges sufficiently to insist that the meeting take place in sight of Essex House, in open boats in the middle of the Thames. And Sir Christopher Blount wanted to use the encounter to eliminate the most vicious of their enemies. In fact, when their boats drew alongside in midstream, Gorges only made explicit to Raleigh what must have been obvious from the growing crowds both inside and outside the gates of Essex House: 'you are like to have a bloody day of it.' And Raleigh's attempt to rescue his relative from the consequences of his involvement in the revolt was cut short by the appearance of a boat with four musketeers that put off from Essex stairs. Sir Ferdinando returned to Essex House, and Sir Walter went back to Court to raise the alarm.

Elizabeth stayed calm in her Whitehall palace. Cecil's informants had kept her up to date on events in the Strand, and the Secretary had sent out a warning to the Lord Mayor and Aldermen of the City of London who were gathering for the first sermon of the day at St Paul's Cross at eight. The councillors who had met the previous night and whose summons had been twice disregarded decided to make one last attempt at peaceful settlement. Lord Keeper Egerton, Essex's not unfriendly former jailer, Sir William Knollys, Essex's uncle, Lord Chief Justice Popham and the Earl of Worcester, a friend of Essex's, were despatched with a small band of servants to Essex House. They were a deputation as well disposed towards Essex as any that could have been selected from the Privy Council, and their mission was to elicit what the Earl's intentions were and to warn him of the consequences of his actions.

They processed up the Strand, and by ten o'clock on that cold February morning they had reached Essex House. Lord Keeper Egerton had brought with him the Great Seal of England. The ever growing crowds made entry through the main gates impossible, and so the party went round to a side 'wicket' entrance. In response to their knocking Sir William Constable, who was commanding a platoon of halberdiers, appeared and asked them their business. They explained that they wanted to speak to the Earl of Essex, and the 'wicket' was promptly opened for them, only to be slammed shut once they were in the courtyard, and their servants were left in the street outside. Alone, except for one servant bearing the Great Seal, the four councillors pushed a way through the jostling noisy crowd that was milling in the courtyard. Some two or three hundred men were preparing their horses and weapons for action and they gathered jeering round this vulnerable little deputation that represented authority.

The councillors found Essex, Rutland, Southampton, Sandys, Mounteagle, Blount and Danvers huddled in a knot, flushed and talking loudly. The Lord Keeper had to raise his voice to ask over the roar of the crowd what the meaning of this assembly was. Essex shouted in a reply that was intended to carry to the crowd – for this was his first and, indeed, his last, formal public explanation of his behaviour – 'that his life was sought, and that he should have been murdered in his bed.'

When the Privy Councillors replied that authorities and due processes of law existed to protect subjects from such dangers Southampton intervened, shouting that he had himself, less than a month before, been murderously set upon by Lord Grey. The Lord Chief Justice pointed out that Grey had been immediately punished for his assault – and suggested that they continue this discussion indoors; he would be most happy to carry to the Queen, and help secure the redress of, any legitimate grievances that Essex might care to lay before him.

It was a civil suggestion but the fidgety crowd disliked it. 'Away, my Lord!' 'They abuse you!' shouted some. Others were more to the point: 'You lose time,' 'they betray you!' The situation was getting ugly – and Egerton decided to act. He had taken off his hat in greeting to Essex, but now he replaced it as a sign that as Lord Keeper of the Great Seal of England he was speaking for the Queen. 'I command you all upon your allegiance,' he cried to the ever more restive crowd, 'to lay down your weapons and to depart, which you all ought to do being thus commanded, if you be good subjects and owe that duty to the Queen which you profess.' It was the Elizabethan equivalent of reading the Riot Act. If Essex continued the assembly and if men marched with him then they were breaking the law and, having been warned, they had no complaint against any punishment they incurred.

Essex said nothing, but put on his own hat and marched into the house with his colleagues. The Lord Keeper and his deputation followed, chased indoors by cries of 'Kill them!' and 'Cast the Great Seal out of the Window!' If there had ever been any doubt that this was a rebellion in real earnest it was removed when the two rival groups reached Essex's study. All through the house and up the stairs Essex, Blount, Southampton and Davies had been whispering together. This royal deputation was something they were totally unprepared for, and their solution to the dilemma was a crude one. Arrived at his study, Essex abruptly gave orders for the Privy Councillors to be locked inside and left Sir John Davies to keep an eye on them. Outside the study door was placed a guard of musketeers, with loaded weapons and fire ready to ignite them, under the command of another Welshman, Owen Salusbury.

'My Lords,' ran Essex's parting words to his prisoners, 'be patient a while and stay here and I will go into London and take order with the Mayor and Sheriffs for the City and be here again within this half hour.'

Then he strode out again to the courtyard. 'To the Court! To the Court!' the mob cried as Essex headed for the City. And the mob were right. For the Court was less than twenty minutes distant and still unprepared for fierce defence. The Privy Council were awaiting the return and report of the now imprisoned deputation. There were no militia summoned. The only force available to protect the Queen was a few score of the royal guard and as many courtiers as could be persuaded to unsheath their ceremonial swords. In the courtyard of Essex House there were at least 200 rough, armed and desperate men.

At half past ten on the morning of 8 February 1601 the Earl of Essex had England at his mercy, but he turned out of Essex House east instead of west – and his chance was lost.

His supporters followed him, but they were confused, for they knew their enemies were in the palace of Whitehall. No one had bothered to explain the strategy of the march to the City for reinforcements, nor why the merchants there might be expected to deviate from their longstanding and well tried loyalty to the Queen. As the cavalcade clattered off the Strand down Fleet Street through the Lud Gate in the City walls and up Lud Gate Hill, its cries for support lacked conviction. It was here Lord Cromwell joined the procession, but the promised assistance of the Earl of Sussex never materialized, and Bedford, Cromwell and Mounteagle were also to make good their escapes before the day was out.

'For the Queen! For the Queen!' cried Essex. 'A plot is laid for my life!' A few citizens cheered in a desultory fashion, but no one seemed anxious to join in the march, let alone rush to arms. The plan had been to catch the vast crowd who gathered for the mid-morning sermon at St Paul's Cross, but the conference and imprisonment of the royal deputation had delayed the timetable. By the time Essex reached the top of Lud Gate Hill the sermon was over and the vast congregation had dispersed. The somewhat less jaunty cavalcade rode through the homegoing East Enders thronging down Cheapside. Somehow neither Essex nor the other leaders could convey the urgency of the situation to the crowds. They smiled, waved and cheered, but seemed to regard the procession as a genteel Sunday outing, not the last throw of a group of desperate men whose lives were now at stake.

Essex rode faster down Poultry Street and Lombard Street in the direction of Fenchurch Street where Sheriff Smyth lived. His home was the object of the whole exercise, for it was to collect the thousand armed men the sheriff was reputed to have promised that Essex had marched east and not west. Lord Cromwell and an advance guard went on ahead to warn Sheriff Smyth of the Earl's arrival – and arrived just in time to catch him slipping out of the back door. He had no men. He disclaimed all knowledge of promising any men, and he asked that the good Earl would not bring his company into the house. Then mumbling something about fetching the Lord Mayor he vanished in the direction of the Mansion House.

It was a cruel disappointment, but one that was of Essex's own making. He had not secured the agreement of Smyth in person, and had simply trusted to the vague assurances of an intermediary that troops would be available. And as he shuddered under that blow news came through that the Privy Council had started to take action. The Earl of Cumberland had been despatched towards the City with a small detachment of troops and had ordered a chain to be drawn across the Lud Gate in the City walls where Essex and his followers had entered. The rebels were suddenly cut off. They would have to fight their way through armed resistance if they wanted to regain Essex House – let alone march even further west to the Court.

Essex came out in a cold and heavy sweat. Things were hopelessly out of control. Concentrating on trivia, he called for another shirt because his own was soaked through with perspiration. Then he tried another battle cry: 'powder and muskets!' for his men; England had been sold to the Spaniard and he, Essex, with only a handful of men armed with swords and rapiers were crusading in her defence. He needed proper weapons. But there were none available, and the best Christopher Blount could manage were a half dozen old halberds commandeered from a local shop. The rebels milled around Fenchurch Street shouting and threatening, but prudent citizens like Sheriff Smyth were heading in the opposite direction.

The total lack of forethought and planning of the whole enterprise was becoming desperately obvious. Essex deserted all pretence at leadership and called for food. While his followers drank the Sheriff's ale, Essex, Southampton, Rutland, Bedford, Cromwell, Sandys, Mounteagle, Danvers, Blount and the other leaders solemnly sat down to a meal pirated from the Sheriff's kitchen.

For three hours the cavalcade that was to save England remained stuck in Fenchurch Street taking its midday refreshment – while the Privy Council acted. Cecil's elder brother, the second Lord Burghley, was sent out into the streets with a royal proclamation denouncing Essex as a traitor and promising complete pardon to those of his followers who were prepared to desert him. No coward, Burghley rode into the City and advanced with his herald as far as Fenchurch Street where Essex's followers were still stuck. Mounteagle's men attacked them – but not before the proclamation had been read. And though Essex sneered from his dining room that a herald would proclaim anything for a couple of shillings, the erosion of support began. The Earl of Bedford took advantage of the general confusion to head for home, and Lord Cromwell also showed a clean pair of heels down a sidestreet.

Essex suddenly realized how grave his position had become. Not before time he jumped up from the table, and with his napkin still round his neck he rushed out into Fenchurch Street. Renewing his cry that he was acting for the good of Queen, City and Crown against atheists in the pay of Spain, he led his sadly decreasing band into Gracechurch Street. And here he met again with Sheriff Smyth. The worthy Sheriff had been in consultation with the Lord Mayor, who had in turn had discussions with the Privy Council, and as a result the Earl of Essex was now asked to ride to the Mansion House and surrender to the City authorities.

It was as though the Earl did not hear a single word addressed to him, for he completely ignored the Sheriff's request and simply repeated the order he had first given on arriving in Fenchurch Street. The Sheriff was to rally his company and ride with Essex. With the air of one talking to a drunkard or idiot the Sheriff patiently explained that he had no company with which to follow Essex or anyone else. The Earl's best course was to surrender to the Lord Mayor.

There was clearly no future in the City. Essex's one last desperate hope was to carve a passage back to Essex House and then to bargain, using the hostages that he had imprisoned there. He turned back down Lombard Street and Cheapside, passed St Paul's and came cantering fast down Lud Gate Hill. But there he was checked, for across the Lud Gate stretched the chain put up by the Earl of Cumberland, and defending it were a small but resolute group of pikemen under the command of a veteran captain, Sir John Leveson. The pikemen were mostly servants of the Bishop of London, co-opted by Cumberland, hastily armed and dressed in breastplates and helmets. Essex halted four pike's lengths from them and asked whose soldiers they were. 'My Lord of Cumberland's,' came the answer. Recognizing Leveson, Essex sent Ferdinando Gorges to request peaceable passage to his house. Leveson refused. Essex then sent one of his captains, Bushell, with a concocted story of a free pass granted by the Lord Mayor and Sheriffs. Leveson was adamant. If the Lord Mayor or Sheriffs cared to appear and affirm the truth of that statement then he would lower the chain; but until they appeared it would stay blocking the gate. Gorges was sent back with yet another request – that one gentleman alone be allowed through with a message to the Queen. The plan was for Gorges to get back to the councillors and use them to negotiate with Elizabeth. But Leveson was a simple and stubborn fellow. He had only by chance fallen in with these pikemen as they marched from the Bishop's palace to the City, but having been given the Lud Gate to defend he was determined to hold it to the bitter end. He refused Gorges' second request – and he refused two more even more grovelling petitions.

Eventually one of Essex's followers lost patience. Like most of the captains, he had joined the rebellion to fight, and was heartily disgusted with traipsing round the City of London. Here at last was a chance for some action, and without more ado he discharged his pistol. It was the signal the other swordsmen and adventurers had been waiting for. With cries of 'Shoot! Shoot!' they fell on Leveson and his little band of episcopal attendants. The defenders fired back, some shot passing through Essex's hat. His page, Henry Tracy, fell dead and two citizens casually watching the scuffle paid a heavy price for their curiosity. But with Leveson's second-in-command, Waite, they were the only fatalities.

The volleying had left the two sides where they were before, and reloading was too complicated a task. Essex called for a charge, and Christopher Blount rushed in bravely, hacking at the line of pikes that defended the chain. The line did not buckle, and Blount was badly gored in the cheek. While still reeling from the blow he was struck smartly on the head, to fall on the cobbles unconscious. Leveson gave the order to charge. The pikemen lowered their weapons. And Essex turned tail and fled, leaving his stepfather felled at the enemy's feet.

The rebels retreated back up Lud Gate Hill in confusion. At St Paul's Cathedral they rallied, and now little more than fugitives, skidaddled down Friday Street to the river. Essex himself was in a state of collapse, sweating and fainting, and pitying citizens raised the chain across Friday Street to let the pathetic band of stragglers down to the Thames. There they discovered boats moored to the river bank, and in the undignified scramble to escape in them, Lord Mounteagle fell into the water and almost drowned. If Essex and Southampton had had time, or been capable of clear thought, they might now have realized how manifestly futile their cause was and could have taken advantage of the boats and flowing current to ride downstream and begin an escape to the Continent. But they were not men to reflect rationally at the quietest of moments, and they still pinned high hopes on the hostages held in Essex House. They might still force the Queen and Council to negotiate.

The Queen and Council might have needed to negotiate that morning, but by the middle of the afternoon they were in a clear position of strength. Messengers had called out villagers from Chelsea, Vauxhall and Westminster who had surrounded the royal palace with arms. A barricade of coaches had been drawn across the Strand at Charing Cross to halt any raiding party that might have designs on Whitehall. And after the initial alarm the Queen had gone about her day's routine as usual, eating a hearty lunch and observing that He who had placed her in her throne would most certainly preserve her in it. When a little force was mustered to make a sally from Whitehall, as if for an afternoon's hunting, she was with great difficulty dissuaded from joining in the sport. And all the while the Lord Mayor, Bishop of London and Earl of Cumberland had been organizing the bands of pike-men and musketeers, one of which had repulsed the rebels so decisively at the Lud Gate.

The Earl of Essex got back to his house as dusk was falling, to suffer his final cruel deception on a day of cruel deceptions. The hostages who were his last faint hope of salvation had vanished. Left in the custody of Sir John Davies they had soon asked why Essex was not returning from the City with the speed he had promised, and not a little embarrassed, Davies had called in the Countess of Essex and Lady Rich to beguile away the tedium of waiting with such small talk as was possible in the circumstances. After a morning and afternoon of strained and improbable social conversation the long ordeal, which would have been comical in less tragic circumstances, was ended by Sir Ferdinando Gorges.

He had made rapid time upstream and was now intent on saving his own skin. He falsely told Gelli Meyrick and Davies that he had orders from Essex to take the hostages to negotiate with the Privy Council, and hustled them out of the door to freedom only minutes before Essex himself arrived.

There was no time to lose in bemoaning such treachery, for already Essex House was surrounded by loyalist forces under the command of Nottingham, the Lord Admiral. Along the Strand were companies of cavalry and infantry under the Earl of Cumberland, the Earl of Lincoln, Lord Thomas Howard, Lord Burghley, Lord Compton and Southampton's old enemy, Lord Grey. Entrenched in the gardens that lay between Essex House and the river were troops under the Lord Admiral himself, Lord Cobham, Sir John Stanhope, Sir Robert Sidney and Sir Fulke Greville. After their unpreparedness that morning the authorities had struck back with a vengeance, and it was now obviously only a matter of time before they broke into the house. Cannon were on their way from the Tower which would make nonsense of the hasty barricades of books and furniture that had been thrown up by the remaining defenders.

Essex set about preparing for arrest, emptying his private drawers and chests and burning all the documents relating to the conspiracy. Destroying the evidence would to some extent protect his friends, and might make easier his defence against charges of malicious premeditation. He unlocked a great iron chest that contained his most private papers, burned its contents, destroyed the list of supporters he had carried with him to the City and, most dramatic of all, ripped off and flung into the flames the little black pouch he had hung round his neck ever since he had received a certain letter from James, King of Scotland. He burnt his diary and all the private letters he could lay his hands on, then drew his sword for the final battle.

The attackers had already broken into the courtyard where Lord Burghley, with the loss of two men, had forced through the gates. The infantry were sniping at the windows, and the sound of their gunfire and the smashing glass jangled with the screams and cries of the terrified womenfolk in the house. One of

Southampton's footmen was shot, and Captain Owen Salusbury, the Welshman who, with Sir John Davies, had guarded the Privy Councillors all day, was mortally wounded when he ventured too near a window. When the cannon came up there would be the most awful carnage, so the Lord Admiral called a halt to the assault and sent forward Sir Robert Sidney, the brother of Sir Philip and the man Essex had advanced as his candidate for the governorship of the Cinque Ports, to urge his friends to surrender peacefully. Southampton came out on to the roof to barter for terms. Essex and the others meant no harm to the Queen, he maintained, and had taken up arms only to defend themselves against their enemies. They were quite ready to present themselves before Her Majesty if the Lord Admiral would give them hostages to guarantee their safe return: 'if not, we are every one of us fully resolved to lose our lives fighting.' Essex had by now joined Southampton on the roof and echoed these sentiments. He declared he was seeking to do his country and sovereign good service by rooting out those 'Atheists and Caterpillars' who were his enemies. Better die now like men with swords in their hands than live a fortnight to perish on a scaffold.

Sidney carried these battling words back to the Lord Admiral, who replied shortly that rebels could not bargain with princes or their representatives, but that he was prepared to grant safe conducts for any womenfolk who wished to leave the house. Southampton thanked him kindly, but claimed it would take an hour to unbarricade the doors, and that would leave a passage that the attackers could exploit. Would the Admiral grant a ceasefire allowing time to open the doors and refortify them again?

In the two-hour truce that Nottingham unexpectedly agreed to, furious arguments broke out amongst the defenders. Once the women were out Essex was willing to be blown to high heaven. Old Lord Sandys, who really had very little to lose, was ready for a similarly honorable end. It was, he declared 'more commendable for Men of Honour to die by the Sword, than by the Axe or Halter.'[1] But not all his colleagues were so Homeric, and Essex and Southampton eventually returned to the roof promising to yield on three conditions: that the Lord Admiral arrest and treat them in a civil fashion; that they would be granted a fair and impartial trial; and that Mister Ashton, a clergyman in whom Essex had special faith, should join Essex in prison and minister to his spiritual needs. The Earl was preparing already for another – and definitely final – bout of religious melancholia.

The conditions were agreed to, and in the fitful, flickering light of torches the conspirators came out of Essex House one by one, fell on their knees, and presented their swords to the Lord Admiral. It was after ten on a dark and chilly night. A storm was brewing. The Thames was rising fast. It was out of the question to risk 'shooting' the rapids of London Bridge and rowing the prisoners down to the Tower of London. And the streets were still too disturbed for them to be conveyed by horse or carriage. Essex and Southampton were taken to Lambeth Palace, and then moved secretly at three in the morning into the Tower. The Queen had sworn she would not sleep till she knew them safely under lock and key – and eventually she could sleep soundly. The Earl of Essex's rebellion had lasted but twelve hours.

30

The Trial

The violence was not quite over. Captain Thomas Lee was a soldier of fortune who had fought in Ireland and was one of the little band that had galloped pell mell down to Nonsuch back in September 1599. A desperado with an unsavoury reputation, he had approached Cecil and the Lord Admiral on the day of the rising and offered to murder Essex on their behalf. The offer was rejected, and Captain Lee had promptly switched his loyalties completely – despite the obvious futility of the Essex cause.

As darkness was falling on the evening of Thursday, 12 February 1601, four days after the rising and the arrest of Essex and Southampton, Captain Lee sidled up to two courtiers, Sir Henry Neville and Sir Robert Cross. He complained violently against the injustice of recent events – and suggested a remedy. It needed but half a dozen men of courage who had access to the Presence Chamber boldly to confront the Queen and force her to sign a warrant summoning the two imprisoned earls to her side. Once there they could explain precisely the noble motives that had impelled them on last Sunday's enterprise, and all misunderstandings would be cleared away. Neville and Cross muttered something noncommittal to this suggestion, and vanished rapidly to report the whole matter to Cecil.

Later that evening Captain Lee was discovered lurking

suspiciously around the Queen's apartments, and on being arrested cheerfully confessed to his intention of breaking in upon Her Majesty while she sat at supper. He was going to lock the doors and force Elizabeth to sign a warrant for Essex's release. Condemned out of his own mouth, Lee was despatched to join the eighty or so of Essex's other followers already behind bars, was tried at Newgate the following Monday and was executed promptly on Tuesday morning.

The government were taking no chances. London in the weeks following the rebellion took on the appearance of an armed camp. Five hundred men levied in Middlesex were stationed at Charing Cross, 400 men from the county of Essex were set to watch the eastern outskirts of the capital, 300 men levied in Surrey were brought up to keep order among the cockpits, playhouses and beargardens of Southwark and Lambeth, and 400 men of Hertfordshire marched into Holborn. Two companies were posted at the Exchange. The proclamation of Essex's treason which had been drawn up on Sunday morning and announced on Sunday afternoon was printed on Monday and distributed on Tuesday. On Wednesday the country's most expert lawyers were called together to organize the work of examining the prisoners and preparing an almost immediate prosecution. After Thomas Lee's abortive coup on Thursday letters were sent out on Friday to summon the peers of the realm selected to try the traitors: there was no pretence that the trial would be a fair or impartial one in the letters that promised the jurymen 'all the particularities not only of their secret practices of treason against the Kingdom but of their actual rebellion within the City of London, where they assembled great forces on Sunday last and killed divers of Her Majesty's subjects.' And on Saturday, 14 February were published the government's elaborate instructions to preachers, for holiday crowds would be gathering on Sunday after a week of rumour, and church sermons, at which attendance was compulsory for all and enforceable with a fine, were the obvious vehicles for stating the Privy Council's point of view. They covered the nation more comprehensively than modern party political broadcasts.

The more idle ministers needed to do little except read out the memorandum that the Privy Council sent them. The Earl of Essex had for the last six or seven years deliberately courted popularity in order to make himself king. His hypocrisy was proved by the piety with which he would attend church services – plotting the downfall of her Majesty the Queen all the while. The analogy with Richard II was not farfetched or accidental. Essex saw himself as another Bolingbroke deposing his sovereign. Special prayers of thanksgiving were ordered to praise God for delivering England, her Queen and people from the consequences of his wicked rebellion.

It was an impressive and deceitful piece of propaganda – though certainly more truthful than anything Essex would have put out had he been victorious – but it was not entirely successful. Loyalist preachers embroidered on the story so heavily that it sounded ridiculous, and ministers favourable to Essex managed to make their sympathies plain enough. A detachment of 500 troops was stationed by St Paul's Cross that Sunday morning in case of demonstrations.

On Tuesday, the day of Thomas Lea's execution, formal indictments were published charging Essex with an attempt to usurp the Crown and charging Essex together with Southampton, Rutland and Sandys with having conspired to depose and slay the Queen and to subvert the government. On Wednesday the lawyers were still working furiously, Francis Bacon prominent among them, to secure from the confessions of the various prisoners the evidence they needed to pin the crucial charge of premeditation on Essex; and next day, Thursday, 19 February 1601, less than two weeks after the conspirators had decided definitely to go ahead with their rising, the Earls of Essex and Southampton were brought up river from the Tower of London to Westminster Hall to be tried for treason by their peers.

It was a short trial, lasting but a day, not attempting to conceal, as the letters to the noble jurymen had made clear, that the verdict was a foregone conclusion. Sixteenth-century treason trials were not concerned with justice but with treason, and once the decision to proceed was taken then their chief function was ritualistic – like the tribunals of the Stalinist purges. The State wished to justify the elimination of those elements dangerous to its safety, and so a law court was taken, filled with men of worth and eminence who were treated to a series of pious exhortations and denunciations, and the understood verdict of guilty was agreed upon. The prosecution could deploy as many lawyers and witnesses as it wished, though it normally took the precaution of securing the witnesses' statements in advance, editing them carefully to remove anything that did not advance the case to its prearranged conclusion, and then reading the altered statement without the witness being present to confirm or deny the truth of the remarks being attributed to him: while the defendants had no legal assistance either in advance or in the court, were given no sight of the charges against them before they stood in the dock, and, conducting their own impromptu defence, had to rely for corroboration of their case on odd questions to such witnesses as the prosecution allowed into court. Small wonder that Essex's speeches at his trial were a strange mixture of self-justification and resignation to the fate he knew he could not escape.

The grandiose staging of this final drama left no doubt as to the care with which the Privy Council had prepared the condemnation. At the end of the court, which had been arranged in the form of a square, was the high canopy of state with a chair and footstool for Lord Treasurer Buckhurst who had risen from his sickbed to preside over the proceedings. In front of him sat a row of eight judges headed by Popham, the Lord Chief Justice. The fact that both Buckhurst and Popham had come into contact with Essex during the rebellion and that Popham had been one of the deputation threatened and imprisoned in Essex House was held to be no bar to their sitting in judgement. Opposite the justices were the Queen's Counsel charged with prosecuting the case, Sir Edward Coke, the Attorney General, Fleming, the Solicitor General, Yelverton, the Queen's Sergeant, the Recorder of London, two Sergeants-at-law, and the unashamed Francis Bacon. Lining the two sides of the court between the judges and the prosecution were the nine earls and sixteen barons summoned to pronounce their verdict. Spectators were set at the back of the court behind a long bar to the rear of the prosecution. The two accused, Essex and Southampton, were to sit inside the square, close to their accusers.

Just before nine the pageant began. Buckhurst was escorted into the court by seven sergeants-at-arms and forty of the Queen's guard under their captain, Sir Walter Raleigh. No one was missing out on the fun, with the exception, apparently, of Cecil, who was nowhere to be seen and whose whereabouts were unknown. Then the Lieutenant of the Tower was commanded to produce his prisoners, and a second procession entered the court – the two accused Earls preceded by the Gentleman Porter of the Tower bearing an executioner's axe with its blade, for the present turned away from the prisoners. Essex was dressed in black; Southampton in a dark-coloured suit and flowing cloth gown in whose long sleeves he kept his hands hidden all day.

Now the roll of the peers sitting as a jury was called, and when the Clerk read out the name of Thomas, Lord Grey, Essex twitched Southampton by the sleeve and laughed. He asked whether the privilege of challenge, which was granted to private people at their trials, applied in this case: not that he wished to contest the suitability of any of the peers set in judgement over them, but his companion, the Earl who stood by him, might well wish to do so. Lord Chief Justice Popham replied that peers of the realm were above such challenges. The charges were read and both earls pleaded 'not guilty'. 'I call God to witness, before Whom I hope shortly to appear,' added Essex, 'that I bear a true heart to her Majesty and my country, and have done nothing but that which the law of nature commanded me to do in my own defence, and which any reasonable man would have done in the like case.'

The prosecution was opened by Sergeant Yelverton, who had no hesitation in using political rhetoric. The prisoners' crime, he maintained, was as heinous as Catiline's notorious conspiracy in ancient Rome. Nor was it considered out of order for him suggestively to speculate in the course of his accusation that there must exist even more damning evidence than had so far come to light: 'overweening ambition is like the crocodile, which is ever growing as long as he liveth ... I can conjecture nothing hereby, but that there is some further matter in it than as yet appears.'

Attorney General Coke, who followed him, was, to modern eyes, equally heedless of legal niceties. He began by most properly and necessarily establishing from precedent that treason could lie simply in resisting royal authority with force. Though proof of deliberate premeditation or stated revolutionary intent was substantial, it was not essential: treason could be implied from any actions liable to bring about the death and destruction of the Queen, he demonstrated. Riotous apprentices who had proposed in 1595 to whip the Lord Mayor had been declared treasonable by learned judges. But Coke went on from this to launch a vicious diatribe against Essex's Catiline, popish, dissolute and desperate company which had proposed, among other things, to summon a Parliament: 'a bloody Parliament would that have been, where my Lord of Essex, that now stands all in black, would have worn a bloody robe: but now in God's last judgement, he of his earldom shall be Robert the Last, that of a kingdom thought to be Robert the First. Why should I stand upon further proofs?'

It was a vicious and illegal smear, for the charges against Essex made no mention of him seeking the Crown for himself, and Coke's previous legal arguments made clear that the prosecution would be producing no evidence to justify any such accusation. Essex was quick to his own defence against such tactics: 'Master Attorney playeth the orator and abuseth your lordships' ear with slanders against us. These are the fashions of orators in corrupt states and such rhetoric is the trade and talent of those who value themselves upon their skill in pleading innocent men out of their lives. . . .'[1] After some argument Buckhurst agreed that Essex should have the right to answer each piece of evidence as it was produced.

The first testimony was the deposition of one Henry Widdington which was read out by the Clerk. It described events in Essex House on the morning of Sunday, 8 February

1601, but Essex dismissed it all as hearsay. He could not be so cavalier with the next piece of evidence which was the testimony of Lord Chief Justice Popham, sworn and delivered in person. He described in lurid detail, corroborated by the Earl of Worcester, how the Queen's deputation had been insulted and imprisoned. The real objection to his account was not the facts, which were undeniable, nor Essex's lame excuse that he had shut up the councillors for their own safety, but the fact that the judge was giving evidence in the very case he was trying.

The next witness was Sir Walter Raleigh. 'What booteth it to swear the fox?' remarked Essex loudly as his old enemy took the oath. Raleigh described his interview on the water with Sir Ferdinando Gorges, and Gorges' warning that 'you are like to have a bloody day of it'.

The testimony of Gorges himself was the next piece of evidence, and having detailed the debates in Drury House it went on to maintain that Sir Ferdinando had urged Essex on his return from the City to submit immediately to the Queen. In fact, Gorges had been fully occupied saving his own neck by spiriting away the councillors, and Essex asked to cross-examine the craven knight in person. Sir Ferdinando was produced, confused and pale.

'Remember your reputation and that you are a gentleman,' warned Essex. 'I pray you answer me, did you advise me to leave my enterprise?'

'My Lord, I think I did,' came the reply.

'Nay,' cried Essex, 'it is no time to answer now upon thinking: these are not things to be forgotten.'

Gorges grew more definite before he stood down. But then it was Southampton's turn to make an undignified bid for his own safety. He admitted he had participated in all the alleged plottings to capture the Court and Tower, but pointed out that none of those plans had been adopted. He claimed to have known nothing at all about Essex's intentions when he came to Essex House that Sunday morning: he had never been close enough to the Herald to hear the proclamation of treason: he had never drawn his sword once in the course of the day. When Coke interrupted to point out the Earl had been seen with a pistol, Southampton maintained he had confiscated it from a man in the street, and that in any case it had no flint. It was a crawling performance, greeted with the silent scorn it deserved. The judges did not take long to rule that the constant adherence of Southampton to Essex in the City could only yield one interpretation.

Then followed confessions read out by the Clerk from Sir Charles Danvers, Sir Christopher Blount, the Earl of Rutland, Lord Sandys and Lord Mounteagle. Coke sententiously remarked how miraculously all these different testimonies concurred to produce the same truth: to which Essex retorted that the selfsame fear and the selfsame examiner could make the most distant accounts come together.

Francis Bacon rose, and his was the unkindest cut of all, for he had used not only the evidence at the Crown's disposal but his own knowledge of his former friend's personality to loose the most deadly shaft shot so far. He had anticipated the defence Essex would offer, and had prepared the very argument to counter it:

My Lord of Essex, I cannot resemble your proceedings more rightly than to one Pisistratus, in Athens, who, coming into the city with the purpose to procure the subversion of the Kingdom, and wanting aid for the accomplishing his aspiring desires, and as the surest means to win the hearts of the citizens unto him, he entered the city, having cut his body with a knife, to the end they might conjecture he had been in danger of his life. Even so your Lordship gave out in the streets that your life was sought by the Lord Cobham and Sir Walter Raleigh, by this means persuading yourself, if the City had undertaken your cause, all would have gone well on your side. But the imprisoning of the Queen's Councillors, what reference had that to my Lord Cobham, Sir Walter Raleigh and the rest?

Essex's wounds at the hands of Cobham and Raleigh had indeed been self-inflicted. And Bacon very craftily insinuated malice, not hysteria, as the reason for this. His speech was the more hurtful for being so personal, and Essex struck back wildly in even more personal terms. In an effort to discredit his persecutor he recounted the tale of the correspondence Bacon had counterfeited between Anthony Bacon and Essex in order to deceive the Queen. Francis was not in the slightest discomforted, indeed he turned his past efforts on Essex's behalf to his own credit.

This is no crimination [he answered coolly]. I confess I loved my Lord of Essex as long as he continued a dutiful subject, and I have spent more hours to make him a good subject to her Majesty than ever I did about my own business. But since you have stirred up this matter, my lord, I dare warrant you these letters of mine will not blush in the clearest light; for I did but perform the part of an honest man, and ever laboured to have done you good, if it might have been.

Essex was losing his temper, and getting more and more heated by Bacon's cool performance. Under stress he was revealing a strange reversion to his former hysteria. Lashing out in a fury of self-justification he repeated his old delusion about Cecil and the Spanish conspiracy: 'as for that I spake in London that the Crown of England was sold to the Spaniard, I speak it not of myself, for it was told me that Mr Secretary should say to one of his fellow Councillors, that the Infanta's title comparatively was as good in succession as any other.'

It was a fierce accusation that touched a very tender spot, for all present suspected Cecil of conducting negotiations with Spain, and all must have had doubts of their own about the content of them. If Essex could at least partially sustain the truth of his statement then his conspiracy fears would appear to possess some substance. And his rising would have to be seen in a new light.

It was a tense, dramatic moment; and suddenly, in the silence, came the sound of a curtain pulling back, and to the front of the court limped the little crookbacked Secretary in person. He had been hidden, listening to the proceedings, and his unexpected almost magical appearance from nowhere had all the drama – and significance – of a last-act dénouement. With an extravagance he seldom allowed himself he fell on his knees before Buckhurst and begged leave to answer Essex's foul and false report. He was roused to a fury few had seen before.

'My Lord of Essex, the difference between you and me is great,' he cried with all the passion of an ugly, unloved little hunchback unloosing his long pent-up hatred, fear and jealousy of gilded mortals like Essex.

For wit I give you the pre-eminence – you have it abundantly. For nobility also I give you place – I am not noble, yet a gentleman; I am no swordsman – there also you have the odds; but I have innocence, conscience, truth and honesty to defend me against the scandal and sting of slanderous tongues, and in this Court I stand as an upright man, and your lordship as a delinquent. I protest, before God, I have loved your person and justified your virtues: and I appeal to God and the Queen, that I told her Majesty your afflictions would make you a fit servant for her, attending but a fit time to move her Majesty to call you to the Court again. And had I not seen your ambitious affections inclined to usurpation, I would have gone on my knees to her Majesty to have done you good; but you have a wolf's head in a sheep's garment. . . . Ah, my Lord, were it but your own case, the loss had been less; but you have drawn a number of noble persons and gentlemen of birth and quality into your net of rebellion, and their bloods will cry vengeance against you. For my part, I vow to God, I wish my soul had been in heaven and my body at rest that this had not been.

Essex was amazed by this sudden burst of passion. 'Ah, Master Secretary,' he sneered, 'I thank God for my humiliation, that you in the ruff of all your bravery, have come hither to make your oration against me this day.'

But Cecil had not revealed himself simply to bandy insults. He returned to Essex's allegation about the Spanish intrigues. Which councillor had repeated that Cecil supported the Infanta's claim to the English throne? 'Name him if you dare. If you do not name him, it must be believed to be a fiction.'

'Nay, my lord,' replied Essex, triumphantly sure of himself, 'it is no fiction, for here stands an honourable person, the Earl of Southampton, that knows I speak no fables, for he heard it as well as I.'

Southampton looked uncomfortable at being dragged into this white-hot dispute. He muttered noncommittally, then said grudgingly that the councillor in question was the Comptroller, Essex's own uncle, Sir William Knollys.

There was no going back. The confrontation had reached the point of final resolution. The fate of Essex – and even perhaps of Cecil himself – hung on the old councillor who was sent for immediately, and who had already suffered imprisonment at his nephew's hands on the day of the rising. A loyal family man, he had stayed away from the trial that day precisely to avoid being asked to give evidence against his sister's son. Now he had no choice. The court greeted him with a buzz of fevered expectation.

Cecil had specifically instructed the messenger sent to summon Knollys that 'as you are a gentleman and you do tender your reputation, that you do not acquaint Mr Controller with the cause why you come for him.' So old Sir William took the stand totally ignorant of the question that was to be put to him. And Buckhurst wasted no time. He repeated Essex's accusation and asked if Knollys had ever heard Cecil express such sentiments in his hearing or to his knowledge.

The whole court hung upon his answer. And he did indeed remember the Secretary saying some such thing. But Cecil had been discussing at the time the tract *Conference on the Next Succession*, by the Jesuit Parsons who took the pen name Doleman. 'Is it not a strange impudence in that Doleman,' the Secretary had remarked, 'to give as equal right in the succession of the Crown to the Infanta of Spain as to any other?'

Essex's case had collapsed in fragments – and his morale with it. For it was on his vast conspiracy theory that he had based the justification for all his plottings – and his eventual rebellion. He could only stutter that the remark had been reported to him in another sense.

It was Cecil's turn to play Bacon and to pierce through the Earl's most vulnerable defences. 'Your malice,' he exclaimed 'whereby you seek to work me into hatred amongst all men, hath flowed from no other cause than from my affection to peace for the good of the country, and your own inflamed heart for war.' It was undeniable that Essex had read into the report of

Cecil's remark the meaning that best suited his own purposes and delusions. The rough, greedy, insensitive ambition that lay beneath his rationalizations had been stripped bare not only before the eyes of the court but also, more hurtfully, before his own eyes. His spirit cracked. When Cecil moderated his denunciation to conclude that 'I forgive you from the bottom of my heart,' Essex meekly responded 'And I, Mr Secretary, do clearly and freely forgive you with all my soul; because I mean to die in charity with all men.'

The trial was over in all but form. After another speech by Coke and further protestations of good intent by the two prisoners, the lords withdrew to consider their verdict. It was now well into the afternoon, and there had been no break taken for food or refreshment. Monsieur de Boissise, the French ambassador, sent back to Henri IV a somewhat jaundiced description of the jury: 'while the Earl and the Counsel were pleading my lords guzzled as if they had not eaten for a fortnight, smoking also plenty of tobacco. Then they went into a room to give their voice: and there, stupid with eating, and drunk with smoking, they condemned the two Earls.'[2] The verdicts were pronounced individually. One by one each of the nobles rose, bowed, placed his left hand upon his right side and declared 'Guilty, my lord, of high treason, upon mine honour': once right through the ranks for Essex, and then the same procedure all over again for Southampton. In each case it was Lord Thomas Howard as the most junior noble who began the declarations.

Essex replied briefly, obviously resigned to his death, but making a quiet plea for clemency for Southampton. Southampton was less courageous, and his grovelling petition for mercy betrayed his fears. It remained only for Buckhurst to declare the terrible sentence the law required in such cases:

. . . you both shall be led from hence to the place whence you came, and there remain during her Majesty's pleasure; from thence to be drawn upon a hurdle through the midst of the city, and so to the place of execution, there to be hanged by the neck and taken down alive – your bodies to be opened, and your bowels taken out and burned before your face: your bodies to be quartered – your heads and quarters to be disposed of at her Majesty's pleasure, and so God have mercy on your souls.

As Essex and Southampton returned in procession to the Tower of London the blade of the Gentleman Porter's axe now pointed towards them.[3]

31

'I have nothing left but that
which I must pay the Queen'

> Little Cecil trips up and down
> He rules both Court and Crown,
> With his brother Burghley clown
> In his great fox-furred gown,
> With the long proclamation,
> He swore he sav'd the town.[1]

London gossiped over and over the tumultuous events of 8 February and the sad confusions that had led up to them. Some blamed Cecil; others, the Queen. But Francis Bacon, now treated as a pariah even by his new allies, had the truth of the matter: 'A great officer at court,' he recounted, 'when my Lord of Essex was first in trouble and he and those that dealt with for him would talk much of my Lord's friends and of his enemies, answered to one of them, "I will tell you, I know but one friend and one enemy that my lord hath; and that one friend is the Queen, and that one enemy is himself".'

Lord Essex had no one to blame for his ruin but himself – his own insatiable over-reaching. He was Icarus, Tamburlaine, Faust. And as he lay in the Tower of London he realized finally how colossal his errors and his presumption had been. Preparing himself for the axe and block – the dreadful sentence of hanging, disembowelling and quartering was, as usual for nobles, commuted to simple execution – the Earl fell into the same manic religious depression that had characterized his long imprisonment in York House. And he was aided and abetted in his remorse by his Puritan chaplain, the Reverend Abdy Ashton, whose ministrations had been one of the three conditions the Earl had placed on his surrender on the roof of Essex House that black Sunday night only two weeks previously.

Essex had no wish to see his wife, or mother, or children, or sisters, or friends. Only his chaplain and his God were proper companions for these last precious days on earth when he could revel in the misery of his heroic failure. Yet by bitter irony, while we will never know how faithfully he was treated by the God to whom he dedicated the strange twisted contradiction of his life, it is certain that his chaplain was false to him. The day after the trial Essex had been visited by Doctor Thomas Dove, the Dean of Norwich, who had tried unskilfully to extract from the condemned earl a confession that could incriminate more fully his fellow conspirators. For the only prosecutions to date had been of Southampton, Essex and the unfortunate Captain Lea. Blount, Danvers, Cuffe, Meyrick, Davies, Sandys, Cromwell, Gorges and the others arrested on and after 8 February 1601 were still awaiting trial, and Essex's swift burning of the documents in his study had left the investigators very little to go on. A full confession from the leader of the whole project would be of enormous assistance, and now the verdict was pronounced he could hardly be afraid of incriminating himself.

Essex was obviously not afraid, but he was a man of honour and he sent Doctor Dove and his tentative enquiries swiftly packing. Yet when the Reverend Ashton came to visit him, the Earl's defences were down. The man had counselled him through some of his most crucial moments of spiritual stress and he trusted him implicitly. His own chaplain's insistence that he must confess all to purge his soul from its weight of guilt met with no resistance. 'You are going out of this world,' Ashton warned him sombrely; 'but yet you know not what it is to stand before God's judgement seat, and to receive the sentence of eternal condemnation. Leave therefore all glorious pretences; free your conscience from the burden of your grievous sins.'

Essex was taken in completely, and to the po-faced Puritan he confessed all: his intentions, his plots, and all who were with him.

The chaplain pounced. 'These be great matters your lordship hath opened unto me,' he remarked sorrowfully, 'and concealing them may touch my life. Also I hold myself bound in allegiance to reveal them.' And so, with Essex's agreement, the priest went hot foot to repeat all he had heard to the Privy Council who had, with hints both of punishment and promotion, previously suborned him. He had done more than extract the story from his victim, he had persuaded Essex to invite Cecil, Buckhurst, Egerton and Nottingham to hear the tale for themselves.

On Saturday, 21 February 1601, just two days after the trial, the Lord Admiral and Secretary went scurrying down to the Tower of London. And there the Earl of Essex freely confessed again the many details that had made him 'the greatest, the most vilest and most unthankfullest traitor that ever was born.' When Cecil asked more questions and then invited Essex to write all the names and facts down in his own handwriting the Earl most readily obliged. And on four close-covered sheets of paper he scrawled out everything, the rôles played by his colleagues now in jail, and the shady activities of more eminent personages whom the government had never suspected, chief among them being Lord Mountjoy. He spared no one – least of all his sister, Penelope, and her philanderings with Mountjoy. 'I must accuse one who is most nearest to me, my sister who did continually urge me on with telling how all my friends and followers thought me a coward, and that I had lost all my valour. She must be looked to, for she hath a proud spirit.'

Memories of Penelope's taunts recalled the sneers of others. Cuffe was sent for, and to his face Essex blamed him for his provocations and scheming: 'I that must now prepare for another world have resolved to deal clearly with God and the world, and must needs say this to you: you have been one of the chiefest instigators of me in all these my disloyal courses into which I have fallen.'

It was a sorry, sorry performance. And all that can be offered by way of explanation, if not of excuse, is the similar hysteria of Essex on other occasions and the desperate abandon that piety could drive him to. He had nothing to gain from confessions, and much reputation as a man of honour to lose. But he seems to have revelled in his faithlessness to the loyalties of this world, as he had rejoiced in the mortification of his confinement in York House. And he was conscious how great a contradiction of his previous values his confessions constituted. 'But now I am become another man,' he told a visiting preacher proudly. The Reverend Ashton had convinced him completely to scorn the baubles of this world and to think only of heavenly things.

He said not one word about Elizabeth – or if he did, the various chroniclers of his last week on earth thought it prudent not to mention it. And the Queen is recorded as saying nothing about the one man whose compulsive attractions had alternately delighted and tortured the waning years of her life. She waited, perhaps to see if he would plead for his life, reconfirming the power of an ageing woman over a handsome young man, then she signed the writ for his execution. Later a romantic legend was spun around these last sad six days between trial and block.

In happier times, the story went, Queen Elizabeth and her Essex were reconciled after a lover's quarrel. And reflecting on the tragic consequences of a real rift between the two, Elizabeth gave the Earl a ring. If Essex were ever to send it back to her, the Queen said, he could be sure of forgiveness. No matter how fierce her anger she would soften at the sight of the ring and the recollections it brought of happier days. It had once saved her from her father Henry VIII's anger.

So locked in the Tower and condemned to death the Earl decided to take his sovereign at her word. He leant out of his cell window, took the ring from his finger, and entrusted the talisman to a page boy. He was to take the ring to Lady Scrope, said the prisoner, and implore her to present it to the Queen.

But the pageboy made a fatal mistake and instead of carrying the ring to Lady Scrope carried it instead to that lady's sister, Lady Nottingham, the wife of Charles Howard, the Lord Admiral and Essex's sworn foe. Lady Nottingham knew just what significance the ring held, but kept it to herself and said nothing while Essex lay waiting in the Tower for Elizabeth's reprieve, and while Elizabeth herself waited sleepless and weeping for her Earl to send the ring that could save his life and restore their relationship. So Essex was executed.

It was not until two years later, when Lady Nottingham lay on her deathbed, that the ring's fate was revealed. For unable to die happily without clearing her conscience, Lady Nottingham confessed all to her Queen. 'God may forgive you, Madam,' sobbed Elizabeth, 'but I never can!' And her will broken by the deception, the Queen of England languished, pined and died.

It is a fine story, but definitely not of contemporary origin.[2] Yet it captures exactly the spirit of false romance that succeeding centuries have woven around the Earl of Essex and Elizabeth, forgetting the vast gulf between their ages, glossing over the deficiencies of personality that each suffered from, and ignoring the economic realities of Court politics at the end of the sixteenth century. For theirs was not a love affair but a relationship of convenience founded initially perhaps upon passing infatuation but drawing its real life from the profit motive of one, the ageing insecurity of the other and the vanity of both. When the profit vanished, when age proved inescapable and when the vanity exhausted itself then the relationship collapsed.

And so on Ash Wednesday, 1601, the third blow of an executioner's axe severed the head of Robert Devereux, second Earl of Essex, from his body. He was buried in the Tower of London but a few yards from Ann Boleyn, the mother of the woman with whom his life and death had been so tragically intertwined. He was thirty-three years old.

What of the others who had lived, loved and fought with him? The Earl of Southampton survived in the Tower of London to win his freedom on the accession of James I in 1603 and became the ornament of that new sovereign's Court which Essex would dearly have loved to dominate. And, ironically, the new King from Scotland demonstrated his affection for the young Earl by bestowing upon him the profits from the Farm of Sweet Wines.

But his fellow conspirators were not so fortunate. On 5 March 1601 Sir Christopher Blount, Sir Gelli Meyrick, Henry Cuffe, Sir John Davies and Sir Charles Danvers all stood their trial for high treason. All were found guilty. Davies was reprieved, but on

13 March 1601 Meyrick and Cuffe were taken to Tyburn and there subjected to the cruel torture of hanging, disembowelling and quartering. Meyrick's knighthood had been granted by Essex and was not considered substantial enough to qualify him for the exemptions from which Sir Charles Danvers and Sir Christopher Blount benefited. They suffered less long-drawn executions five days later on Tower Hill. Blount conceded that 'if we had failed in our ends, we should, rather than have been disappointed, even have drawn blood from herself [the Queen]'[3] Danvers' head 'was cut off at one stroke, saving a little which an officer cut off with his knife.'[4] He had offered to pay £10,000 in lieu of his life, but the authorities were too infuriated by his resolute silence under examination to spare him.

Poor Gelli Meyrick was punished even after death, for he had set aside for his tomb some Spanish sculptures captured on the Cadiz raid of 1596. But the Earl of Lincoln submitted to the Privy Council that such marble pillars were ornaments too fine to grace a traitor's resting place, and so Gelli had to lie beneath a gravestone as simple as those which had covered his ancestors.[5]

Others were more fortunate. The young Earl of Rutland bought his freedom for a £20,000 fine, only part of which he paid. And the other conspirators who were fined – Bedford £10,000, Sandys £5,000, Mounteagle £4,000, Cromwell £3,000 – also escaped simply by paying a few of the instalments which they owed the Exchequer, for within two years King James was on the throne anxious to heal up past animosities.

The non-titled conspirators were also released for fines whose size reflected less their guilt than the amount the government thought they could afford. And towards Essex's widow Frances the Queen was more than generous. When the Earl had returned from Ireland and been imprisoned, Frances, fearing Essex House would be searched and incriminating documents discovered, entrusted a casket of her husband's letters to a former servant, Jane Daniel. The letters set out the Earl's anger with his Queen and the rebellious thoughts against her that were whirling through his mind. And when Jane Daniel's husband read them he realized their value. He refused to return the more incriminating documents to Lady Essex until he was paid £3,000, and receiving only £1,720, he retained the originals and surrendered forged copies.

When the Privy Council's investigators uncovered the sordid little bye-plot they repeated the facts to the Queen, who ordered the immediate arrest of the blackmailer, vowing she would keep 'her winding sheet unspotted'. Daniel was prosecuted in Star Chamber, fined £3,000, and £2,000 of that was passed on to the widowed Frances.

Francis Bacon did not profit greatly from his treachery, as he was compelled to admit: 'the Queen hath done somewhat for me, though not in the proportion I hoped.' He had to be content with pocketing the £1,200 fine levied on Sir William Catesby, and felt so oppressed by general disapproval of his actions towards his former master that he had published an *Apology* justifying his behaviour. It was not until the reign of James that he achieved the eminence for which he had always been prepared to sacrifice so much self respect, becoming Solicitor General, Lord Chancellor and Viscount St Albans – though not without cost. In 1621 he was impeached by Parliament for bribery and corruption after a prosecution instigated by his old rival, Sir Edward Coke, was fined £40,000, was imprisoned briefly in the Tower and died in 1626 deeply in debt. His crippled brother Anthony had died in May 1601, equally alone, equally in debt but mourning with rather greater sincerity the master who had raised the Bacons to the centre of national affairs, only foolishly and fatally to ignore their advice.

Robert Cecil, of course, prospered, stage-managing the transfer of power from Elizabeth to James in 1603, negotiating peace with Spain in 1604 and winning for himself as James' chief minister the Earldom of Salisbury, whose holders have remained discreetly close to the centre of English power ever since. He died in 1612, as hardworking and as understandably but unfairly unloved as ever.

What of the people of London on whose support the Earl of Essex had counted and who had failed him so tragically? Eighteen months later a German visitor discovered them singing nothing but *Essex's Last Good Night*, even at the gates of the Court: he was pointed out the spot in the Tower where 'the brave hero' was beheaded, and in Whitehall itself he was shown the shields which 'the great and celebrated noble warrior' had presented to the Queen.[6]

The Essex strain and those connected with it seemed to live out its contentiousness to the last. Tresham, Catesby and the other Catholics who had marched with the Earl in 1601 came finally to grief in 1605 with Guy Fawkes. Essex's son, another Robert, was restored to his titles by King James to become the third Earl of Essex, grew up as a friend of Charles I but then, like his father, turned against his sovereign to become a Parliamentary general in the Civil War. It was no coincidence that his Adjutant-General was one Sir John Meyrick, a nephew of Gelli's; but, again like his father, Robert the 3rd Earl did not outlive the sovereign against whom he took up arms. He died in 1646 childless, and the title died with him, not to be revived until 1661 by the Capell family who have held it to this day. His mother Frances, Essex's widow, was married again in 1603 to the Earl of Clanrickard, becoming a Roman Catholic. And his aunt, the wanton Penelope, became Catholic too, though not before she was finally divorced from Lord Rich in 1605 to marry the man whose children she had already borne. But Lord Mountjoy, untroubled for his flirtation with Essex and created Earl of Devonshire as a reward for his Irish triumphs, died in 1606 and, broken-hearted, Penelope survived him but a year. It was Essex's old mother, Lettice, who proved hardiest of all. Having seen her third husband, Christopher Blount, executed only a few weeks after the death of her sole surviving son, she quickly regained her old style of existence, to die in 1634 at the ripe old age of 94.

She long outlived Queen Elizabeth, whose demanding wilful spirit had been at the heart of the whole tragedy and who proved to have the least power of recovery. She lived on but 25 months after Essex's death, a quieter, saddening woman who was seen to weep whenever the name of the red-haired young Earl was mentioned – though whether she wept for him or for her own delusions that died with him was uncertain. When she opened her last Parliament at the end of 1601 she was seen to stagger under the weight of her ceremonial robes, and she would have fallen had not her councillors held her up. It was noted how few members saluted her with the customary 'God Save Your Majesty', and when she left the House of Lords no one obeyed when the gentlemen ushers called for room to let her pass. It was a troublesome assembly, the first of a century of troublesome assemblies, and Elizabeth was fortunate to escape comparatively lightly from its hostility. She was not at home in the seventeenth century. She began to lose her appetite and to sleep badly. 'My Lord,' she told Howard, the Lord Admiral, 'I am tied with a chain of iron about my neck.'

When Marshal Biron, sent to the English Court by Henri iv of France, brought up the sad history of the Earl of Essex in the course of conversation, the Queen reproved him angrily. Then she weakened and said that if only the Earl had taken the advice of his wiser friends and made obvious his submission then all might have been well. But she had obviously forgotten much.

She was a lonely, declining old woman and could no longer hide from herself the evidence of her own decay. The Court became a mournful, empty place. Few courtiers could be persuaded to stay there for the Christmas festivities of 1602. The Coronation ring Elizabeth had refused ever to remove from her finger had to be sawn off, for it had grown into her flesh – and shortly after the ring was cut, Queen Elizabeth fell ill as though struck down by the symbolism of the ring's severing. She was dying, but she refused all medicine and food. She sat alone for hours on end saying nothing to those who tried to break her reveries. And as she sat alone she played from time to time with one ring that did still fit her swelling ageing fingers, for it was one the Earl of Essex had given her.

Her godson, Sir John Harington, came to Court. 'Our dear Queen,' he wrote to his wife, 'doth now bear show of human infirmity.' He had fought in Ireland with Essex, and the Queen remembered that, shedding a tear and smiting her bosom. 'Oh, now it mindeth me that you was one who saw this man elsewhere,' she sobbed. Harington tried to cheer her with some epigrams, but she had no time for laughter. 'When thou dost feel creeping time at thy gates, these fooleries will please thee less,' she reproved him. 'I am past my relish for such matters.'

Whitgift, the Archbishop of Canterbury, whom she had in happier times nicknamed her little 'black husband', was called to pray long hours by her bedside. His old knees creaking, he knelt beside his Queen mumbling psalms and incantations, once making as if to rise but being instructed to continue with his ministrations with a gesture that held but a pale reflection of its former imperiousness. And then Queen Elizabeth turned her face to the wall, said nothing more and, between the cold dark hours of two and three in the morning of 24 March 1603, she passed quietly away 'as the most resplendent sun setteth at last in a western cloud'.

Did she perhaps sigh in her last chill hours for Robert Devereux, Earl of Essex? She gave no sign. Her last thoughts were a mystery.

Notes

Abbreviations

A.P.C.	Acts of the Privy Council
B.M.	British Museum
C.S.P.Dom.	Calendar of State Papers (Domestic)
C.S.P.I.	Calendar of State Papers (Ireland)
Charterhouse	The Charterhouse, Founders' Papers
E.H.R.	*English Historical Review*
Essex R.O.	Essex Record Office
Hants R.O.	Hants Record Office, Wriothesley Manuscripts
H.M.C.S.	Historical Manuscripts Commission Salisbury (The Cecil Papers at Hatfield House)
Lambeth	Lambeth Palace Manuscripts
S.P.Dom.	Public Record Office; State Papers Domestic; Elizabeth
V.C.H.	Victoria County History

1 'He desired nothing more than to die in public'

1 Winwood, R., *Memorials of Affairs of State in the Reigns of Queen Elizabeth and King James I* (London, 1725), I, p. 309.

2 Anon., *A Lamentable Ditty Upon the Death of Robert Lord Devereux, late Earl of Essex, who was beheaded in the Tower of London, on Ash Wednesday in the morning, 1600. To the tune of Welladay. Printed for Cuthbert Wright* (London, c. 1625).

2 The Devereux

1 *Devereux Papers, with Richard Broughton's Memoranda,* Camden Society Miscellany 13 (London, 1923).

3 The Boyhood of Essex

1 Stone, L., *Crisis of The Aristocracy* (Oxford, 1965), p. 680.

2 Devereux, W.B., *Lives and Letters of The Devereux, Earls of Essex* (London, 1853), I, p. 165.

3 *ibid.,* I, p. 166.

4 *ibid.,* I, p. 167.

5 Harrison, W., *An Historical Description of the Ilande of Britain* (1577), edited by L.Withington (London, 1876), p. 249.
6 Clarke, Samuel, *The lives of Sundry Eminent Persons in this Later Age* (London, 1683).
7 H.M.C.S., v, 323.
8 *ibid., op. cit.,* I, xi, 44.
9 Devereux, *op. cit.,* I, p. 171.

4 *At the Court of Queen Elizabeth*

1 Mathew, D., *The Celtic Peoples and Renaissance Europe* (London, 1933), p. 339.
2 Cited in Hurstfield, J., *The Queen's Wards. Wardship and Marriages under Elizabeth I* (London, 1958), p. 343.
3 *ibid.,* p. 366.

5 'To my beloved and much honoured lord, the Earl of Essex, my best sword'

1 Greville, F., *The Life of The Renowned Sir Philip Sidney*, edited by N.Smith (Oxford, 1907), pp. 129–30.
2 Lant, T., *Funeral of Sir Philip Sidney* (London, 1587).

6 'Till birds sing in the morning'

1 Tanner MSS (Bodleian Library), 79, 89.
2 Stone, *op. cit.,* p. 464.
3 Devereux, *op. cit.,* I, p. 185.
4 *ibid.,* I, pp. 187–9.

8 'A lady whom time hath surprised'

1 Cited in Hurstfield, J., *Elizabeth I and the Unity of England* (London, 1960), p. 176.
2 *ibid.,* p. 190.
3 Harington, J., *Nugae Antiquae*, edited by T.Peck, 2 vols. (London, 1769), II, p. 215.
4 Corbett, J.S., *The Successors of Drake* (London, 1900), p. 41.
5 Harington, *op. cit.,* II, pp. 140–1.
6 C.S.P.Dom., Eliz., cclxiv, p. 77.
7 Foley, H., *Records of The English Province of The Society of Jesus* (London, 1877), I, pp. 21–2.
8 *ibid.,* I, p. 8.

9 Maisse, André Hérault, Sieur de, *Journal, 1597*, translated by G.B. Harrison and R.A. Jones (London, 1931).
10 Cited by Nichols, J., in *The Progresses of Queen Elizabeth* (London, 1823), III, p. 552.
11 Harington, *op. cit.*, II, p. 186.
12 C.S.P.Dom., Eliz., cclxxiv, p. 40.
13 Dietz, F.C., *English Public Finance, 1558–1641* (New York, 1932), p. 298.
14 Hurstfield, *Elizabeth I, op. cit.*, p. 341.
15 Cruickshank, C.G., *Elizabeth's Army* (Oxford, 1966), p. 283.
16 Naunton, R., *Fragmenta Regalia*, edited by E. Arber (London, 1895), p. 50.
17 Hurstfield, *Elizabeth I, op. cit.*, p. 337.
18 Stone, *op. cit.*, p. 165.
19 *ibid.*, p. 410.
20 *ibid.*, p. 411.
21 *ibid.*, p. 410.
22 *ibid.*, p. 452.
23 *ibid.*, p. 453.
24 *ibid.*, p. 453.

9 *Shepherd of Albion's Arcadia*

1 Birch, T., *Memoirs of the Reign of Elizabeth* (London, 1764), I, p. 56.
2 Harleian MSS, 6395.
3 Devereux, *op. cit.*, I, p. 197.
4 *ibid.*, I, p. 202.
5 Speed, J., *The History of Great Britain* (London, 1611), p. 1190.
6 Henry, L.W., 'The Earl of Essex as Strategist', *E.H.R.* LXVIII, 268 (July 1958), p. 363.
7 Wilson, E.C.K., *Elizabeth's Eliza* (Harvard, 1939), p. 144.

10 *'I will adventure to be rich'*

1 Wilson, E.C.K., *op. cit.*, p. 144.
2 Devereux, *op. cit.*, I, p. 206.
3 Mathew, *op. cit.*, p. 339.
4 Except for the rare quantifications of patronage cited in Chapter 8, evidence that would allow any evaluation of these and other perks of office is by its nature scarce and insubstantial.
5 Stone, *op. cit.*, p. 456.
6 *ibid.*, p. 569.
7 *ibid.*, p. 568.
8 *ibid.*, p. 569.
9 H.M.C.S., v, 137, 252.

10 S.P.Dom., 12/46/39.
11 B.M., Lansdowne MSS, 69/41.
12 Devereux, *op. cit.*, I, p. 208.
13 *ibid.*
14 Simon, A., *A History of The Wine Trade in England* (London, 1906), II.

11 *First Command*

1 Stone, *op. cit.*, p. 665.
2 Devereux, *op. cit.*, I, p. 214.
3 Stone, *op. cit.*, p. 456.
4 Corbett, *op. cit.*, p. 19.
5 Devereux, *op. cit.*, I, pp. 234, 239, 240.
6 Stone, *op. cit.*, p. 71.
7 Devereux, *op. cit.*, I, p. 244.
8 *ibid.*, I, p. 245.
9 *ibid.*, I, p. 247.
10 *ibid.*, I, p. 250.
11 *ibid.*, I, p. 269.

12 *New Directions, New Friends*

1 Spedding, J., *Collected Works of Francis Bacon* (London, 1857–74), I, p. 6.
2 Lambeth, Bacon MSS, v, 659, g.21.
3 Birch, T., *op. cit.*, I, pp. 80–6.
4 Devereux, *op. cit.*, I, p. 295.
5 Birch, *op. cit.*, I, p. 93.
6 Corbett, *op. cit.*, p. 24.
7 Cited in Williamson, G.C., *George, Third Earl of Cumberland* (Cambridge, 1920), pp. 98–9.

13 *The Parliament of 1593*

1 Devereux, *op. cit.*, I, p. 280.
2 *ibid.*, I, p. 283.
3 Spedding, *op. cit.*, I, p. 208.
4 *ibid.*, I, p. 215.
5 *ibid.*, I, p. 222.
6 Birch, *op. cit.*, I, p. 97.
7 Spedding, *op. cit.*, I, p. 240.
8 Birch, *op. cit.*, I, p. 20.
9 Spedding, *op. cit.*, I, p. 230.

14 *The First Setback*

1 Birch, *op. cit.*, I, p. 108.
2 *ibid.*, I, p. 125.
3 Mathew, *op. cit.*, p. 405.
4 Heffner, R., *The Earl of Essex in Elizabethan Literature* (Baltimore, 1934), p. 20.
5 Cited in Strachey, G.L., *Elizabeth and Essex* (London, 1928), p. 57.
6 Birch, *op. cit.*, I, p. 152.

15 *The Sad Case of Doctor Lopez*

1 This account is based on C.S.P.Dom., 1591–4, pp. 390–1, 394, 411–14, 422. Birch, *op. cit.*, I, pp. 150–60. Harleian MSS, 871, 34 and 39.

16 *Violent Courses*

1 This account is based on the evidence pieced together by Akrigg, G.P.V., in *Shakespeare and the Earl of Southampton* (London, 1968).
2 Stone, *op. cit.*, p. 225.
3 Devereux, *op. cit.*, I, p. 317.
4 *ibid.*

17 *Winters of Discontent*

1 Shakespeare, W., *Midsummer Night's Dream*, II.1.93.
2 Harrison, G.B., *Elizabethan Journal* (London, 1938), I, p. 132.
3 Hurstfield, *Elizabeth I*, *op. cit.*, p. 184.
4 Abbott, E.A., *Bacon and Elizabeth* (London, 1877), p. 34.
5 Pickering, D., *The Statutes at Large* (Cambridge, 1763), 39: Eliz. I: c.1: c.2.
6 Lambarde, cited in Nichols, J., *The Progresses and Public Processions of Queen Elizabeth*, *op. cit.*
7 Stone, *op. cit.*, p. 38.
8 S.P.Dom., 230, 26.
9 S.P.Dom., 259, 22.
10 Donne, J., *An Anatomy of The World* (London, 1611).
11 Abbott, *op. cit.*, p. 9.
12 Williams, N., *Elizabeth, Queen of England* (London, 1967), p. 324.

18 *The Fall of Calais*

1 Edwards, E., *Life of Sir Walter Raleigh* (London, 1868), I, p. 245.

2 A.P.C., xxx, 496.
3 B.M., Lansdowne MSS, 73, no. 55.
4 Cruickshank, *op. cit.*, p. 253.

19 *The Capture of Cadiz*

The account given in this chapter has been based on: Hakluyt, R., *The Principal Navigations etc. (1589)*, 12 vols., edited by W. Raleigh (London, 1903–5); Harrison, W., *An Historical Description, op. cit.*; Monson, W., *Naval Tracts*, edited by M. Oppenheim (London, 1902–14); Corbett, J.S., *op. cit.*

1 See, for example, Privy Council transactions for 30 April 1594.
2 Grierson, H.J.C., ed., *The Poems of John Donne* (Oxford, 1912), II, 5a.
3 Harleian MSS, 167, no. 209.
4 Lambeth MSS, 250, 348–9.
5 Grierson, *op. cit.*, 'A Burnt Ship'.
6 'late Island', meaning 'in that island of the late events', refers to the fact that the Cadiz peninsula stands almost totally cut off from the mainland.

20 *'A dangerous image'*

1 H.M.C.S., vi, 327.
2 *ibid.*, vi, 321.
3 *ibid.*, vi, 329.
4 See H.M.C.S., vi, vii and viii for the continuous correspondence this diamond provoked.
5 Cited in Strachey, *op. cit.*
6 Birch, *op. cit.*, ii, 61.
7 Henry Cuffe's *Examination*, 2 March 1601: Camden Society, lxxviii, 88.
8 Devereux, *op. cit.*, I, 392.
9 Naunton, *op. cit.*, p. 51.

21 *The Islands Voyage*

The account given in this chapter has been based on: Hakluyt, R., *The Principal Navigations etc. (1589)*, 12 vols., edited by W. Raleigh (London, 1903–5); Harrison, W., *An Historical Description, op. cit.*; Monson, W., *Naval Tracts*, edited by M. Oppenheim (London, 1902–14); Corbett, J.S., *op. cit.*

1 Cited in Strachey, *op. cit.*, p. 139.
2 S.P.Dom., 466.
3 *ibid.*, 473.
4 *ibid.*, 469.
5 Henry, *op. cit.*, p. 381.
6 Cheyney, E.P., *History of England from the Defeat of the Armada to the Death of Elizabeth* (London, 2 vols., 1914 and 1926), II, p. 429.

7 H.M.C.S., vii, 368.
8 *ibid.*, vii, 361.
9 *ibid.*, vii, 386.

22 *Lord Essex's Sickness*

1 *ibid.*, vii, 446.
2 *ibid.*, vii, 449.
3 Stone, *op. cit.*, p. 99.
4 Goodman, G., *The Court of James I* (London, 1839).
5 S.P.Dom., 532.
6 Neale, J.E., *The Elizabethan House of Commons* (London, 1949), pp. 239–43.
7 H.M.C.S., vii, 520.
8 Maisse, *op. cit.*, p. 116.

23 *Felix and Bolingbroke*

1 Guilpin, E., *Skialotheia* in Shakespeare Association Facsimiles (London, 1931), vol. 2, Satire 1.
2 Birch, *op. cit.*, II, p. 389.
3 *ibid.*, II, p. 385.
4 Devereux, *op. cit.*, I, 493.
5 Birch, *op. cit.*, II, p. 390.
6 H.M.C.S., ix, 6.

24 *The Irish Enterprise*

1 Moryson, F., *Itinerary* (London, 1617), IV, p. 191.
2 Falls, C., 'The Elizabethan Soldier in Ireland', *History Today* (London, February 1951), p. 40.
3 Campion, E., *History of Ireland* (London, 1633), Chapter 1.
4 C.S.P.I., ccv, pp. 362–3.
5 *ibid.*, 7.
6 Gainsford, T., *The Glory of England* (London, 1618), p. 144.
7 Irish Archaeological Society Tracts (Dublin, 1842), p. 35.
8 Harington, *op. cit.*, p. 278.
9 *ibid.*, I, p. 280.
10 S.P.Dom., 151.
11 A.P.C., xxix, 120.
12 C.S.P., ccvi, 3.
13 C.S.P., cciv, 172.
14 *ibid.*, 231.
15 C.S.P., ccv, 38 and 52.

16 C.S.P.I., ccvi, 10.
17 *Annals of the Four Masters* (Dublin, 1599), pp. 2119–21.
18 C.S.P.I., ccv, 113.
19 *ibid.*, ccv, 124.
20 *ibid.*, ccv, 129–31.
21 *ibid.*, ccv, 155.

25 *'A hatred in her as will never be reclaimed'* and 26 *Confinement*

These chapters are based on A.P.C., C.S.P.Dom., H.M.C.S., Devereux, *op. cit.*, Chamberlain, *op. cit.*, Winwood, *op. cit.*, and Birch, *op. cit.*

27 *'The licence of sweet wines lies at anchor aloof'*

1 Shakespeare, W., *Macbeth*, III.4.137.
2 S.P.Dom., 468.
3 Chamberlain, J., *Letters during the reign of Queen Elizabeth* (London, 1861), p. 86.

28 *The Rebels*

1 H.M.C.S., xi, 141.
   Belvoir Castle, Rutland MSS, 90, 95, 97, 100, 309, 310, 312, 378.
2 H.M.C.S., viii, 357.
   S.P.Dom., 12/278/132.
   Hants R.O., 58, 169, 283, 430, 441, 442, 582.
3 S.P.Dom., 14/26/33/34.
4 H.M.C.S., vi, 294; viii, 421; x, 9, 126.
   S.P.Dom., 12/278/135.
5 V.C.H., Lancs, viii, 183.
   V.C.H., Herts, iv, 95, 102–3.
6 B.M. Lansdowne, 84/72.
   Essex R.O., D/DPF, 240.
   Charterhouse, F, 4/28; D 3/233; E 123/23/60.
7 Spink, H.H., *The Gunpowder Plot and Lord Mounteagle's Letter* (London, 1902), p. 22.
8 S.P.Dom., 648–9.
9 Shakespeare, W., *King John* (1594), II.1.66.
10 Mathew, *op. cit.*, p. 423.
11 H.M.C.S., x, 250.
12 S.P.Dom., 577–8.
13 S.P.Dom., 580.

29 *The Rebellion*

1 Camden, W., *Annals* (London, 1630), II, p. 632.
This account of the rebellion has been based on A.P.C., C.S.P.Dom., H.M.C.S., Devereux, *op. cit.*, Chamberlain, *op. cit.*, Winwood, *op. cit.*, and Birch, *op. cit.*

30 *The Trial*

1 Jardine, D., *Criminal Trials* (London, 1832), I, p. 321.
2 Winwood, R., *op. cit.*, I, p. 299.
3 This account of the trial was based on Jardine, *op. cit.*, C.S.P.Dom., A.P.C., and H.M.C.S.

31 *'I have nothing left but that which I must pay the Queen'*

1 Cited in Harrison, *Journals*, *op. cit.*, III, p. 174.
2 *The Secret History of the most renowned Queen Elizabeth and the Earl of Essex, by a person of quality* (London, 1695) sets the story out in full. The first recorded reference to it is in a pamphlet *c.* 1620 ('The Devil's Law Case').
3 Hargrave, F., *State Trials* (London, 1776), I, p. 212.
4 Stow, J., *A General Chronicle of England* (London, 1631), p. xxxlv.
5 H.M.C.S., x, 38.
6 Neale, J.E., *Queen Elizabeth* (London, 1934), p. 379.

Index

INDEX

Norris, Sir John, 67, 82
North, Lord, 17, 59, 73, 244
North Hall, Elizabeth at, 44
Northern England, 129, 267; Catholic
rebellion of, 9, 283–4
Nottingham, Earl of, see Howard of
Effingham, Charles, Lord
Nottingham, Lady, 314–15

O'Byrnes, of Wicklow, 220, 231
O'Connor, Sir Donogh, 233–4
O'Donnell, Hugh Roe, Prince of Donegal,
224, 234
offices of state, 28–9
O'Hagan, Henry, 235
O'Moore, MacRory, 230
O'Neill, Hugh, see Tyrone, Earl of
O'Neill, Tyrlong, 224
Ordnance, Mastership of the, 175–6, 215,
279
Ormonde, Earl of, 229, 230
Overall, Dr John, 252
Oxford, bishopric of, 75
Oxford, Earl of, 58, 125

Panama, isthmus of, 138
Parliament, 33, 100, 132; election to, 101;
state opening of, 200;
of 1593; composition of, 99, 100–2;
opening, 102–3; business of, 103–6;
of 1597, 206; of 1601; opening, 319
Parma, Alexander, Duke of; in Nether-
lands, 34, 36; negotiates with Elizabeth,
47–8; in France, 81, 89
Parsons, Robert (R. Doleman), 127, 308
patronage system, 132, 134
Paulet, Sir Amyas, 94
Pembroke, Earl of, 17, 275–6
Percy, Sir Charles, 282
Percy, Sir Jocelyn, 282
Perez, Antonio, 201
Perkinson, Capt, at Calshot Castle, 123
Perrot, Tom, 9, 23, 44
Philip II, King of Spain, 34, 47, 96, 115,
137, 264; plans to invade England, 47,
138, 173, 197–8
Picardy, 198
Platt, Hugh, 131
Plymouth; Essex escapes from, 1589, 65–6;
1596 camp at, 143–4, 147–8, 153; de-
parture from, 150; blown back, 152;
return to, 164, 165–6;
1597 exp. at, 179, 180, 181;
return to, 198
Poland, ambassador from, 181–2
Poole, Sir Germaine, 126
Popham, Lord Chief Justice; in deputation
to Essex House, 287–8; at trial of Essex,
301, 302, 303
Portsmouth, Elizabeth at, 85

Portugal; Don Antonio claims throne of,
63–4, 67–8; 1589 exp. to, 67–9; plot to
kill Don Antonio, 116–18; 1596 raid on,
163–4
Prestwood, cattle driven from, 126
Privy Council; of Edward VI, 8; of 1560,
and troops, 145; of Elizabeth, 31, 49,
63, 88, 89, 123, 132–3, 139, 141, 142,
148–9, 162, 167, 183, 208, 216, 225, 226,
234, 238; and Mary Queen of Scots,
39–40; and Parliament, 102, 103–4; Essex
sworn in, 102; and Essex, 129, 198, 215;
examine Essex, 244–5; denounce in Star
Chamber, 248–9; trial postponed, 253–3;
Special Commission, 253–6; and rebellion, 274, 276, 277, 283–4, 290, 291, 294;
deputation to Essex House, 287–8, 294–5;
after rebellion, 299–300, 301, 313, 316,
317
Protestants; Essex and, 253, 274; in France,
81, 96, 140; and Netherlands, 253; persecution of, 8; Reformation, 10, 73;
Spain and, 140, 208
Puckering, Lord Keeper, 59
Puerto Rico, Spanish treasure at, 138
Puritans; attack Church, 20, 106; preach at
Essex House, 274, 277, 278

Raleigh, Sir Walter; and Elizabeth, 30, 31,
41, 52, 138; marriage of, 97–8; and
Essex, 3, 31, 44–5, 63, 181, 186–92,
194–6, 203, 207, 263; on 1592 pirate
exp., 98; naval ability, 98; on Cadiz
exp., 140, 150, 151, 156, 157; on Azores
exp., 180, 181, 183, 184, 185–92, 194–6;
Governor of Jersey, 266; on day of
rebellion, 286–7; at trial of Essex, 302,
304; mentioned, 169, 242, 262, 281,
305
Rathlin, Isle of, captured, 12
rebellion, Essex's, 1601; plotted, 262–7;
motives for, 268–77; conferences, 278–
282; last two days before, 282–5;
Elizabeth and, 269–70; day of, 286–97;
reprisals, 277, 309–10, 315–16
Reformation, the, 10, 73, 274
religious; disputes, 20, 97; persecution, 8,
52; wars, 81, 96; tolerance, 96, 266, 274;
see also Catholics, Protestants, Puritans
Reynolds, Edward, 101, 109
Rich, Lord; marriage of, 23, 318; and
Essex, 65, 242, 243
Rich, Lady, see Devereux, Penelope
Richard II, King of England, 56, 276; see
also Bolingbroke, Henry and under
Shakespeare
Ridd, Anthony, Bishop of St David's, 53
Robsart, Amy, death of, 16
Roman Catholics, see Catholics
Roman Church in England, 8